The End of
Soviet Politics

The End of Soviet Politics

Elections, Legislatures, and the Demise of the Communist Party

Brendan Kiernan

Westview Press
BOULDER • SAN FRANCISCO • OXFORD

This Westview softcover edition is printed on acid-free paper and bound in library-quality, coated covers that carry the highest rating of the National Association of State Textbook Administrators, in consultation with the Association of American Publishers and the Book Manufacturers' Institute.

All rights reserved. No part of this publication may be reproduced or transmitted in any form or by any means, electronic or mechanical, including photocopy, recording, or any information storage and retrieval system, without permission in writing from the publisher.

Copyright © 1993 by Westview Press, Inc.

Published in 1993 in the United States of America by Westview Press, Inc., 5500 Central Avenue, Boulder, Colorado 80301-2877, and in the United Kingdom by Westview Press, 36 Lonsdale Road, Summertown, Oxford OX2 7EW

A CIP catalog record for this book is available from the Library of Congress.
ISBN 0-8133-8275-0

Printed and bound in the United States of America

∞ The paper used in this publication meets the requirements of the American National Standard for Permanence of Paper for Printed Library Materials Z39.48-1984.

10   9   8   7   6   5   4   3   2   1

For Lyuda and Masha

Contents

Acknowledgments	xi
1 Introduction	**1**
The End of Soviet Politics	1
Analyzing *Demokratizatsiia*	2
Comparative Politics and Soviet Studies	5
Notes	12
2 Democratization?	**17**
Soviet Power and Lenin's Legacy	17
Stalin and the Post-Stalin Consensus	19
Soviet Power in the Early 1980s	23
Theoretical Frameworks	26
'Soviet Power' and the Transition	32
Notes	33
3 Power to the Soviets?	**37**
Gorbachev and the Soviets	37
Gorbachev as General Secretary	39
The 19th Party Conference	44
Final Session of the Old Supreme Soviet	48
Notes	48
4 The 1989 Elections	**53**
Creating a New Electoral System	53
The Campaign	57
The Results: Accountability Reborn	67
Notes	69

5	**The Congress of People's Deputies**	73
	Preparing the Congress	73
	The First Session of the CPD	77
	The CPD and Political Leadership	85
	Notes	85

6	**Creation of the New Supreme Soviet's Committees**	89
	The 1988 Constitutional Amendments	89
	Commissions and Committees	91
	Standing Rules and Procedures	95
	Chairmen and Members	97
	Staff and Infrastructure	99
	Procedure and Debate	101
	Formation of the Defense Committee	102
	The Interregional Deputies' Group	104
	Politics, Policy, and Leadership	106
	Notes	106

7	**The Committees at Work**	113
	Committee Responsibilities	113
	Confirmation Hearings	114
	Monitoring Implementation	118
	The Legislative Process	119
	'Specialist' Committees and Political Leadership	123
	Notes	125

8	**Development of the Supreme Soviet**	129
	The Supreme Soviet's First Year	129
	Committees and the Secretariat	132
	The Soviet Presidency	136
	The Supreme Soviet's Second Year	140
	Notes	150

9	**The 1990 Elections**	159
	The Electoral Law	159
	Links Between the 1989 and 1990 Campaigns	161
	Electoral Blocs	164
	The CPSU's Preparations	167
	The Campaign	171
	Results: Accountable Again	181
	Notes	182

10 Politics in the RSFSR CPD — 189
Preparing the Congress — 189
The First Session of the RSFSR CPD — 192
Development of Russian Legislative Politics — 201
Notes — 204

11 'Soviet Politics' and the End of the Soviet Era — 209
Demokratizatsiia and Democratization — 210
Electoral Politics — 213
Legislative Politics — 218
The End of the Soviet Era — 228
Notes — 232

Index of Names — 239

Acknowledgments

Funding and other support for this study were provided by the International Research and Exchanges Board (IREX), Fulbright Hays, Indiana University, the Center on Global Change and World Peace at Indiana University, the Henry M. Jackson School of International Studies at the University of Washington, the Social Science Research Council (SSRC), the Center on East-West Trade, Investment, and Communications at Duke University, Duke University's Political Science Department, and the Comparative Property Rights Project in the W. Allen Wallis Institute of Political Economy at the University of Rochester.

I am indebted to Darrell P. Hammer, Robert W. Campbell, Jeffrey Hart, Bernard S. Morris, and Dina R. Spechler for their patient guidance throughout my graduate career at Indiana University. I also thank Sharon LaRoche and other friends and colleagues at Indiana's Political Science Department, Russian and East European Institute, and Summer Slavic Workshop.

While an IREX scholar in the USSR in 1988-89, I was hosted by D.L. Zlatopolskii and G.V. Barabashev at Moscow State University's Law Department. These two distinguished scholars and my other Soviet colleagues provided a friendly atmosphere and interesting work environment. I am grateful to Burton Miller and Michael Urban, fellow IREX exchangees, for their friendship and support. Stephanie Ratmeyer and Paul Richardson provided logistical and other aid for follow-up trips to Moscow in 1990 and 1992. This project could never have been completed without their help.

Daniel Chirot and the Henry M. Jackson School of International Studies at the University of Washington were gracious hosts during my postdoctoral year in 1990-91 in Seattle. Nancy Acheson, Mikhail Chernysh, Steve Hanson, Lawrence Lerner, Sabrina Ramet, and Karen Walton helped make my stay at the Jackson School's Soviet and East European Studies Program both pleasant and productive.

Jerry F. Hough and the Center on East-West Trade, Investment, and Communications at Duke University supported my research in 1991-92 through a postdoctoral fellowship. I had the opportunity to share my ideas both with center fellows and a series of visiting scholars. Kathleen Watters, Christina Lubert, Mindy Marcus, and Sylvia Rogers, the Center's staff, cheerfully helped me over many hurdles. Ronald Archer and Herbert Kitschelt from Duke's Political Science Department organized and ran a joint Duke University and University of North Carolina seminar on democratization that served as both a challenge to rethink my ideas and a forum to defend them. Allen Kornberg and the Political Science Department gave me the opportunity to test some of my thoughts on Duke's students in the fall of 1991, for which I am grateful. I thank John Aldrich for letting me sit in on his seminar on American political parties, especially the sections on the early US Congress, which helped me think about the birth of political parties in the ruins of the USSR.

The Social Science Research Council awarded me a postdoctoral fellowship that allowed me to devote the summers of 1991 and 1992 to research and writing. Thanks to this support, I spent June and July 1992 in Moscow and Kiev interviewing Supreme Soviet deputies. Some of that research is reflected here, but I hope to publish more later.

William Riker and David Weimer deserve special thanks, not only for sponsoring the closing stages of this research through the auspices of the Comparative Property Rights Project at the University of Rochester in the fall of 1992, but also for helping open new intellectual horizons to me, most especially comparative political economy and positive political theory. I also am happy to have the opportunity to thank Richard F. Fenno, who let me sit in on a graduate readings course on the US Congress. His enthusiasm for legislative politics in general and interest in the peculiarities of the Russian case offered real encouragement during the final stages of this project.

Rebecca Ritke, my editor at Westview, patiently helped me through the painful process of finishing a first book. I am grateful to Robert W. Campbell, Darrell P. Hammer, Jeffrey Hart, Jerry Hough, Herbert Kitschelt, Steve Lewis, Bernard Morris, Damon Palmer, Patricia R. Pauly, William Riker, Peter Rutland, and David Weimer for reading and commenting on the manuscript at various stages of its development.

Finally, hearty thanks to the following individuals for countless good deeds that enabled me to complete this project: Brett Adolfson, Rafael Akopov, Dominique Arel, Melissa Bokovoy, Robert Clough, Virginia Clough, Renee Despres, Olga Diuzheva, Steve Flinn, Daniel Green, Barbara Hicks, Barbara Hopkins, David Hunter, David Johnson, Olga Kareva, Michael Katz, Konstantin Kuranov, Vladimir Kuznetsov, Elizabeth Martineau, John McClellan, Ihor Ostash, Kristen Paris, Patricia Pauly, Neda Shashani, Laurie Skirkanich, Regina Smyth, Ireneusz Sipowicz-Hicks, Maria Solomon-Arel, Jeremy Snow, Michael Treitler, Thomas Vellenga, Erik Whitlock, and Andrew Wilson.

Brendan Kiernan

Chapter 1

Introduction

The End of Soviet Politics

Politics everywhere involves a struggle for power and leadership. After elbowing his way to the top of the Communist Party of the Soviet Union, Mikhail Gorbachev faced a dilemma: he was powerless to lead. He described this situation in terms once used by Lenin: running the USSR was like driving a car with a broken steering wheel.[1] In January 1987, after two years of economic tinkering and political preparation, Gorbachev launched a reform program designed to re-empower the Communist Party and allow him to lead the Soviet Union into the 21st century. He told the CPSU's Central Committee that perestroika was in trouble, that *demokratizatsiia*, the rebirth of soviet socialist democracy and the creation of a truly *Soviet* Union, was the only way to save it, and that Communists should lead the way by democratizing internal party relations and relearning the art of political leadership.

Gorbachev proposed that the USSR return to its soviet roots as part of the "logic of the development of socialism."[2] The significance of this *soviet* cachet should not be underestimated—it touches both the roots of the revolution and the heart of *demokratizatsiia*. In 1917, the Bolsheviks exercised their self-proclaimed right to leadership of the working class by seizing power in the name of the soviets, a revolutionary system of popularly-elected self-government councils. 'Soviet government,' an allegedly superior solution to the universal political problems of power and leadership, was for seventy years the formal foundation of the USSR's political system.[3] The term 'soviet politics' was, however, an oxymoron. The soviets were intended to *eliminate* the fig leaf politics that allegedly hid bourgeois domination in the capitalist world. 'Soviet power' was another contradiction in terms: the soviets never expressed the sovereign will of the people but were instead rubber stamps controlled by the CPSU.[4]

This book, an analysis of Gorbachev's brand of Soviet socialist democracy, tells the story of his attempt to revive the soviets and, through them, the Soviet Union. Throughout the text, readers should keep in mind three principal conclusions. First, *demokratizatsiia* is best viewed as an attempt to reempower the party leadership politically and economically, not an attempt to share or divide power, i.e. extricate the party from its monopolistic position. Today, republican leaders face much the same economic and political problems of empowerment that Gorbachev faced in 1985. Second, the institutional structures that the party selected to implement its strategy strongly influenced outcomes. Paradoxically, the CPSU was unsuited as an organization to the semi-competitive electoral and legislative institutions that it created. These same institutions, the legacy of 'soviet-style' government, will, however, serve as a brake on further political development. Third, the *sequence* of electoral and legislative reforms that Gorbachev and his comrades selected strongly influenced outcomes. If electoral reform had started with controlled contests for 15 republican Supreme Soviets instead of creating a focus for discontent in the USSR Congress of People's Deputies—with the added promise of republican elections to come—the national elites that tore the USSR apart with the help of Supreme Soviets based on the doctrine of legislative supremacy may have been forced to choose different routes to power, perhaps in a more legitimate federal Congress.

Analyzing Demokratizatsiia

Theoretical Approaches

What is the best way to analyze *demokratizatsiia*? This study starts from two related assumptions. First, since power and leadership in the USSR were concentrated in the Communist Party, any study of political reform should examine the changing role and nature of the CPSU. Second, legislative and electoral institutions provide the incentive structures that shape party organizations and party systems in any democratic polity. One fruitful way to study a reform program allegedly dedicated to recreating Soviet democracy, therefore, is to examine the CPSU's role in electoral and legislative politics. Both Leninist theory and the literature on authoritarianism and transitions to democracy provide theoretical frameworks to structure such an investigation.

Leninism. Early studies of Leninism and later studies of totalitarianism pointed to the importance of Lenin's organizational and institutional innovations. In 1959, Leonard Schapiro anticipated Gorbachev when he pointed out that a generation of leaders who matured politically after 1945 would eventually come to power. Concluding his classic study of the CPSU with a question, Schapiro pointed to the issue that is at the heart of this book: "When, and if, [this new generation] comes to rule through the medium of the party, will [its] political horizon still remain limited by the rules for an underground conspiracy as once formulated by Lenin?"[5]

This study explores, in Schapiro's words, the limits of Gorbachev's "political horizon." In 1988, he claimed to be returning to Leninism and an original kind of Soviet socialist democracy that, he said, was distorted by Stalin. It seems logical, therefore, that Gorbachev's reforms be judged by these criteria. This study uses the core of Leninist theory on the relationship between the party and the soviets to create a benchmark to measure the depth and breadth of change. Because Leninism was an explicit rejection of 'bourgeois parliamentarism,' this method also allows explicit comparisons with western democratic systems.

Democratization Theory. Although a 'Leninist' framework can help identify the principal elements of the reform program and measure its depth and breadth in diachronic terms, evaluating the relationship between Gorbachev's *demokratizatsiia* and democratization more broadly defined is a separate task. Neither Western eagerness to see the Soviet Union democratize, assumptions built into the modernization literature, nor the surprising ease of the political transition in Eastern Europe should prejudice our answer to one question: Can the term '*demokratizatsiia*' as Gorbachev defined it be translated sensibly as democratization? While some scholars rushed to judgement, Stephen Cohen warned of the dangers inherent in "the American habit of interpreting Russia through the prism of our own ideology...For decades it was an alien 'Communism'...Now it's an American-style 'free market' and 'civil society.'" Samuel Huntington also has argued that it is wise to be cautious: while true democratizers often try to reassure conservatives that they want liberalization to defuse opposition, mere liberalizers often seek support by creating the impression they want to democratize.[6] In short, a hasty analysis of the meaning of *demokratizatsiia* obscures elements of both Gorbachev's political strategy and the course of Soviet political development.

The comparative politics literature on transitions from authoritarian rule, particularly studies of what Huntington calls the "third wave" of democratization, transformations in the past fifteen years in Southern and Eastern Europe, Latin America, and Eastern Asia, provides a theoretical basis for some tentative conclusions about the relationship between *demokratizatsiia* and democratization.[7] In particular, this literature helps resolve alternative interpretations: 'Gorbachev the revitalizer' and 'Gorbachev the democratizer.' The transitions literature also helps place Gorbachev's *demokratizatsiia* into the larger patterns of political changes that gripped the USSR.

This study uses a model of 'democratic crafting' proposed by Giuseppe Di Palma, but also uses work done on democratization by scholars such as Juan Linz, Guillermo O'Donnell, Adam Przeworski, and Philippe Schmitter. Di Palma's model was chosen for two reasons. First, *To Craft Democracies* was one of the first books in the democratization literature to specifically explore the Soviet case: it appeared when I needed help thinking about *demokratizatsiia*. Second, Di Palma's self-conscious optimism concerning the success of democracy in post-communist countries and his insistence that clearly-defined institutional forms are less important than the crafting of an initial agreement to compete for office offered an open-minded approach to institutional change in the Soviet case. Wary of charges of prejudice or non-objectivity, I wanted to at least consider the possibility that Gorbachev really wanted to create a revolutionary new form of democratic institution by reviving soviet-style government. Despite its application of Di Palma's model, this book lays no claim to comprehensive application or testing of democratization theory. This literature merely provides an analytical guide, a way to order and evaluate the complex political and institutional changes of *demokratizatsiia*.

Methods

The broad scale of this study was a conscious methodological choice. Elections and legislatures cannot be understood independently. Elections set the context for legislative politics. Legislative action influences representatives, the electorate, and the electoral system in both direct and indirect ways. Moreover, electoral and legislative reform are related over time: electoral campaigns and legislative reforms at the federal, republican, and local levels in both 1989 and 1990 were closely interconnected. A book more narrowly focussed on either legislative or electoral politics might fail to identify some of the fundamental elements of *demokratizatsiia*. A book focussed on 1989 or 1990, or on federal or republican politics, would be misleadingly incomplete.

Students of the final days of Soviet politics face a confusingly complex task; thus, readers deserve a series of methodological caveats. First, traditional Kremlinological analyses of shifting alliances in the party leadership are largely ignored here, not because the author considers the political maneuvers of Politburo members such as Yegor Ligachev or Alexander

Yakovlev unimportant, but because theoretical considerations make this type of evidence secondary for the questions at hand. Second, international aspects of democratization, processes referred to elsewhere as diffusion and demonstration effects, are not an explicit part of this study.[8] The influence of the fall of communism in Eastern Europe on the USSR, the effects of President Bush's speeches in Moscow and Kiev in 1991 shortly before the coup, or the echoes in Russian politics of change in Lithuania, deserve a type of in-depth attention that cannot be given here. Third, considering the fundamental nature and extended time frame of the changes at the federal level and in each of 15 widely different republics, this book can do little more than scratch the surface. Attention here is concentrated on Russia and, more specifically, Moscow. Any generalizations from Moscow to Russia or from Russia to any of the former republics of the USSR must be done with the greatest caution.[9]

Sources

The majority of the research for this study was completed during two trips to the USSR totalling fifteen months in 1988-1990. The political atmosphere created by perestroika allowed me to get unprecedented access to the political system, both its actors and institutions. In the summer of 1989, I found myself in a position unthinkable only a short time earlier: I was able to cold-call Supreme Soviet committees and, sometimes, be invited in. While in Moscow, I observed the 1989 and 1990 elections and conducted an interview program. I spoke with candidates, voters, deputies, campaign team members, electoral commission members, and a broad spectrum of other participants. Most crucially, I was able to explore the transformation as a process by following individual and organizational progress over the course of two campaigns. I collected a number of unpublished documents and electoral materials, including stenographic records of the first session of the USSR Supreme Soviet, campaign posters, leaflets, and other programmatic handouts. I was fortunate to have access to the stenographic records of the new USSR and Russian legislatures that are available at the Center on East-West Trade, Investment and Communications at Duke University. Last, and certainly not least, this book benefits from the flood of new information in the official and unofficial press.

Comparative Politics and Soviet Studies

Both the sweep of this study and the complexities of analyzing Soviet legislative and electoral politics call for at least an introductory discussion of three broad problems: the applicability of democratization theory to the Soviet case; the link between legislative and electoral institutions and the politics of the transition; the personalization of Soviet politics as reflected by Gorbachev, Yeltsin, and the fights between them.

The Democratization Literature and the Soviet Case

Students of Soviet politics, like the Soviet Union a short time ago, are at a crossroads. We desperately need to understand the processes of political change that have taken place in the USSR and will continue in coming decades in the shards of Gorbachev's reforms. Unfortunately, we were caught unprepared both theoretically and methodologically for the striking changes that have taken place. Who could have imagined even five years ago that real democratic change would soon be on the agenda? Moreover, the data now available across the spectrum of the social sciences, from politics to economics, from sociology to demography, are mind-boggling. Competent use of social science theory is the only way to take advantage of this unexpected bounty.

Theoretical and conceptual clarity, as Giovanni Sartori and others have argued, is a *sine qua non* of comparative politics. Thus, if studies of the new politics in the former republics of the USSR are to contribute to the accumulation of knowledge in comparative politics, we must maintain intellectual rigor. This is an especially vexing problem when discussing the relationships among democratization, the transformation of the Soviet system, and the fall of communism. Elements of three strands of the democratization literature demand special attention: structural prerequisites of democracy; regime-society interaction and the politics of transformation; and, attempts to construct a comparative logic of democratic transformation.

Structural preconditions of democracy such as wealth or levels of education have been the object of scholarly attention for several decades. Despite widespread disenchantment with the prerequisite-focused modernization approach, and although the movement toward the study of human agency and political possibilism inherent in later studies offer a more optimistic perspective on the problems and possibilities for democracy (while also suggesting explanations for the failure of democratization, one of the principal weak points in analyses arising out of the modernization school), it is important to remember that strong correlations exist between, for example, wealth and democracy, or democracy and market economies.[10] Those who reverse accepted wisdom and abandon the "language of prerequisites," assume a heavy burden of proof.[11] As Huntington argues, the importance of political factors should not "lead to a total rejection of broader, contextual, social, economic, and cultural factors in explaining democrat-

Introduction

ic development... all operate, often in conflicting ways, either to facilitate the creation of democracy or to sustain authoritarianism."[12] In short, if we ignore the conclusions of this literature, we may overestimate the chances for democratic change.

A second strand of the democratization literature explains outcomes by the political 'mode' of the transition, i.e. the type of politics that characterized regime-society interaction during the move away from authoritarianism. Huntington briefly summarizes terminology used to describe the modal types:

> For analytical purposes it is useful to group the cases into three broad types of processes. Transformation (or, in Linz's phrase *reforma*) occurred when the elites in power took the lead in bringing about democracy. Replacement (Linz's *ruptura*) occurred when opposition groups took the lead in bringing about democracy, and the authoritarian regime collapsed or was overthrown. What might be called transplacement or *"ruptforma"* occurred when democratization resulted from joint action by government and opposition groups. In virtually all cases groups both in power and out of power played some roles, and these categories simply distinguish the relative importance of government and opposition.[13]

Democratization, in the modal view, is a self-conscious political process based on the interaction of regimes and societies.

There are at least two problems with modal explanations that are especially troublesome when applying them to the Soviet case. First, focussing on regime-society interactions and the politics of democratization demands careful attention to problems of comparability. Although Soviet politics and society were far different from those in Latin America and Southern Europe upon which much of the democratization literature is based, some authors have uncritically applied these models to *demokratizatsiia*.[14] The contributions of modal explanations, perhaps best exemplified in the volume on transitions edited by O'Donnell and Schmitter, surely can help analysts of the Soviet case, but only if the peculiarities of the former USSR and its constituent republics are taken into account. At a minimum these peculiarities include a formal federal structure, a centralized, socialized economy and a population that only now is taking concrete organizational steps toward creating a civil society through the trade unions and political parties that are a key element of many modal explanations. A second, more troubling problem with this literature is its failure to explain outcomes. A growing number of analysts are starting to suggest that elements other than the mode of the transition, particularly institutional structure, may be more important to the success or failure of transitions from authoritarian rule.[15]

A third strand of democratization literature grew out of modal analysis and the literature's focus on political strategies of interested elites. Adam Pzerworski, perhaps the best-known advocate of this approach, calls for application to the study of transitions of a "formalistic, ahistorical approach inherent in the abstract theory of games." While searching for a comparative logic of democratic transformation, and starting to apply elements of formal game theory to the transition period, we cannot neglect to explore carefully the programs and politics of those elites and their 'democratization' programs.[16] Even if direct comparisons of the societies involved in the "third wave" of democratization and the USSR are questionable, it is, of course, legitimate and useful to entertain the possibility that Gorbachev wanted to democratize the USSR, or was forced down that road by a 'logic' to which he could only submit. Surely, we must try to identify the strategic elements of his political environment. We cannot, however, remain at the level of strategy. We need to explore implementation, muck around in the trenches of the political struggle. The temptation to posit logical alternatives, hidden strategies, and long-term strategic vision is great, yet dangerous. This study starts from the assumption that a sophisticated, in-depth understanding of goals and the institutional menu that influences them are just as significant as an appreciation of the strategies and tactics used to pursue them. Although one might argue, like Russell Bova, that "the goals of the old regime often become irrelevant" because "most efforts to transform authoritarian regimes take on a life and dynamic of their own," such an approach denies, at least in part, the very elements of human agency and institutional structure that are at the core of political explanations of democratization.[17] While purporting to identify the logic of democratization, such an approach encourages a tendency to start down a slippery slope into unclear language that obscures rather than explains. If Gorbachev's intentions do not matter, it seems, less attention need be paid to the concrete elements of his reform intitiatives. In short, an approach based on the 'logic' of democratization risks falling into the same trap that weakened old-time Kremlinology: stringing together selected quotations on official positions cannot identify the true politics in any system. Strategy divorced from goals and both the constraints and opportunities provided by institutional structure is irrelevant.

Elections, Legislatures, and the Transition

Most contemporary theories of democratization focus on the politics of the democratization process and suggest that the transition should be viewed as an open and open-ended game. In a study that concentrates on elections, legislatures, and the institutional basis of democracy, four elements of this game are important: first, the focus of the political approach to democratization is the self-interest of individuals; second, the role of legislative institutions in accounting for these interests during democratization is a matter of some debate; third, the rebirth or creation of civil society plays a central part in democratization efforts and is connected to both electoral and legislative politics; fourth, the role of economic power in the democratization game suggests that analysts should pay special attention to the transformation of centralized socialist economies.

Democratization and Personal Interests. A democratic system is a compromise about procedures and not about outcomes. Interests involved in the democratic compromise battle through the newly constructed institutions of a procedural democracy. Thus, the multiple, interconnected incentive structures of the modern party-state, where legislative, executive, and electoral politics are closely related in a complex net, are the only basis for genuine political democracy. The problem of democratization is to design and install a political incentive structure that is flexible enough to encourage career-minded politicians and elites to identify alternative approaches to solving pressing problems and adjust to shifting coalitions while being stable enough to stand the pressures that are an inevitable product of fundamental change. In short, institutional choices matter because they focus individual interests.

Democratization and Institutions. Adam Przeworski reminds us that democratic institutions must be adopted from a limited set: human imagination has produced a finite number of tested and workable models. He argues that during the transformation "the problem that thrusts itself to the center of the political agenda...is whether any institution that will allow open-ended, even if limited, contestation will be accepted by the relevant political forces."[18] Legislatures, executives, electoral systems, and party systems are the basic building blocks of democracies. The relationship of political institutions, and particularly the role of parliamentary politics, in the democratization process itself is, however, an open question. Liebert and Cotta, in a study of the legislatures of Southern Europe, phrase the question most directly: can parliament be a "central site of democratic instauration?"[19]

A simplified version of the debate over the role of institutions would identify two schools, one headed by Di Palma and one by Przeworski. Di Palma argues that institutions are irrelevant until after the creation of an agreement in principle by all concerned parties to compete democratically. This founding agreement can evolve over time, but specific institutional structures are not necessarily relevant to its creation. Indeed, a certain 'fuzziness' in institutional structures offers political advantages: participants who see what they want to see in any given institution are less likely to exit the game. "Poor institutional coherence may give democratic institutions a peculiar value in the eyes of opposing players." Przeworski, on the other hand, argues that the essence of any democratic agreement can be found in a nation's political institutions. Because democratic procedures are reflected in political institutions, constitutional decisions about legislatures, elections and parties are essential elements of any democratic transformation. The transition depends on clarity and vision: "institutions adopted as temporizing solutions will turn out to be just that." "The game [of democratization] is solved," he argues, "if a sytem of institutions that engenders spontaneous compliance is an equilibrium of the transition."[20]

The political role of the institutions of the party-state suggests four general guidelines for any study of democratization in the USSR. First, constitutions are important as the basis of concrete political agreements that reflect the basic elements of complex political patterns. Second, legislatures can tell us something about the intentions of constitutional architects. This is especially true in the Soviet case at the federal level, where the central party apparatus played the principal role in drafting and ratifying constitutional amendments that drastically altered the USSR's institutional structure. Third, the constitutional design of legislatures and their interface with electoral systems can tell us something about the possible outcomes of reform efforts.[21] Fourth, negative findings in the study of democratization and legislative politics are just as significant as positive findings. That is, if an analysis of the interwoven incentive structures of legislative and electoral politics does not lead one somewhere near the heart of the political organism, one is forced to ask why. Legislative and electoral politics serve as excellent foils to examine the key elements of any purportedly democratic political system.

Democratization and Civil Society. A third principal element of the democratizations literature is a focus on civil society and the importance of the birth or resurrection of civil society in the transformation from authoritarian rule. One should note, however, that the rebirth of civil society in a politically constructive sense, especially in the atomized populations of post-communist regimes, must eventually lead to the creation of political organizations. While central authorities wield liberalization as a tactical tool in political reform, new political groups, parties and other organizations can attempt to organize the electorate and push democratic change.

Despite the importance of the rebirth of civil society for arguments advanced in the democratization literature, as Daniel Levine has noted, it "is treated in general and abstract terms, with insufficient attention to specific

Introduction

groups and to the *organized* relations that bind sectors and movements to the leaders, structures, and institutions of national life."[22] This study of democratization in the USSR starts from the assumption that if individuals and groups are to be politically relevant in a nation that has made a commitment to the procedural forms of the democratic game, they must organize society and, eventually, react to its demands through electoral links. Thus, it becomes crucial to study the birth or rebirth of electoral politics.

Democratization and Economic Reform. While it would be an exaggeration to say that too much attention is paid in the literature to the problems of economic reform and the terrors that economic distress holds for proponents of democratization, it also would be accurate to note that too little attention is paid to the *institutional politics* of economic reform and democratization. Reading Przeworski, for example, one is struck both by his argument that democratic solutions can only be found in a limited number of institutions and his observation that we know little about their relative merits. Clearly, an exploration of electoral and legislative politics in the Soviet case can contribute to this important new discussion.

If one starts from the assumption that transitions in post- communist societies involve both political *and* economic re- empowerment, a focus on the institutions points to the importance of two key problems. First, if democracy and democratization are about procedures and about redesigning incentive structures to insure that all interests are accounted for, one needs to design an institutional system that will work efficiently to reflect those interests. At the same time, however, the system should not preclude painful economic choices that will rebuild empowering economic institutions like property rights, monetary systems, or tax codes. Second, institutional change highlights the existence of what one might call separate political and economic cycles of reform. Presidents, for example, are elected with a degree of public support for a constitutionally-defined period of time. If a president squanders that 'mandate' before his formal political tenure is over, political stagnation in the form of a lame duck executive threatens. In parliamentary systems the problem is often the opposite. Governments fall repeatedly over the fundamental questions of reform while nothing gets done. The problem that post-communist states face in the transition is to find an institutional solution or set of solutions that will help the political and economic cycles of transformation mesh or, at least, interfere minimally with each other.

Personification and Soviet Politics

A process that one might call the personification of Soviet politics was one of the most noticeable elements of the transition period. Both in the

USSR and around the globe, Gorbachev personified perestroika. Yeltsin's startling 1989 campaign for the USSR Congress of People's Deputies was successful in large part because he became a human symbol of defiance of the party apparat. In August 1991, Yeltsin embodied Russian democracy as he denounced the coup and rallied support from the turret of a tank. The fierce personal and political struggle between Gorbachev and Yeltsin from October 1987 through December 1991 captured unprecedented media attention as the world watched the disintegration of the USSR.

Great personalities almost always play a role in historically striking political transformations. Unfortunately, however, the personification of Soviet politics encouraged both voters and analysts to forget that the interwoven incentive structures of a modern political democracy depends on the creation of a party-state. This problem was magnified by Gorbachev's successful bid, through his program of *demokratizatsiia*, to invoke the symbols of democracy and thereby define the terms of debate for the entire globe. 'Gorbomania' was a reality: it helped tear apart the Communist order in Central Europe.

Personal political choices, for example Gorbachev's shift to the right in the fall of 1990 and rejection of the radical '500-days' plan for economic reform, are not merely a result of tactical movements on a standard political spectrum, but are strongly influenced by institutional possibilities and political inertia arising from institutional choices made in previous rounds of the transition game. Indeed, one of the key problems of the transition is to produce a political incentive structure that will limit personification and encourage the growth of democratic political organizations. Analysis of the institutional elements of the transition period is one way to avoid the temptation to focus exclusively on interesting personalities and their tactical maneuvering. This book, a study of the political transformation of the USSR, cannot ignore Gorbachev, Yeltsin, or other politicians; nonetheless, the focus here is on institutional changes that were aimed at the political and economic empowerment of the former USSR.[23]

Notes

1. See *Perestroika i novoe myshlenie dlia nashei strany i dlia vsego mira*, Moscow: Politicheskaia literatura, 1988, pp. 18–19, 44–45, and esp. pp. 51–52. Thane Gustafson presents a similar argument in "The Crisis of the Soviet System of Power and Mikhail Gorbachev's Political Strategy," in Seweryn Bialer and Michael Mandelbaum, eds., *Gorbachev's Russia and American Foreign Policy*, Westview: Boulder, 1988. pp. 200–210. See also I. Kliamkin, "Logika vlasti i logika oppozitsii: Pochemu Gorbachev

soglasilsia na prezidentskuiu sistemu?," *Cherez ternii,* Moscow: Progress, 1990, pp. 701-719. T.H. Rigby addresses the problem of power, or the absence of it, in *The Changing Soviet System,* Vermont: Edward Elgar, 1990, p. 222.

2. *XIX Vsesoiuznaia konferentsiia kommunisticheskoi partii sovetskogo soiuza, Stenograficheskii otchet,* Vol. 1, Moscow: Politizdat, 1988. For a discussion of the reality of 'soviet power' see "Chto takoe sovetskaia vlast, i byla li ona u nas?," *Narodnyi Deputat,* No. 14, 1990, pp. 53-58. F.M. Burlatskii offers some bitter backstage commentary on the decision to revitalize 'soviet-style' government in "Alternativa drobleniiu levykh sil— dvizhenie k sotsialnoi demokratii," *Literaturnaia gazeta,* 1 January 1991, p. 5.

3. For a discussion of theoretical and practical differences between soviets and parliaments see V. Sirotkin, "Sovety i parliamentarizm," *Narodnyi Deputat,* No. 17, 1991, pp. 4-7. For a discussion of the foundations of the Soviet system see Barrington Moore, *Soviet Politics: The Dilemma of Power,* New York: Harper and Row, 1970.

4. On the question of power in a comparative political context see Jerry F. Hough, "The Soviet Experience and the Measurement of Power," *The Journal of Politics,* Vol. 37, No. 3, pp. 685-710. William E. Odom reflected on the relationship between political power and political analysis in "A Dissenting View on the Group Approach to Soviet Politics," *World Politics,* No. 28, 1976, pp. 542-567.

5. Leonard Schapiro, *The Communist Party of the Soviet Union,* New York: Random House, 1959, p. 590. On the applicability of Leninist standards to *demokratizatsiia* in the party see Ronald J. Hill, "The CPSU: From Monolith to Pluralist?," *Soviet Studies,* No. 2, 1991, pp. 217-237.

6. Stephen F. Cohen, "What's Really Happening in Russia?," *The Nation,* 2 March 1992, p. 259. Samuel P. Huntington, *The Third Wave: Democratization in the Late Twentieth Century,* Norman: University of Oklahoma Press, 1991, p. 129.

7. For reviews of the transitions literature as it relates to Soviet politics see Russell Bova, "Dynamics of the Post-Communist Transition: A Comparative Perspective," *World Politics,* Vol. 44, No. 1, pp. 113-139 and Thomas F. Remington, "Regime Transition in Communist Systems: The Soviet Case," *Soviet Economy,* Vol. 6, No. 2, 1990. Georger W. Breslauer discusses the transformations literature and applies it to the Soviet case in "Evaluating Gorbachev as Leader," *Soviet Economy,* Vol. 5, No. 4, 1989.

8. For Di Palma's discussion of diffusion and demonstration effects, see *To Craft Democracies,* pp. 14-17. Larry Diamond discusses international strategies for democratization in "Beyond Authoritarianism and Totalitarianism: Strategies for Democratization," *The Washington Quarterly,*

Winter 1989, pp. 141–163.

9. Material that would have made the description of new institutions more complete can, thankfully, be found elsewhere. Robert T. Huber and Donald R. Kelley edited a volume that stands as the best introduction to legislative and executive institutions at the all-union level. See *Perestroika-Era Politics: The New Soviet Legislature and Gorbachev's Political Reforms*, New York: M.E. Sharpe, 1991. Ed A. Hewett and Victor H. Winston compiled a number of the best articles on politics at the end of the Soviet era in their edited volume, *Milestones in Glasnost and Perestroyka: Politics and People*, Washington: Brookings, 1991. Reports published by the Radio Liberty/Radio Free Europe Research Institute are most helpful in following institutional changes. Some textbooks do a good job. See, for example, D.P. Hammer, *Politics of Oligarchy*, third edition, Boulder: Westview Press, 1991.

10. See Huntington, *The Third Wave*, esp. p. 37.

11. G. Di Palma, "Why Democracy Can Work in Eastern Europe," *Journal of Democracy*, Vol. 2, No. 1, Winter 1991, p. 28.

12. Huntington, p. 39.

13. Ibid., p. 114.

14. For a discussion of the economic and political peculiarities of the Soviet case see A. Migranyan, "Dolgii put k evropeiskomu domu," *Novyi Mir*, No. 7, 1989, pp. 166–184.

15. This was one conclusion reached at a session of the Duke-UNC seminar mentioned in the acknowledgments.

16. For a classification of adherents of this approach see David Collier and Deborah L. Norden, "Strategic Choice Models of Political Change in Latin America," *Comparative Politics*, Vol. 24, No. 2, 1992, pp. 229–244.

17. Bova, "Political Dynamics of the Post-Communist Transition," pp. 113-138. Daniel H. Levine discusses the problems of definition of democracy and democratization in a review of O'Donnell and Schmitter's *Transitions....* See "Paradigm Lost: Dependence to Democracy," *World Politics*.

18. Adam Przeworski, *Democracy and the Market: Political and Economic Reform in Eastern Europe and Latin America*, New York: Cambridge University Press, 1991, p. 39.

19. Ulrike Liebert and Maurizio Cotta, *Parliament and Democratic Consolidation in Southern Europe: Greece, Italy, Portugal, Spain, and Turkey*, New York: Pinter, 1990.

20. Przeworski, pp. 94, 39.

21. Work by Michael Mezey and Marvin Weinbaum, for example, outlined the role that legislatures play in developing democracies around the world. Jewell's, Lijphart's, and Horowitz's studies of the role of electoral

Introduction

systems in divided societies can also play a key role in analyzing the transformation of the political systems in the former republics of the USSR. A series of volumes published by Duke University Press in the early 1970s is the best place to start to explore this literature. See, for example, Durham: Duke University Press, 1972.

22. Levine, "Paradigm Lost...," p. 379.

23. A collection of speeches and commentary, organized chronologically, documents the confrontation between Gorbachev and Yeltsin. This is an outstanding resource for anyone interested in the final days of the Soviet era. See *1500 Dnei Politicheskogo Protivostoianiia*, Moscow: Terra, 1992.

Chapter 2

Democratization?

It is difficult to understand *demokratizatsiia* without a firm base in the *old* Soviet politics: Gorbachev's reform program, particularly his institutional choices, milked the taproot of Soviet political history. The first three sections of this chapter set an historical context for subsequent analysis by discussing Lenin's view of the soviets, Stalin and the post-Stalin consensus on the soviets, and soviet-style government in the early 1980s.[1] Historical analogies, however, cannot clarify completely the problems confronted by students of Soviet politics. This chapter, therefore, takes two additional steps. First, it creates a Leninist benchmark to measure the depth and breadth of change.[2] Second, it outlines some contemporary thought on democratization and suggests how such work can be applied to the Soviet case.

Soviet Power and Lenin's Legacy

Peasants, soldiers, and workers formed the first soviets during the Russian Empire's 1905 revolution. Local strike committees developed into councils, or soviets, that took control of work collectives and, later, of urban and rural areas. Deputies were elected to the soviets in both direct and indirect elections and could be recalled by popular demand. Although the situation was chaotic and electoral procedures poorly developed, the soviets clearly were a nascent form of popular representation.

Lenin's attitude toward the soviets was formed between 1905 and 1907 and changed little in the period up to 1917. "The soviet of workers' deputies," he argued, "is not a workers' parliament nor any instrument of proletarian self-government...but a militant organization for the attainment of specific goals." He insisted on the Bolsheviks' claim to leadership of the revolutionary movement and, consequently, in the soviets. Noting this instrumental view of the soviets, Oskar Anweiler argued that "the basic contradiction of the Bolshevik system, which purports to be a democracy of all working people but in reality recognizes the rule of only one party, is already contained in Lenin's interpretation of the soviets during the first Russian revolution."[3]

The revival of thousands of soviets in the revolutionary upheavals of 1917 demonstrated the hold on popular consciousness they achieved in 1905. A Congress of Soviets, composed of representatives of local soviets from across the empire met for the first time in Petersburg in June 1917. The Congress elected a Central Executive Committee (CEC) that exercised all powers of the larger body between sessions. Until October 1917, the Congress of Soviets and its CEC shared power with the Provisional Government. The two institutions cooperated for a time, but mutually exclusive claims to legitimacy destabilized the system. Lenin probably issued his famous slogan, "All power to the soviets!" in April 1917 to hasten its collapse.[4] As Leonard Schapiro pointed out, "it is unlikely that [the Bolsheviks'] emphasis on winning over a majority in the soviets [was] anything more than a tactical recognition of the popular support which the soviets enjoyed."[5]

After taking power, Lenin could no longer consider the soviets "organs of the insurrection," so he redefined them and argued that, "Soviet power is nothing but the organizational form of the dictatorship of the proletariat." In reality of course, the 'dictatorship of the proletariat' soon became a Bolshevik dictatorship as the party moved to control the new government. On 8 November 1917, the Congress of Soviets created a new executive body, the Council of People's Commissars (*Sovnarkom*). Lenin used Bolshevik predominance in the *Sovnarkom* to reinforce his party's position elsewhere. The CEC gave the *Sovnarkom* the right to issue without prior approval decrees "within the general framework of the program of the Congress of Soviets." This decision established the executive's, and by extension the party's, power to dictate decisions to the CEC.

The 8th Party Congress in 1919 decided the fate of the soviets. Lenin acknowledged that "the soviets, which by virtue of their program are organs of government by the working people, are in fact organs of government for the working people by the advanced section of the proletariat, but not by the working people as a whole." Despite this inconsistency of theory and practice, and in part because of it, he stressed two themes. First, Soviet democracy was an immeasurably higher and more progressive form of democracy than bourgeois parliamentarism. Second, a division of functions should be established between the party and the soviets.[6] Finessing the question of whether it would be necessary to choose between the party and the soviets, Lenin argued that "the solution is without doubt both the soviets of workers deputies *and* the party. The question...consists only in what ways to divide and in what ways to share the tasks of the soviets and the tasks of the party."[7]

The problem of dual power was resolved quite easily—the soviets became rubber stamps. On 10 July 1918, the Congress of Soviets ratified the RSFSR's first constitution, which institutionalized the soviets as the basic building block of government while saying nothing about the role of the Communist Party. This constitution abandoned the 'bourgeois' concept of separation of powers, further strengthening the power of the party and the executive over the soviets. Addressing the Congress, Lenin argued that bourgeois constitutions, which take into account, "the internal struggle of separate groups of bourgeois society, have set up an artificial separation between individual elements of power (legislative, executive, judicial)." "We," he argued, "aim to concentrate as far as possible all these elements."[8] On 31 January 1924, just days after Lenin's death, the Congress of Soviets ratified a constitution that established the Union of Soviet Socialist Republics. The structure of power outlined in this new document, like the one ratified in 1918, did not reflect the way that the system actually worked. The 1924 constitution, as Merle Fainsod argued in his classic study of Soviet government, hid "the dominating role of the party...behind an elaborate array of pseudo-representative institutions."[9] In short, Lenin founded a nation based on the slogan "All power to the soviets!" while systematically undercutting the ethos of soviet power, popular rule.

Stalin and the Post-Stalin Consensus

In 1935, Stalin decided to institutionalize the status quo with a new constitution. According to the so-called *Short Course*, Stalin's fabricated history of the Communist Party, the new constitution "gave legislative embodiment to the epoch-making fact that the USSR had entered a new stage of development, the stage of the completion of the building of a socialist society and the gradual transition to Communist society." Ratified in 1936, this constitution revised the institutional structure of the political system. The unicameral Congress of Soviets was replaced by a Supreme Soviet, an institution whose two chambers were created to provide at least formal recognition of the USSR's federal, multinational structure. Although the Supreme Soviet was declared the highest organ of state power, like its predecessor it played only a symbolic role.[10] Summarizing the relationship between Stalinism and soviet-style government, Anweiler concluded that

"Stalinism, with its coercive machinery, police, army, and bureaucracy, was the final denial of the original Soviet idea."[11]

Khrushchev

The CPSU's 20th Party Congress in 1956 usually is remembered for Khrushchev's so-called 'secret speech.' This congress, however, played a less-noticed role in de-Stalinization by starting the formal activization of the soviets, a process that would continue for decades with few tangible results. Khrushchev criticized party supervision of the soviets in a long list of "grave shortcomings" and "outright deviations from the Soviet Constitution." These shortcomings included deputies' failure to report to their constituents, the absence of recall campaigns for deputies who failed to "justify the trust placed in them," and the failure of the Supreme Soviets of the union and autonomous republics to meet twice per year as constitutionally required. Khrushchev claimed it was necessary "to put an end to these defects in the work of the soviets, to strengthen their ties with the electorate, and to observe strictly all the provisions of the constitution." He argued that the soviets should attend to concrete questions of development. "It is through the soviets that economic, organizational, cultural, and educational functions of the socialist state are exercised... That is why it is the duty of our party organizations to keep close to the soviets."[12] Arguing that the masses should participate in managing the state, he concluded that, soviet democracy should be developed "in all possible ways." Resolutions ratified at the congress directed party organizations to activate the soviets and demanded that they "decisively strengthen [their] role in economic and cultural construction."[13]

On 22 January 1957, in accordance with resolutions of the 20th Party Congress, the Central Committee published a decree that instructed party committees and the ministerial apparatus to revitalize the soviets. The decree urged CPSU party committees to activate the leadership of party members and party groups in the soviets and their executive committees. Party groups in the soviets, it claimed, "unsatisfactorily fulfill their functions defined by the party statute. Their work... has a formal character, they rarely meet, and they do not discuss the work of the party members in any given soviet. Such a situation... does harm to the task of party leadership of the soviets."[14] The directive encouraged party members in the soviets to exercise their powers to draft legislation and monitor policy implementation. During the next two years, a series of legislative acts were passed to more clearly define and regulate the Supreme Soviet's rights.[15]

In 1961, the 22nd Party Congress ratified revised versions of the party program and the party statute. Both documents called for the activization of the soviets. Discussing the view of the development of the political system set out in these documents, Khrushchev claimed that "proletarian democracy" was becoming "socialist democracy of the whole people."[16] He argued that "tens of millions of Soviet people" should participate in government adminstration and advocated "perfecting the forms of popular representation," i.e. the soviets.[17] The socialist state, he said, was entering a new stage of development. Instead of serving the dictatorship of the proletariat, the state would become an organization "embracing the entire people." The soviets, therefore, would eventually "be transformed into organs of public self-government." The new program called for the activization of the soviets, including both their deputies and standing commissions. Deputies should be freed from other employment "to promote improvement in the work of legislative organs, and the strengthening of their monitoring of executive organs.' Khrushchev argued that "the standing commissions of the Supreme Soviets should systematically monitor the activity of [the executive] and actively promote implementation of decisions."[18] The program called for expanding the role of the soviets "to make final decisions on all questions of local significance." To promote participation, at least one-third of all deputies were to be replaced at each election. To strengthen control over the executive, the soviets' standing commissions were to be enlarged.

Khrushchev emphasized "the task of steadily perfecting government bodies and reorganizing [the soviets into] bodies of self-government." He argued that they should become "working corporations performing the practical function of managing the economic and social processes that Marx and Lenin had in mind when analyzing the nature of truly popular power," and that "many of the matters which are today allotted to the competence of the executive should be handled directly by the soviets and their committees."[19] However, despite Khrushchev's wide-ranging proposals concerning the soviets, no meaningful changes were made. Like many of the developments promised in the 1961 party program, the transfer of power to the people through participation in the soviets never happened. By October 1964, Khrushchev was a pensioner.

Brezhnev

The transition from Khrushchev to Brezhnev in 1964 did not halt the formal activization of the soviets; however, the process acquired a different conceptual basis. During the Brevhnev era, the soviets and their deputies were no longer expected to replace the executive and create a people-run government; instead, they were asked, at least in theory, to play a role in helping monitor the implementation of public policy. In this sense, they fit into the broad outlines of Brezhnev's campaign for scientific management and political and economic stability. In practice, of course, the soviets never played a significant role.

Brezhnev's first 18 months in office were dedicated to the abolition of Khrushchev's 'hare-brained schemes.' In March 1966, the 23rd Party Congress renounced the rotation of cadres, a policy that threatened the positions of party officials.[20] At the same time, this congress continued the formal activization of the soviets, encouraging them both to exercise dormant powers, and to take the initiative in resolving issues within their competence.[21] Brezhnev argued that the soviets could be improved through a process that he called *demokratizatsiia*: longer, more significant sessions, strengthened standing commissions, and more active deputies. The USSR Supreme Soviet and the union republic Supreme Soviets should play a more substantial role through the formation of new standing commissions.[22]

In a campaign speech for elections to the Supreme Soviet in June 1966, Brezhnev called for strengthening the soviets and improving their ties with workers.[23] Soon thereafter, in accord with the decisions of the 23rd Party Congress, the party started a sweeping set of changes in the Supreme Soviet. On 3 August 1966, the number of its standing commissions was increased from 4 to 11. Seven industrial 'branch commissions' were added to the Supreme Soviet's original four commissions (mandate, legislative proposals, budget, foreign affairs).[24] Brezhnev called for improved ties between the commissions and executive organs, strengthening their monitoring powers, and improving their work by making it easier to add specialized personnel to check policy implementation.[25]

Formal recognition of the role of the soviets continued throughout the Brezhnev era, and was not limited merely to his acquisition of the chairmanship of the Supreme Soviet's Presidium. In June 1977, for example, the Presidium met to discuss its own activities and the work of the standing commissions and the Supreme Soviet. Addressing the meeting, Brezhnev argued that "it is useless to write laws if they are not fulfilled." He called for the Supreme Soviet, its Presidium, and its standing commissions "to monitor...the implementation of economic plans and state budgets."[26] The 1977 Constitution strengthened the formal standing of the Supreme Soviet's standing commissions. On 22 May 1979, the Supreme Soviet's Presidium published a decree that emphasized the need to improve sessions of the soviets, strengthen the work of the standing committees and executive committees, and "stubbornly excise formalism and the practice of keeping quiet about insufficiencies and problems." In February 1981, the 26th Party Congress called for the activization of the soviets' powers to monitor the implementation of legislation and the observance of the law. The congress emphasized the necessity of each meeting of a soviet's standing commissions to become a "group of people in a collective search for correct decisions."[27] Shortly after this congress, the Central Committee published a decree calling for the further activization of the soviets' monitoring functions. Party committees were criticized for poor efforts in coordinating and directing the work of the soviets.[28]

Andropov and Chernenko

The formal activization of the soviets continued throughout the tenures as General Secretary of Iurii Andropov and Konstantin Chernenko. The Central Committee Plenum that elected Chernenko simultaneously ratified a statement that called for revitalization. This document undoubtedly was prepared while Andropov was still alive; therefore, it is not unlikely that Gorbachev, Andropov's right-hand man, played a major role in drafting its principal arguments. In any case, information distributed exclusively to Supreme Soviet deputies emphasized that the April 1984 CPSU Central Committee plenum demanded that "the nationwide realization of a definite turning-point in the work of the soviets." The improvements in the soviets were viewed as one part of a larger plan to "strengthen and develop positive tendencies in the economy."[29] Although Chernenko, like his immediate predecessor, died long before these so-called positive tendencies could develop, a "definite turning point" was not far off. Indeed, the definition of the turning point sounded suspiciously like proposals Gorbachev would soon advance.

Soviet Power in the Early 1980s

The difference between the theory of soviet government and the reality of the early 1980s is well demonstrated by a brief review of the Supreme Soviet's activities. According to the 1977 Constitution, the Supreme Soviet was the USSR's highest body of state authority. Despite an impressive list of constitutional responsibilities, it exercised no real power. The Secretariat of the Commuist Party's Central Committee and the Council of Ministers prepared virtually all legislation, only a fraction of which was given to the Supreme Soviet to be rubber-stamped.[30] Perhaps the clearest indication of the gap between theory and practice in the Supreme Soviet's work was provided by its commissions.

In 1984, the Supreme Soviet's two chambers, the Soviet of the Union and the Soviet of Nationalities, elected identical systems of 17 standing commissions oriented around traditional matters of state, economic affairs, and major facets of social and cultural life.[31] Aside from the credentials, legislative proposals, foreign affairs, and planning and budget commissions, neither the number of commissions nor their bailiwicks were prescribed by law. Approximately 60% of Supreme Soviet deputies in each convocation were standing commission members and served throughout their five-year terms. At the first Supreme Soviet session after elections, nomination lists of commission members, chairmen, vice-chairmen, and secretaries were presented to each of the chambers and ratified unanimously. The commissions had 35 members each, except for the planning and budget commissions, which had 45 members.

The commissions never exercised their formal powers, and, on average, met only once or twice per year. The Central Committee apparat controlled them in two principal ways. First, there were limits to the subjects within their jurisdiction. For example, there were no commissions for national security matters or defense and the armed forces. Second, the Secretariat of the Supreme Soviet's Presidium managed the commissions, which had no staffs or budgets of their own.[32] All work was done by consultants from the Secretariat and was carefully planned ahead of time, usually two questions per year.[33] A.A. Logunov, chairman of the youth affairs commission in the Soviet of the Union during the final convocation of the old Supreme Soviet, often went weeks without doing any commission work. He never exercised his formal rights and powers. When necessary, he would travel downtown from his job as rector of Moscow State University to speak with consultants from the Secretariat who provided "advice" on preparations for commission meetings.[34]

Like chairmen, commission members had no power. Robert Siegler, in one of the only western analyses of the old Supreme Soviet, argued that commission membership was best analyzed in terms of two sub-groups, 'the practical support group' and 'leadership collegia people.' The 'leadership collegia,' composed of intellectuals, specialists, and leadership elites from various sectors of society, consisted almost invariably of party members and were responsible for most of the commissions' work. According to Siegler, commissions benefitted from the work experience of the 'practical support group,' which consisted of the approximately two-thirds of the membership of each commission who were working-class deputies.[35] Interviews with Presidium consultants suggest that this interpretation of the committees was off target. Workers rarely played an active role in commission work and sometimes were not allowed to participate at all. Often, they were handed a script to read. Scripted parts were not, however, confined to workers. In some commissions, the consultants wrote the speeches and presentations for *all* participants.[36]

The standing commissions' powers fell into two spheres, drafting legislation and monitoring policy implementation. The work done in 1987 by the legislative proposals standing commissions concerning the law on individual labor activity is one good example of this process. According to Deputy L.V. Sharova, a commission member, a draft project of the law on individual labor activity, "worked out in accordance with the decisions of the 27th Party Congress and...the constitution," was first discussed by the Politburo and then reviewed by a series of government agencies and ministries. The commissions eventually were given a draft that was not intended to be revised. A special deputorial preparatory group and later the commissions and the Supreme Soviet all played the role of rubber stamps.[37]

The second principal function of the commission system, monitoring policy implementation, was also controlled by consultants from the Presidium's Secretariat. Work plans on any given question generally contained lists of members of the preparatory group, places to gather information, necessary trips, and specialists to invite as well as all deadlines for completion of the work. Sometimes a small group of deputies would make a brief fact-finding trip arranged by the consultants. Prior to the commission meeting, all materials considered relevant by the consultants were mailed to the deputies, although sometimes these materials were sent late, and sometimes not at all. Members of preparatory groups received materials three weeks in advance and were asked to comment by phone. These comments were included in a draft of the commissions' conclusions that was discussed at a meeting of the preparatory group a few days before the meeting of the whole commission.

Commission meetings were always held in the Kremlin. To promote discussion, consultants sometimes arranged confrontations by reading stenograms from past commission meetings, picking out unfulfilled promises by ministers, and giving them to deputies in the form of questions.[38] Although some meetings produced heated debates, one veteran consultant found it difficult to point to specific examples where these debates led to changes. After the meetings, a document that contained the commissions' recommendations was drafted by the consultants, signed by the chairmen, and sent to the Council of Ministers, which distributed it to the relevant executive organs, which in theory, were required to send answers to the commissions. Ministerial reactions were not prompt when they were sent at all. Consultants summarized these answers and wrote speeches that the commission chairmen presented at Presidium meetings.[39]

In sum, the Supreme Soviet was a rubber stamp. Its deputies and commissions played no real role in the creation and implementation of public policy. 'Soviet power' was a Potemkin village.

Theoretical Frameworks

A summary of the growth of 'Soviet power' is useful when placing *demokratizatsiia* into the context of Soviet political history, or when analyzing the political background of choices made by the so-called 'children of the 20th Party Congress,' i.e. Gorbachev's generation. Nonetheless, the analysis of *demokratizatsiia* requires a consistent set of standards. This section sets out a framework based on the advantages that Soviet scholars claimed Leninist 'soviet-style' government had over 'bourgeois parliamentarism.'

A Leninist Framework

Leadership. Until shortly before taking power, Lenin probably never thought that his ambitions could lead so far; instead, he focused his attention on the problem of leading a conspiratorial, revolutionary party dedicated to the overthrow of an autocratic empire. Through a combination of political necessity and internal political skirmishing, the party's organizational principle became democratic centralism, a doctrine that allegedly allowed for full discussion of all problems facing the party organization and for unity of action after a decision was made. Although Stalin destroyed whatever remained of inner-party democracy, Lenin's democratic centralism, in practice, served as the organizational basis for the Soviet political system. As early as 1903, Trotsky pointed out that if one applied Lenin's formula, "the organization of the party takes the place of the party itself; the Central Committee takes the place of the organization; and finally the dictator takes the place of the Central Committee."[40] Lenin's semantic identification of the party's interests with those of the proletariat, and the proletariat and the peasantry's interests with those of the nation, left little room for political leadership understood as a voluntary and contingent relationship between party members, party organizations, private citizens, and the state.[41]

Lenin designed the country's political and economic systems to conform to Bolshevik principles. Early in 1917, for tactical reasons, he advocated 'revolutionary self-government' and radical decentralization. After Lenin took power, economic chaos and civil war encouraged him to abandon this tactic. Confronting a crisis, he turned to a solution that had worked before, democratic centralism. Party political leadership based on the ideology of Marxism-Leninism and implemented through the doctrine of democratic centralism could produce, he argued, unified, decisive administration. This, therefore, was the chief alleged advantage of soviet-style government.

Despite the ideals set out at the 8th Party Congress, party organs never concentrated on strategic 'political leadership,' but were constantly dragged into detailed questions of economic management. Indeed, politics in any system is in the details. Thus, political inertia led to constant undermining of the soviets. 'Political leadership' became the responsibility of party committees from outside the soviets, whose meetings became a type of absurd political theater.

Accountability. Lenin justified his political decisions, at least formally, on a class basis. The state was an instrument to be used by the working class in the defense of its own interests. The alleged advantage of soviet government was that, for the first time in history, the state was accountable to and run by the broad masses of the people. From an instrument of oppression of the majority by a minority, the state had become the means for humans and human society to reach their full potential. Through a simple process of self-definition, the Bolsheviks, as the avantgarde of the working class, became an arbiter, accountable to no one.

Lenin split political leadership and accountability. Both existed, but in forms where they no longer harnessed private interest to a contingently-defined public good. The Bolsheviks' monopolism and the absence of accountability at the ballot box led the Soviet Union into the horrors of Stalinism. The lack of accountability and leadership *inside* the party produced the slow decay of Brezhnevism. One important corollary of the self-defined leading role of the party and the split of leadership and accountability, a *de facto* division of labor, was established between party committees and the executive. This division of labor allowed the executive to acquire a life of its own and, eventually, run amok. The system reached its apotheosis under Brezhnev, when its inherent weaknesses led the USSR into socioeconomic stagnation. The party itself grew out of control and became a sprawling umbrella organization of republican and oblast fiefdoms.

Representation. The soviets allegedly provided a type of direct democracy in which the working class governed itself. The membership composition of the soviets was intended to reflect the demographic makeup of the population. These factors promoted the concepts of worker-deputies, i.e. non-professional, part-time representatives. The soviets were 'working institutions' where, in theory, deputies were able both to keep in close contact with their constituencies and bring to bear on policy problems the expertise that they derived from full-time employment. Moreover, the argument went, deputies were not held captive by the type of wealthy special interests who fund the expensive campaigns common elsewhere. In this way, soviet-style government allegedly insured the opportunity for the participation of all interested citizens. Although some effort was made to project an image of representation through the tradition of *nakazy*, a system whereby deputies 'brought home the bacon' by 'ensuring' the construction of housing or the provision of services, in reality the soviets were powerless.

Executive-Legislative Relations. The elimination of the distinction between legislative and executive institutions and a centralized 'planned' economy were seen as other key advantages of soviet-style government. Theoretically, the soviets thereby avoided the negative features of traditional parliaments where "an omnipotent state apparatus actually decides affairs of state behind a facade of representative bodies."[42] The soviets, as the highest organs of state power, not only made decisions but also, in theory, implemented them. Through their deputies, the soviets put laws and decisions into effect. Lenin once pointed out that deputies "themselves have to work, have to execute their own laws, have themselves to test the results achieved in reality, and to account directly to their constituents." Therefore, "there is *no* parliamentarianism here as a special system, as the division of labor between the legislative and the executive, as a privileged position for the deputies."[43]

Legislative-executive interaction in the soviet system was alleged to be superior both to parliamentary systems and systems characterized by a separation of powers. Deputies could see and control the results of their legislative activity because they retained full-time jobs and met infrequently. In theory, the economy was planned and controlled by a system of executive organs that worked in harmony with soviet power. In reality, the soviets were subordinate to party fiat. At national, republican, and local levels soviet deputies were powerless to create or control public policy.

The Transitions Literature

What is the relationship between *demokratizatsiia* and democratization? USSR People's Deputy Iurii Afanasev argued that the two words have nothing in common: *demokratizatsiia*, was an attempt by the CPSU apparat to preserve its privileged position in an altered guise. Conservative Communists shared a different view: *demokratizatsiia* handed government to a rabble of power-hungry pseudo-democrats and led to the disintegration of both the socialist camp and the USSR.[44] The comparative politics literature on democratization is one place to turn for help in sorting out these interpretations and understanding the overall process. The best place to start is by defining briefly three concepts: democracy, liberalization, and democratization.

In one principal work in the transitions field, O'Donnell and Schmitter argue that modern political democracy is based on a type of contingent consent among political actors who "agree to compete in such a way that those who win greater electoral support will exercise their temporary political superiority in such a way as not to impede those who may win greater support in the future from taking office." Losers agree to respect the contingent authority of the winners in exchange for a guaranteed right to fight for office in the future. Or, in Przeworski's words, "democracy is a system in which parties lose elections."[45]

Liberalization and democratization, key elements of any transition from authoritarianism, can be related but are not necessarily linked. Authoritarian rulers may support liberalization, "opening up certain spaces for individual and group action," to "relieve various pressures and obtain needed information and support without altering the structure of authority." Democratization, on the other hand, refers to a process by which "the rules and processes of citizenship," a packet of freedoms including the right to compete for office, are acquired by people and institutions." Liberalization and democratization are linked only when political systems are moving toward a standard of political contingency. "Without the guarantees of individual and group freedoms inherent in [liberalization], the [democratization] risks degenerating into mere formalism... Without the accountability... institutionalized under [democratization], liberalization may prove to be easily manipulated."[46]

Democratization and Political Crafting. O'Donnell and Schmitter compare the transition, metaphorically, to a wild three-dimensional chess game: players challenge the rules on every move, push and shove to get to the board, shout out advice and threats from the sidelines, and try to cheat wherever they can. Participants, they claim, become mesmerized by the drama and gradually make committments to play "more decorously and loyally to the rules they themselves have elaborated." The chess analogy, interesting as it is, does not suggest a method for evaluating how or why players become 'mesmerized' by the game or how they cope with uncertainty. As Levine notes, the O'Donnell and Schmitter volume fails to explain the "commitments to institutionalized compromise, accomodation, and mutual guarantees typical of democratic systems."[47] Giuseppe Di Palma offers some useful insights into the development of the democratic game. His basic assumption is that "many set ways of understanding the prospects of democratizing stubborn dictatorships and stubborn societies may well gain from being supplemented and amended by... consideration about the role of human choice."[48]

Democratization *ala* Di Palma is 'political crafting,' a process that addresses the same problem in all transitions, convincing actors of the potential utility of the uncertainty associated with outcomes in the democratic process. The rules of the democratic game, he argues, are "worked out among competitive leaderships and institutions." 'Crafting' consists of four elements: the democratic rules and institutions that are chosen; the mode of decision making leading to the selection of rules and institutions (pacts and negotiations versus unilateral action); the type of craftsmen involved (the alliances and coalitions forged in the transition); and the timing imposed on the various tasks of the transition.[49]

The political nature of democratic crafting consists in manipulating both perceptions of and the reality behind each of these four elements. Di Palma points out, for example, that hesitant actors can be won over to the democratic game by surrounding initial agreements "with substantial fuzziness" that gives democratic institutions "a peculiar value in the eyes of opposing players." "The commitment to mutual adjustments that this implies," he argues, "helps [define] a *modus vivendi*." Time can be used as a tactical resource: clear signals about a speedy reform agenda add credibility to the process. Elections, which can "energize and possibly protect democratization beyond the hopes or fears, and indeed the understanding of the principal actors," can play perhaps the most significant tactical role.[50]

In Di Palma's model, the viability of any transformation rests on making democracy appealing, convenient, or compelling to principal political actors.[51] Dictatorial regimes lose to democracy not because they become delegitimized or because democratic principles garner general acceptance. Democratization wins because it leads to "the emergence of a concretely attractive set of democratic rules" that replace repression with coexistence. As a result, he claims, "genuine democrats need not pre-exist democracy." Instead, they are won over by the benefits they can win in the democratic process. Thus, democratization

> refers to crafting the rules of competition so as to attract players, many of whom may be unconvinced of the game or even opposed to it. More precisely, it refers to crafting those rules so as to remove or render inoperative for the foreseeable future the temptation of essential players, most obviously but not exclusively those who had reservations to begin with, to boycott the game.[52]

That is, the object of democratic crafting is not to convert reluctant participants immediately but to affect their behavior.[53] A first choice that for some participants may be 'second-best' can lead to "other behavioral commitments with further unanticipated consequences of their own."[54] Subsequently, reluctant actors participate in an emerging democratic process because "a move to scuttle the agreement...may leave them out of...the only game in town."[55]

The Rebirth of Civil Society. The birth or rebirth of a civil society is a central element of many theories of democratization. O'Donnell and Schmitter, for example, argue that

> once the government signals that it is lowering the costs for engaging in collective action and is permitting some contestation on issues previously declared off-limits... Former political identities reemerge and others appear *ex novo* to expand, beyond anyone's expectations, the public spaces the rulers decided to tolerate at the beginning of the transition. In the precarious stages of the first stages of the transition, these individual gestures are astonishingly successful in provoking or reviving collective identifications and actions; they, in turn, help forge broad identifications which embody the explosion of a highly re-politicized and angry society.[56]

When liberalization starts and some citizens begin to test its limits, "the whole texture, density, and content of intellectually authoritative discourse changes, giving an enormous impulse to the demise of authoritarian rule."

Di Palma contends that the rebirth of civil society can be used as a tactical element of the crafting process "to pressure reluctant political classes into supporting limited reforms." He points out, however, that reforms intended to revitalize society and thereby save the "political class" can instead "contribute to the latter's disunity and even demise." This point, apparently, is when civil society resurfaces "with a decisiveness that takes the political class by surprise." The leadership is then faced with "previously untested dilemmas on how far to proceed, if at all."[57]

Crafting Democracy in the USSR. Di Palma points to two principal considerations in the analysis of the democratization of Communist regimes, the monopoly of ruling parties and the incompatibility of democracy and socialism. The monopoly of ruling parties fits neatly into the conception of democratic crafting: he argues that "efforts to change Communist post-totalitarian regimes... often take the form of extrication guided by the very core of the regime."[58] In other words, the party leadership is in an effective position if and when it decides to craft a democratic agreement. The incompatibility of democracy and socialism is harder to square with the idea of democratic crafting. Although he points out that liberalization "demands reforming and in large part dismantling party-bureaucratic apparats whose institutional interests are closely connected with the operation of collective economies," Di Palma offers few suggestions on how the transition to a system of institutionalized market-style uncertainty could be made to appear "appealing, convenient, or compelling" for those with a stake in the old economic systems. Members of the economic administrative elite, he conjectures, may find that the transition to a market economy offers irresistible temptations.[59]

At some point, if the party leadership accepts reform in order to maintain a significant position in a democratized system, it can turn what could be perceived as a weakness into a strength.

> The advantage of party reforms that come from the very core of a Communist regime is that, although difficult, they carry greater legitimacy. It is one thing when radical reforms are sought by specific regime fractions...it is another when the same thing is done by the core leadership—that is by the leadership of the very party that is to be reformed. The core cannot be held disloyal or incompetent as easily as a group of secessionists.[60]

Di Palma points out, however, that the leadership faces a dilemma because it "wishes reforms but also wishes to save the political class." The answer to this dilemma, he contends, is that institutional reform can offer "the political class glimpses of how they may survive in a more competitive political order—for instance, [holding] office in elected bodies." "Glimpses and anticipations of alternative institutional roles" supply the incentive needed for elites to take the plunge into political uncertainty. Democratic crafting, he argues, has the potential "for inducting a Communist class, wholly or in part, and willy- nilly, into competitive politics.[61]

'Soviet Power' and the Transition

Soviet political institutions presented a series of problems and possibilities to Gorbachev and his allies. Soviet political history, including the Leninist traditions and myths of the superiority of the soviets, combined with a distrust of parliamentary government, made any movement toward western-style government risky. On the other hand, the soviets provided a convenient medium for political reform and could, perhaps, provide the "glimpses" of an alternative future that Di Palma suggested might lead to democracy. Moreover, the soviets, because of their roots in the revolution, were a tempting arena in which to attempt yet another political experiment in which the Communist Party could maintain its 'leading and guiding role.' After all, soviet power had never really been implemented: there was plenty of room to work with. The following chapter analyzes how Gorbachev filled the empty form of 'soviet power' with new meaning much closer to a type of authoritarian political experiment than to western-style democracy.

Notes

1. The old Supreme Soviet is discussed here not only for its historical relevance: new information, compiled through interviews conducted in the USSR, adds depth to earlier portraits. The three principal works written in the West on the old Supreme Soviet were: S. Minagawa, *Supreme Soviet Organs: Functions and institutional development of federal and republican presidiia and standing commissions*, Nagoya: University of Nagoya Press, 1985; R.W. Siegler, *The Standing Commissions of the USSR Supreme Soviet: Effective Cooptation*, New York: Praeger, 1982; P. Vannemann. *The Supreme Soviet: Politics and the Legislative Process in the Soviet Political System*, Durham: Duke University Press, 1977. A good summary by S. White of the development of the Supreme Soviet from 1937-1979 can be found in S. White and D. Nelson, *Communist Legislatures in Comparative Perspective*, London: Macmillan, 1982. O. Anweiler covers the earliest period of the soviet's existence in *The Soviets: The Russian Workers, Peasants, and Soldiers Councils, 1905-1921*, translated by Ruth Hein, New York: Pantheon, 1974. For Soviet work on the Supreme Soviet see D.L. Zlatopolskii, *Verkhovnyi Sovet SSSR: Vyrazitel Voli Sovetskogo Naroda*, Moscow: Iuridicheskaia Literatura, 1978; O.E. Kutafin *Postoiannye komissii Verkhovnogo Soveta SSSR*. Moscow: Iuridicheskaia Literatura, 1971.

2. George W. Breslauer in "Evaluating Gorbachev as Leader," *Soviet Economy* suggests that such frameworks are useful tools.

3. Anweiler, p. 111.

4. Adam Ulam, *The Bolsheviks*, New York: Collier, 1965, p. 333.

5. Leonard Schapiro, *The Communist Party of the Soviet Union*, New York: Random House, 1959, p. 165.

6. See *Sovetskoe gosudarstvennoe stroitelstvo i pravo. Uchebnik dlia vysshykh partiinykh shkol*, Moscow: Mysl, 1984, pp. 151–156 and P.P. Ukrainets, *Partiinoe rukovodstvo i gosudarstvennoe upravlenie*, Minsk: Belarus, 1976, p. 53.

7. V.I. Lenin, *Polnoe sobranie sochinenii*. Vol. 12, p. 61.

8. See J. Towster, *Political Power in the USSR 1917-1947: The Theory and Structure of Government in the Soviet State*, New York: Oxford University Press, 1948.

9. M. Fainsod, *How Russia is Ruled*. London: Oxford University Press, 1953, p. 368.

10. The Bolshevik's leading role was defined for the first time, at least constitutionally, in Article 126, which stated that the party was the 'leading group' of the country's political system.

11. Anweiler, p. 123.

12. *Report of the Central Committee of the Communist Party of the Soviet Union to the 20th Party Congress*, Moscow: Foreign Languages Publishing House, 1956, pp. 109-110.

13. V.M. Morozov, *Partiia i sovety*. Moscow: Politicheskaia literatura, 1982, p. 161.

14. *Kommunisticheskaia partiia sovetskogo soiuza v rezoliutsiiakh sezdov, konferentsii, i plenumov TsK*, Vol. 7, 1955-1959, Moscow: Politicheskaia literatura, 1971, p. 246.

15. This question is discussed in S.A. Avakian, *Pravovoe regulirovanie deiatelnosti sovetov*, Moscow: Iuridicheskaia literatura, 1980.

16. *On the Communist Programme, Report on the Programme of the CPSU to the 22nd Congress of the Party*, 18 October 1961, Moscow: Foreign Languages Publishing House, p. 101. See I. Senin, "Nekotorye voprosy deiatelnosti biudzhetnoi komissii Soveta Soiuza Verkhovnogo Soveta SSSR," *Sovetskoe gosudarstvo i pravo*, No. 11, 1962, pp. 26–37 and S.G. Novikov, "Uchastie nauchnoi obshchestvennosti v rabote komissii zakonodatelnykh predpolozhenii Verkhovnogo Soveta SSSR po podgotovke zakonoproektov," *Sovetskoe gosudarstvo i pravo*, No. 12, 1963, pp. 56–66.

17. Ibid., p. 83.

18. See D.I. Nikitin, *Sovety narodnykh deputatov: Status, kompetentsiia, organizatsiia, deiatelnost, Sbornik dokumentov*, Moscow: Iuridicheskaia literatura, 1980.

19. *On the Communist Programme...*, p. 82.

20. D.P. Hammer discusses Brezhnev's first months in power in, "Brezhnev and the Communist Party," in Erik P. Hoffmann and Robbin F. Laird, *The Soviet Polity in the Modern Era*, New York: Aldine, 1984, pp. 197–198.

21. On this point see A.I. Lukianov, *Razvitie zakonodatelstva o sovetskikh predstavitelnykh organakh vlasti*, Moscow: Iuridicheskaia literatura, 1978, p. 167.

22. See *XXIII sezd KPSS, Stenograficheskii otchet*, Vol. 1, pp. 101–102, 241–243, Vol. 2, p. 314.

23. George W. Breslauer, *Khrushchev and Brezhnev as Leaders: Building Authority in Soviet Politics*, London: George Allen, and Unwin, 1982, p. 175.

24. Seven branch commissions, industry, transport and communication, construction and the industry for construction materials, agriculture, health and social security, education, science, and culture, and trade and consumer goods were added to the four original commissions: mandate, budget, legislative proposals, and foreign affairs.

25. Kutafin, p. 56.

26. *Pravda*, 18 June 1977, p. 1.

27. A.I. Lukianov, *Sovety narodnykh deputatov: spravochnik*, Moscow: Politicheskaia literatura, 1984, p. 176.

28. See *Sovetskoe gosudarstvennoe stroitelstvo i pravo: Uchebnik dlia vysshykh partiinykh shkol*, Moscow: Mysl, 1984, p. 99.

29. Ronald J. Hill discusses the Chernenko interlude in "State and Ideology," in Martin McCauley, ed., *The Soviet Union Under Gorbachev*, New York: St. Martin's, 1987.

30. N.I. Ryzhkov, Gorbachev's long-time Prime Minister described the relationship between the Council of Ministers and the old Supreme Soviet. See "Realizm prakticheskikh deistvii," *Komsomolskaia Pravda*, 18 June 1989, p. 2.

31. The standing commission's functions were defined in a decree ratified by the Supreme Soviet in October 1966 and amended in April 1979.

32. Interview of Presidium consultant, summer 1990.

33. Consultants sometimes asked deputies to propose questions that they were interested in examining. See also Kutafin, pp. 18, 168-169.

34. Interview of A.A. Logunov, Moscow State University, 3 March 1989.

35. The 'practical support group' was also an attempt by the party to reinforce its legitimacy in the working class. See Siegler, p. 255.

36. Interview of Presidium consultant, summer 1989.

37. "Kto pishet zakony?," *Pravda*, 30 August 1987, p. 2.

38. According to one consultant, members of the Central Committee's apparatus occasionally dropped in out of curiosity to hear what "real" discussion sounded like.

39. One Soviet scholar told me that a minister could tell a commission "to go to hell" in the unlikely event that its conclusions were upsetting.

40. Trotsky, of course, later overcame these misgivings and became Lenin's partner. See M. Fainsod, *How Russia is Ruled*, London: Oxford University Press, 1953, p. 42. Ronald Tiersky provides an informative discussion of these questions and more in *Ordinary Stalinism: Democratic Centralism and the Question of Political Development*, Boston: George Allen and Unwin, 1985.

41. See B.D. Wolfe, *An Ideology in Power: Reflections on the Russian Revolution*, New York: Stein and Day, 1969, p. 38.

42. V. Chkhivadze, *The Soviet Form of Self Government*, Moscow: Progress Publishers, 1972, p. 66.

43. V.I. Lenin, "State and Revolution," in *Sochineniia*, Vol. 25, p. 396.

44. Afanasev's reasoning can be clearly seen in "Perestroika, zadumannaia partapparatom, udalas," *Stolitsa*, No. 1, 1990, pp. 1-3. For a more measured exposition of a similar argument see I. Kliamkin, "Logika vlasti i logika oppozitsii: Pochemu Gorbachev soglasilsia na prezidentskuiu sistemu?," *Cherez ternii*, Moscow: Progress, 1990, pp. 701-719. For an example

of the conservative position see remarks at a Central Committee plenum by V.E. Brovikov, former ambassador to Poland, in *Pravda*, 7 February 1990.
    45. Przeworski, *Democracy and the Market*, p. 10.
    46. Di Palma, p. 66.
    47. Levine, "Paradigm Lost...," p. 394.
    48. Di Palma, p. 9. O'Donnell and Schmitter argue that the challenge in establishing such a political democracy is to find a set of rules which embody "contingent consent."
    49. Di Palma, p. 30.
    50. Ibid., p. 130.
    51. Ibid., p. 31.
    52. Ibid., p. 42.
    53. Ibid., p. 111.
    54. Ibid., p. 112.
    55. Ibid., p. 113.
    56. O'Donnell and Schmitter, pp. 48–49.
    57. Di Palma, p. 113.
    58. Ibid., p. 37.
    59. Ibid., p. 181.
    60. Ibid., p. 42.
    61. Ibid., pp. 175, 177.

Chapter 3

Power to the Soviets?

Perestroika was not an unbroken procession toward the constitutional amendments passed in December 1988; nonetheless, it is clear that many reforms in the early period of perestroika dovetailed neatly with Gorbachev's proposals concerning soviet power. This chapter, which outlines the reform program both in its initial stages and in the more complete form taken at the 19th Party Conference, is a key first step toward understanding why and how *demokratizatsiia* was aimed at turning the USSR into a truly *Soviet* Union.

Gorbachev and the Soviets

Gorbachev graduated from Moscow State University's department of law.[1] Although one cannot draw direct links between education and behavior (remember Stalin's seminary years!), Gorbachev's legal training surely helped shape his political views. As one biographer noted, a legal education gave him an unusual chance to broaden his intellectual horizons. "Gorbachev...heard and read things that would never reach...other students: constitutional law..., the history of political ideas..."[2] While a law student, Gorbachev also had an opportunity to ponder the theoretical underpinnings of the political system by taking required courses about the soviets and their role in the socialist state. Anatolii Lukianov, who later became Gorbachev's point man in the Supreme Soviet, was a student in the law department at the same time and a Komsomol acquaintance of the later General Secretary. Is it merely a coincidence that Gorbachev maintained a relationship with a man who later earned a doctorate in law and wrote books on the theory and origin of soviet-style government?[3]

Gorbachev's legal education is not his only long-term connection with the soviets. As a regional party secretary and Supreme Soviet deputy since 1970, he unquestionably had an inside view of the soviets. During discussions of the draft of the 1977 constitution, Gorbachev addressed a meeting of the constitutional editorial commission, where he advocated expanding the rights of the Supreme Soviet's standing commissions. Gorbachev probably was pleased to learn that his proposal had caught the General Secretary's eye. In fact, Brezhnev's collected works contain a summary of Gorbachev's remarks: "The relationships of the commissions of the Supreme Soviet and its chambers with other state and social organs ought to be more fully articulated and priorities ought to be more clearly defined when putting into practice the commissions' recommendations."[4]

Gorbachev's speech to the constitutional editorial commission marked the beginning of the public phase of his call for the revitalization of the soviets. In addition to normal sessional activities, Gorbachev participated in the Supreme Soviet's work through the operation of its standing commissions. He served as chairman of the youth affairs commission of the Soviet of the Union from 1974-1979 and chairman of the legislative proposals commission of the same chamber from 1979 to 1983. During this period, he came to know the commissions' activities, or lack thereof, from the inside. An event that illustrates this learning process occurred in the late 1970s when he was head of the Central Committee's agricultural section. One commission sent a memo to the Central Committee that stated the problems present in agricultural machine building. The head of the relevant section in the Supreme Soviet's Presidium was unsure whether to give this material to deputies and asked for Gorbachev's approval. Gorbachev called a meeting of relevant staff members and praised the memorandum as an example of the type of objective material that the deputies should work with.[5]

In 1983, when Konstantin Chernenko was elected General Secretary, Gorbachev became chairman of the Soviet of the Union's foreign relations standing commission. Before Chernenko, Mikhail Suslov held this position from 1962 until his death in 1982, a tenure that suggests that at least some symbolic importance was attached to this office by the inner core of the party elite. Although neither Suslov nor Chernenko ever used the commission as an active tool, Gorbachev took a different approach. On 22 June 1984, he presided over a discussion in the foreign affairs commissions concerning training foreign specialists at Soviet universities. This was the first time that the foreign affairs commissions addressed an issue other than a treaty or international agreement. Buried like a shiny nugget in the typically dry, formulaic prose of the Supreme Soviet's weekly bulletin was a report that this meeting was the "beginning of a new stage." The commissions had "gone beyond the bounds" of their previous work and included "a wider circle of deputies as well as many representatives of interested organizations."[6]

Gorbachev as General Secretary

In March 1985, addressing the Central Committee for the first time as General Secretary, Gorbachev stressed moving the Soviet economy "onto the rails of intensive development." Nonetheless, he also identified "the further perfection and development of democracy" as "one of the fundamental tasks of the party's domestic policy." "What I have in mind," he declared, "is the further heightening of the role of the soviets...Ahead lies hard work, both in existing and new directions."[7] Although it is doubtful that even Gorbachev could have predicted accurately the new directions that he would eventually take, it was not long before the broad outlines became clear.

In October 1985, speaking with a group of oblast first secretaries, Gorbachev discussed the relationship between party committees and the soviets. He complained that party committees took upon themselves a significant portion of work of other organizations and stressed that "it is very important that each ...soviet...be occupied with its own tasks, fulfilling the functions given to it by law and the party statute." This summons would soon become a favorite refrain. During the following three years, Gorbachev introduced the principal elements of perestroika. In the period before January 1987, he emphasized *uskorenie*, or the acceleration of economic growth, while political change moved ahead only slowly.[8]

The 27th Party Congress

The 27th CPSU Congress in February 1986 played an influential role in developing an ideological and programmatic foundation for the revitalization of the soviets. Although much of the preparation for the Congress was conducted before Gorbachev became General Secretary, his mark is clear on the documents ratified by the assembled delegates. The new party program and statute called for radically altered relations between the party and the soviets and a new focus on the personal responsibility of individual Communists in their legislative activities.

The party's new program, which replaced a version ratified in 1961, contained several new ideas directly related to the revitalization of the soviets. The most significant of these ideas concerned the nature of development of the socialist political system. The 1961 program was based on the assumption that the functions of the state's managerial apparatus would gradually, in an ever growing number of policy areas, be handed over to the soviets and their standing commissions. Further, it assumed that only simple administrative skills were needed to run a modern economy, that these skills would be acquired by an ever greater number of citizens through their participation in the soviets, and that the demand for professional administrators eventually would disappear. Even if the party program had been taken seriously, subsequent political development failed to validate its assumptions. Neither professional administrators nor their managerial apparatus disappeared. Soviet deputies, occupied only part-time by their legislative responsibilities, were incapable of carrying out the specialized tasks of professional managers.

The party program adopted in 1986 dropped assumptions concerning the withering of the administrative apparatus and called for the full development of the inner potential of all parts of the political system. Discussing this aspect of the program, Gorbachev advocated "using all the constitutional abilities of the all-union and union republic Supreme Soviets, and the local soviets, to increase their role and responsibility before the electorate."[9] The program called for shifting the balance of power between legislative and executive institutions, not for eliminating executive organs or giving the soviets functions that deputies were poorly equipped to handle. The new program called for increasing the responsibilities of the all-union and union republic Supreme Soviets by involving them in key decisions of domestic and foreign policy.

The 1986 program encouraged the activization of the soviets in at least three other ways. First, section seven of the new program, "The Development of the Political System of Soviet Society," stressed the idea that the CPSU should play a role in activating the institutional components of the political system and ensuring that constitutional rights were exercised. The 1961 program did not require party committees or members to act in this manner. Second, the new program stated that the soviets' standing commissions should play a bigger role in a wider circle of questions. Third, the program called for the Supreme Soviet to cultivate, in depth and breadth, its exchange programs with other socialist legislatures.[10]

Revisions in the party statute reinforced the changes introduced in the program. For the first time since 1934, Article 19 of the party statute was amended. The party's organizational principle, democratic centralism, was retained but modified by the addition of a fifth characteristic. The new point stressed collegiality and personal responsibility for the operation of non-party organizations. Article 60 of the statute, in a modified and expanded section, "The Party and State and Social Organizations," required that Communists and party groups in state and social organizations insure that these institutions exercise their constitutional powers. Party organizations were forbidden to undermine the soviets or allow the confusion of party functions with those of soviets, trade unions, and other social organizations. Neither of these two requirements appeared in the old statute.

Gorbachev argued that the new CPSU statute clarified the principles of party leadership. State and social organizations were required to fulfill their own functions while "party leadership of their activity ought to bear a clearly expressed political character, actively aiding the further development of the people's socialist self-management."[11] Gorbachev claimed that the revised statute would help both to strengthen the party organizationally "on the tested principles of democratic centralism" and to reinforce the leading role of the party "in the face of new tasks standing before our country." He admitted that it was difficult to define the point where party leadership starts to undermine the prerogatives of the soviets, but nonetheless argued that every situation could be defined concretely. In this regard, he declared, much depends on the "political culture and maturity of the leaders."[12]

Principles ratified at the 27th Party Congress were reflected in a number of subsequent decisions. On 31 March 1986, the Supreme Soviet's Presidium discussed the soviets' new tasks. Andrei Gromyko, the Presidium's Chairman, declared that the documents ratified by the Congress had strengthened the soviets. He urged deputies to make this new potential a reality. "The principal criteria by which the activities of the soviets and their organs must be judged," he argued, "are not the number of meetings and debates, but practical, real results." The Presidium defined its position the same day in a decree, "Concerning the tasks of the Soviets of peoples' deputies arising from the decisions of the 27th CPSU Congress." A CPSU Central Committee decree published in August 1986, "Concerning the further perfection of party leadership of the soviets of people's deputies," called for the activization of the soviets and the renewal of the content, style, and methods of their work. Party committees were instructed to lead the activization process but were also warned to avoid undermining the soviets through petty intrusions and duplication of effort. In September 1986, Gorbachev asked the Supreme Soviet to review an unprecedented legislative package that contained many of his reform initiatives.[13]

Membership turnover in the Supreme Soviet reached unprecedented levels after 1986, a process that suggested the plans that Gorbachev had for the institution. Two aspects of the turnover were interesting, both the sheer number of changes and the way that Gorbachev assembled allies in the Supreme Soviet. In the ten years prior to 1985, there were, on average, 10 new members elected to the Supreme Soviet *per annum* when deputies died, retired, or were removed. In 1985, there were 20 changes and, in 1986, 67. Several cadres decisions suggest that Gorbachev used this strategy to build a team of supporters into the Supreme Soviet. A.I. Lukianov, who became Gorbachev's first deputy at the first session of the *new* Supreme Soviet in 1989 and E.M. Primakov and R.N. Nishanov, the first chairmen, respectively, of the *new* Soviet of the Union and Soviet of the Nationalities were elected to the *old* Supreme Soviet on the same day in 1987 in a by-election.[14]

The January 1987 Plenum

A CPSU Central Committee plenum in January 1987 played a decisive role in the development of the reform program. The plenum, postponed several times because of opposition to planned changes, was the forum from which the 19th Party Conference was launched: it finally was clear that economic and political change must go hand in hand. On January 29th, the Central Committee issued a decree that summarized the results of the plenum, "On perestroika and the party's cadres policy." As Michael Urban pointed out, the decree supported Gorbachev's ideas, "but in language much tamer than that employed by the General Secretary."[15] In part, it stated that a "clear system of control over the work of leading cadres" should be created through "sessions of soviets of peoples' deputies..., the activities of the standing commissions of the Supreme Soviet of the USSR, the Supreme Soviet of union and autonomous republics, and local soviets."[16] The goal of the reforms was "strengthening the democratic foundations of the activities of the soviets and their executive organs and the fuller and more effective exercising of their powers." To accomplish this task, it would be necessary "to raise the level of the work of party groups in the soviets, to strengthen their influence on the activity of soviet organs."[17]

The reform program gained momentum in several ways after the January 1987 plenum. Mass media focused more attention on the party leadership's role in the soviets. The Politburo, on 12 February 1987, responded favorably to a report by Gromyko on the Supreme Soviet's work during 1986. According to a summary of the meeting, the Politburo called for further activization of the legislature's commissions and deputies.[18] At the same time, the Supreme Soviet's international activities were expanded. Its commissions exchanged visits with foreign legislatures, reportedly to share work experience.[19] Other international activities were expanded, including a satellite link in the fall of 1987 between the Supreme Soviet and the US Congress to discuss human rights. The INF Treaty was reviewed and accepted by the Supreme Soviet's foreign relations committee, a purely symbolic act but one that, at least formally, exercised a right never used before.[20]

In 1987, the Supreme Soviet for the first time exercised its right to question the activities of the ministerial apparatus when six deputies made official inquiries of government officials. One group of three deputies asked the Council of Ministers' Bureau of Petrochemical and Energy Affairs to describe the lessons it learned from the previous year's mistakes. The ministry of light industries was asked to discuss improvements in the quality and assortment of consumer goods. Reports were given on the final day of the session by the chairman of the Council of Ministers and the ministry of light industry.[21]

Publications from party and state organs and scholarly institutions played an intellectual and ideological role in the activization process.[22] A new debate on the roles of the soviets covered a broad spectrum, with suggested changes ranging from measures as mild as increasing the deputies' expense allotments to others as radical as scuttling some fundamental principles of the USSR's political system. Editorial control over *Sovety narodnykh deputatov*, a journal published for deputies, was handed over to the Supreme Soviet's Presidium. The new editorial board dedicated itself to analyzing "the perfection of soviet democracy..."[23]

Despite many signs of activization, the Supreme Soviet's work remained highly formalized. Convincing proof of the legislature's weakness was that its standing commissions barely functioned. Speaking at a joint session of the Supreme Soviet that ratified a new law on state enterprises in June 1987, I.V. Maslennikov, the chairman of the legislative proposals commission of the Soviet of the Union, called for the commissions to start fulfilling their potential. He maintained that the commissions "were not fully active" in the preparation of the law and asserted that they should monitor both preparations for its introduction and its implementation.[24] Maslennikov concluded by calling for "the further activization of the work of the standing commissions."

From March 1985 to the spring of 1988 Gorbachev set the stage for the dramatic reforms announced at the 19th Party Conference. Addressing a Central Committee Plenum in February 1988, he summarized the position that he had developed over the three previous years. The principal goal of political development, he argued, was to create "a mechanism of power and management...based on genuine democratic control." Such a mechanism would "significantly reduce and eventually eliminate...arbitrariness in the decision of state and political questions" and exclude "subjectivism." "It is necessary," he said, to make "all political decisions with the active participation of the people. This would correspond to socialist democracy." Gorbachev went on to argue for "a cardinal increase in the role of the soviets as the core of the political system of our society" and called for the "rebirth of soviet power in a Leninist sense," arguing that this would create genuine "centers of state power and management."

The 19th Party Conference

In June 1988, the CPSU convened the 19th Party Conference to discuss one question: how to make perestroika "irreversible." Gorbachev's answer was a return to the ideals of Leninism through *demokratizatsiia*, the "radical democratization of socio-political life and the reform of the political system."[25] The program that Gorbachev presented to the conference was a synthesis of new and old ideas intended to establish the preconditions for a "qualitatively new type of society."[26] Political reform was the key to resolving the country's remaining problems: without it, perestroika could not succeed. Gorbachev based his proposals on a political and historical analysis of the 'deformation' of the socialist system. He argued that the political system established by Lenin had been disfigured by "the power monopoly held by Stalin and his circle."[27] "We want a type of socialism that, while cleansed of the deposits and distortions of the past, also would inherit all of the best that was built on the creative thought of the founders of [Marxism-Leninism], made a reality by the labor and efforts of the people, and reflects [their] hopes and dreams."[28] The reforms included changes within the party, the soviets, and the executive as well as alterations in the way they interacted.

Reforming the CPSU

Gorbachev's discussion of reforms in the CPSU had two principal parts. First, he affirmed the necessity for party leadership and praised the good will of party members. Second, he called for radical changes in the party that would lead to the "democratization of its leadership activities and inner life."[29] Gorbachev claimed that the source of the party's problems was, "first of all that the principle of democratic centralism, the basis of the structure and the activity of the CPSU, was at a certain stage undermined to a great degree by bureaucratic centralism."[30] Although, he claimed, the essence of a Leninist approach was free discussion of all problems and policies and unity of action after a decision was taken, with the acceptance of the administrative command system "the atmosphere of party comradeship gradually gave way to relationships based on orders..., a division of party members into bosses and subordinates, and on the violation of the principle of the equality of communists."[31] He argued that the party should rejuvenate democratic centralism by returning to first principles, removing Stalinist distortions, and recreating an atmosphere conducive to "discussion, criticism and self-criticism, conscious discipline, party comradeship, unconditional personal responsibility, and businesslike behavior."[32]

Gorbachev noted that reviving democratic centralism in its 'Leninist' form would require more than the establishment of an open atmosphere and called for reinvigorating electoral principles within the party as well as a series of other related changes. The party could not play the leading role in Soviet society unless all party organizations, from the factory floor to the Central Committee, restructured the style, method, and forms of their work. Emphasizing this problem, he pointed out that, "the situation is still such, comrades, that... the Politburo and Secretariat... must resolve [scores] of questions, the majority of which could be handed over to lower organs without any harm at all."[33]

How could the party render political leadership without undermining the state? In addition to an old-fashioned ban prohibiting party organizations ranging from the Central Committee to the local level from interfering with the day-to-day management of government and economic enterprises, Gorbachev proposed several changes, including: (1) renewed reliance on the Leninist principle that the party should lead through the participation of its cadres in key non-party positions (in this case, the revival of party groups in the soviets), (2) abandoning the practice whereby party committees issued direct orders to state, economic, and social organizations, and, (3) reorganizing the Central Committee apparatus to reduce its size and eliminate detailed supervision of the economy and other areas of soviet life. The question of political leadership was also at the root of a surprise announcement: Gorbachev called for party secretaries to run for corresponding soviets and seek office as the chairman of their executive committees. Combining these positions, he claimed would force party leaders to pay more attention to their constituents and, therefore, lead in a manner that accounted for constituent interests.[34]

Lest anyone interpret the strengthening of the soviets and the rebirth of the Supreme Soviet as first steps toward weakening the party's monopoly, Gorbachev warned about attempts to use democratic rights for "undemocratic ends." "Some people," he noted, "think that any question can be resolved in this way." He argued that such a "misuse of democracy... contradicts the tasks of perestroika, and is not in the interests of [our] people."[35] Clearly, Gorbachev reserved to the CPSU, really to the Politburo and central party organs, the right to define the bounds of legitimate political discourse.

Revitalizing the Soviets

The revitalization of the soviets, according to Gorbachev, was part of "the logic of the development of socialist democracy." He noted that CPSU leaders at all levels had often complained about the soviets' inactivity but that little was done to resolve the problem. As a result, "the situation not only failed to improve, but as the years passed got significantly worse." He proposed that "not a single question concerning the state, the economy, or the social fabric can be decided if the soviets are bypassed."[36] To make this vision a reality, Gorbachev maintained that, "in the Supreme Soviets and local soviets the democratic principles of sessional work, the standing commissions, and deputies should be strengthened, while the reporting of officials to the soviets and the asking of questions by deputies should be improved."[37] He expected the soviets to start exercising their constitutional rights through political leadership provided by the participation of Communist deputies.

Activating the soviets would demand shifting the division of functions at the highest level of the USSR's political system. "First of all," Gorbachev argued, "the Central Committee and the Politburo ought to be and act as organs of political leadership... Everything that the USSR Supreme Soviet and the Council of Ministers are supposed to do, should be done by *them*."[38] To strengthen the soviets' position within the political system's division of functions, Gorbachev called for establishing the rule of law on both individual and governmental levels.[39] A correct and firm division of functions, "the constitutional regulation of interactions of the highest echelons of power, including the USSR Council of Ministers,"[40] was indispensable if the reforms were to succeed.

Noting that institutional reorganization was not enough to insure the revitalization of the Supreme Soviet, Gorbachev called for a new set of operating principles, for changing "the very character and style of the Supreme Soviet's activities. Long speeches, self-serving reports, over-organization, and formalism must be eliminated from its sessions. [Sessions] ought to become lively and demanding..."[41] Gorbachev questioned the Supreme Soviet's tradition of unanimity, arguing that disagreement is a "normal manifestation of the democratic process." In short, he argued that a "socialist pluralism of opinions, argument, discussion, the comparison of views" is the "way to search for the best, optimal decisions."[42]

Gorbachev also maintained that soviets would not produce, "necessary results if the initiative of the deputies is not strengthened." "We must do everything necessary so that the law on the status of deputies is unswervingly fulfilled, so that every deputy has all opportunities to actually realize his powers." Electoral reforms would play a role in strengthening the soviets. As a rule, he argued, elections should be conducted on a competitive basis with the strict observance of democratic procedure. He offered no support for a multi-party system, insisting instead that candidates run as individuals, but did step away from the demographic principle of representation. He argued that particular social groups had no priority and that mandates should be fought for and won by "politically literate, active people."[43]

Reforming the Ministerial Apparatus

A third key element of the reform program was based on Gorbachev's argument that an "ossified system of power" stood in the way of perestroika. He identified the central ministerial apparatus, or "administrative command system," as a principal obstacle to change. It had grown in size and power to the point where it "practically dictated its will in economics and politics." Neither the party nor, obviously, the soviets had been able "to control the pressure of executive interests."[44] The administrative-command system was the source of a multitude of problems: (1) an underestimation of the value of socialist democracy and the inability to reform the system, (2) stagnation in economic and social life, (3) the concentration of economic and managerial powers in the hands of the party-political leadership, (4) the hypertrophy of the executive apparatus, (5) the growth of the powers of ministries and the executive apparatus to a point where they were accountable neither to the party nor to the soviets, (6) the excessive governmentalization of society, (7) the growth of an underground economy and culture because of the inability of the state to meet people's needs, (8) a society whose thinking became static because of the bureaucratization of the state structure and the weakening of social creativity, (9) a political system not based on law but on the fulfillment of instructions, and (10) a society democratic in principle but authoritarian in practice.

The conference resolutions declared that the executive should be "completely subordinate to elected organs, Soviet power, and the people."[45] The reforms were aimed at subordinating executive power to politically accountable soviets controlled by the party while radically improving executive performance through the introduction of a market-type mechanism and a "rational combination of centralization and decentralization." Gorbachev called for a series of changes aimed at holding the ministerial apparatus accountable for its actions. First, he claimed, combining the posts of party secretary and chairman of the corresponding soviet would strengthen the soviets and help reestablish a correct balance of power between executive and legislative organs. Simplification of the administrative apparatus by merging managerial organs in industrial branches, decreasing the number of ministries and state administrations, and liquidating 'unnecessary' organizations was another key goal. Third, he advocated greater democratic control, both from workers' collectives on the factory floor, and from the soviets.[46]

Final Session of the Old Supreme Soviet

In December 1988, the final session of the old Supreme Soviet ratified constitutional amendments designed to implement the political reforms outlined at the 19th Party Conference. These amendments were, as Michael Urban noted, prepared by a narrow circle of legal specialists with the participation of the Politburo.[47]

The old Supreme Soviet's final session, despite an agenda full of complex constitutional questions, required only two days. Gorbachev claimed in his opening address that the amendments included changes in the USSR's governmental structure and electoral laws that would "not only preserve, but strengthen the principal elements which from the beginning characterized soviet-style organization...and makes it the optimal form for a socialist state and democracy."[48] The new legislation, he claimed, would create "democratic instruments for the free expression and coordination of many different opinions and interests." He argued that longer sessions with full-time deputies would strengthen the Supreme Soviet and help reverse the *de facto* dominance of the executive apparatus. The constitutional amendments provided for legislative sessions of 6–8 months as well as the possibility of full-time deputies. Retreating from traditional arguments for unified power in a socialist state, Gorbachev argued that a socialist system of "checks and balances" was needed to help ensure that no part of government acquired enough power to threaten "socialist legality." Within this system of checks and balances, the Supreme Soviet would be expected to define and defend the people's interests.[49]

Perhaps the most exciting piece of legislation passed at the session was a new electoral law that foresaw the possibility of multi-candidate elections. Debated widely throughout the fall of 1988 for a number of innovative elements and convenient loopholes, this bill eventually created a situation where the Communist Party could no longer completely control electoral outcomes. This process, the subject of the next chapter, started a series of events that sent *demokratizatsiia* careening out of the control of the party leadership.

Notes

1. For an account of Gorbachev's law school years see G. Sheehy, *The Man Who Changed the World: The Lives of Mikhail S. Gorbachev*, New York: HarperCollins, 1990. Jerry F. Hough describes Gorbachev's unique characteristics in *Russian and the West: Gorbachev and the Politics of Reform*, New York: Simon and Schuster, 1988.

2. C. Schmidt-Hauer, *Gorbachev. The path to power*, translated by E. Osers and C. Romberg, London: I. B. Tauris, 1986.

3. For some thoughts on Gorbachev's relationship with Lukianov see, "Slishkom seryi kardinal dlia perestroiki," *Stolitsa*, No. 2, January 1991. pp. 9-12. Gorbachev's Komsomol connection with Lukianov is also described in Gerd Ruge, *Gorbachev: A Biography*, translated from the German by Peter Tegel, London: Chatto and Windus, 1991, pp. 37-39. For Lukianov's academic work see *Razvitie zakonodatelstva o sovetskikh predstavitelnykh organakh vlasti*, Moscow: Iuridicheskaia literatura, 1978, p. 167. F.M. Burlatskii discusses Lukianov's role in deciding to restore 'soviet-style' government rather than turning to a western model. See "Alternativa drobleniiu levykh sil–dvizhenie k sotsialnoi demokratii," *Literaturnaia gazeta*, 1 January 1991, p. 5.

4. For Brezhnev's remarks see *Leninskim kursom*, Vol. 7, pp. 250-254. For Gorbachev's ideas see *Vneocherednaia sedmaia sessiia verkhovnogo soveta SSSR (deviatii sozyv), Stenograficheskii otchet*, Moscow: 1977, pp. 250-254. I thank D.P. Hammer for giving me this citation.

5. A consultant from the Presidium told me this story in the summer of 1989. For a discussion of this period in Gorbachev's career see, Zh. Medvedev, *Gorbachev*, Oxford: Basil Blackwell, 1986, pp. 94-118.

6. *Vedomosti verkhovnogo soveta SSSR*, No. 27, 4 July 1984, p. 587.

7. M.S. Gorbachev, *Izbrannye rechi i stati*, Vol. 2, Moscow: Politicheskaia literatura, 1987, p. 130. On this point see also Archie Brown in "Power and Policy in a Time of Leadership Transition," in *Political Leadership in the Soviet Union*, Bloomington: Indiana University Press, 1989, p. 186. Robert Kaiser points out an interesting speech that Gorbachev made before his trip to Britain in 1984. See *Why Gorbachev Happened: His Triumph and his Failure*, New York: Simon and Schuster, 1991, pp. 75-79.

8. Gorbachev, *Izbrannye...*, Vol. 3, p. 19. The agendae of all significant party meetings from March 1985-April 1990 can be found in "Partiinye forumy perestroiki," *Izvestiia TsK KPSS*, April 1990, pp. 140-150. Changes in the top CPSU leadership are listed in "Sostav rukovodiashchikh organov tsentralnogo komiteta partii—Politbiuro (prezidiuma), orgbiuro, sekretariata TsK (1919—1990 gg.)," *Izvestiia TsK KPSS*, No. 7, 1990, pp. 69-82.

9. M.S. Gorbachev, *Izbrannye...*, Vol. 3, p. 414.

10. *Sovety narodnykh deputatov*, No. 11, 1987, p. 10.

11. M.S. Gorbachev, *Izbrannye...*, Vol. 3, p. 12.

12. Ibid.

13. Gromyko's new attitude was relected in a speech he made to the Gorky oblast soviet published in *Sovety narodnykh deputatov*, No. 12, 1985, pp. 7-19. The legislative package consisted of 38 laws, the institutions responsible for drafting them, and a timetable. There was no evidence,

however, that the Supreme Soviet's procedures changed to accommodate the review.

14. *Vedomosti verkhovnogo soveta SSSR*, No. 13, 1 April 1987, p. 179.

15. Michael Urban, *More Power to the Soviets: The Democratic Revolution in the USSR*, England: Edward Elgar, 1990.

16. *Izvestiia*, 30 January 1987, p. 2.

17. Ibid.

18. *Izvestiia*, 12 February 1987, p. 1. *Izvestiia*, 15 January 1988, p. 1. During Andropov's tenure as General Secretary, the period when accounts of Politburo meetings were first published, no progress report on the Supreme Soviet's work was ever discussed in the press. For a report of another Politburo meeting that discussed this issue see *Pravda*, 8 January 1988, p. 1.

19. In the fall of 1987, for example, the legislative proposals commission of the People's Republic of China visited Moscow. *Sovety narodnykh deputatov*, No. 11, 1987, p. 10. Reporting on foreign legislatures also changed. See, for example, "Deputat bundestaga," *Pravda*, 17 June 1988, p. 6.

20. See "Na puti realnogo razoruzheniia," *Pravda*, 24 May 1988, p. 4.

21. *Sovety narodnykh deputatov*, No. 8, 1987, pp. 7–8.

22. For an interesting discusion of the changes in published attitudes toward the soviets see Michael Urban, *More Power to the Soviets*, pp. 19–30. See also Ronald J. Hill, "State and Ideology," in Martin McCauley, ed. *The Soviet Union Under Gorbachev*, New York: St. Martin's, 1987, pp. 45–46.

23. *Sovety narodnykh deputatov*, No. 6, 1987, p. 6. In July 1987, the journal published a special issue, dedicated to helping deputies deal with the 'revolutionary new winds' that were changing the demands placed on them.

24. *Izvestiia*, 30 June 1987, pp. 4–5.

25. *XIX Vsesoiuznaia konferentsiia kommunisticheskoi partii sovetskogo soiuza, Stenograficheskii otchet*, Vol. 1, Moscow: Politizdat, 1988, p. 45.

26. Ibid., p. 57.

27. Ibid., p. 46.

28. Ibid.

29. Ibid., p. 47.

30. Ibid., p. 48.

31. Ibid.

32. Ibid.

33. Ibid., p. 31.

34. For a discussion of this issue see "Sekretar i predsedatel v odnom l-itse," B.P. Kurashvili, *Izvestiia*, 22 July 1988, p. 3, and I. Kliamkin, "Logika

vlasti i logika oppozitsii: Pochemu Gorbachev soglasilsia na prezidentskuiu sistemu?," *Cherez ternii*, Moscow: Progress, 1990, p. 708. Kurashvili offered some other thoughts on the institutions proposed at the party conference in "Kakoi byt strukture vlasti," *Izvestiia*, 28 July 1988, p. 3.

35. *XIX Vsesoiuznaia konferentsiia kommunisticheskoi partii sovetskogo soiuza, Stenograficheskii otchet*, Vol. 1, Moscow: Politizdat, 1988. See Ye.K. Ligachev's opinion on the effects of the 19th Party Conference in his review of Gorbachev's policy, *Zagadka Gorbacheva*, Novosibirsk: Interbuk, 1992, esp. pp. 38, 69–116.

36. Ibid.
37. M.S. Gorbachev, *Izbrannye...*, Vol. 4, p. 93.
38. Ibid., p. 53.
39. Ibid., p. 41.
40. Ibid., p. 66.
41. Ibid., p. 35.
42. Ibid.
43. M.S. Gorbachev, *Izbrannye...*, Vol. 6, p. 362.
44. Ibid., p. 47.
45. Ibid., p. 76.
46. Ibid., p. 37.
47. Michael Urban, *More Power to the Soviets*, p. 44. Both Urban and Jeffrey W. Hahn offer useful outlines of the new structures. For Hahn see, "The Soviet State System," in Stephen White, Alex Pravda and Zvi Gitelman eds., *Developments in Soviet Politics*, Durham: Duke University Press, 1990, pp. 87–103.
48. *Sovetskaia Rossiia*, 30 November 1988, p. 2.
49. For a discussion of a socialist system of checks and balances see B. Lazarev, "Razdelenie vlastei i opyt sovetskogo gosudarstvo," *Kommunist*, No. 16, 1988. A roundtable on the topic, with the participation of Politburo member A.N. Iakovlev was published in "Razdelenie vlastei: teoriia i praktika," *Narodnyi deputat*, No. 15, 1990, pp. 7–27.

Chapter 4

The 1989 Elections

Electoral politics, a principal source of power and leadership in any democratic political system, played a different role during seventy years of 'Soviet power.' One way to a clearer understanding of the depth and breadth of change inherent in the 1989 elections is to compare them to the traditional electoral system. Elections to the old Supreme Soviet were non-competitive, single-party contests that played a symbolic role involving all four core elements of old-fashioned soviet-style government: party leadership, accountability, representation, and executive-legislative relations.

Creating a New Electoral System

For Stalin and his successors, the drive for universal electoral participation was an attempt to propagandize the party, its leaders, and its leading role. Party leadership was reflected in an electoral platform as well as the nomination of leading party members to run for deputy in a number of districts: those higher on the party 'totem pole' received more nominations in a wider variety of locations. Leading members of the party elite made campaign speeches in the days leading up to the election in reverse rank order: junior members spoke early and far from the capital, senior members addressed their electors just before the big day in their Moscow electoral districts.

Traditional Soviet elections, for three reasons, had little to do with accountability. First, of course, no opposition party was allowed to compete; indeed, the creation of an opposition would have been unthinkable. Although non-party members were included as candidates in most districts, and even became a majority in many local soviets, those running for office were referred to as the 'unsplittable bloc of Communist and non-party candidates.' Second, the elections allowed only one candidate on the ballot. Third, the elections were not secret. To vote against a candidate citizens were forced to publicly act out their defiance by walking to an assigned booth and crossing off the name of the candidate on the ballot. Abstaining by staying home and refusing to vote was also sure to attract attention. Although public intimidation did not always work, it clearly discouraged both dissenting votes and abstention.[1]

A third symbolic element of the traditional electoral process was a theory of representation based on the ideals of soviet-style government: workers participating in and controlling the activities of the state. The party ensured that the membership composition of the soviets reflected, imperfectly, but to a degree unknown in other systems, the demographic makeup of the population. Soviet theorists claimed that it was better to be represented by people who understood 'real life' through immersion in it. Although deputies were supplied with instructions (*nakazy*) from their electors (actually by local party organs) concerning particular public works projects or other concrete objectives, political questions were left to the party.

Traditional Soviet elections reflected the belief that executive and legislative organs should cooperate and that a separation of powers was a wasteful conceit. Although executive officials made up a large part of the membership of soviets at all levels, this was not a parliamentary system where ministers served at the consent of a party that enjoyed a temporary electoral majority. Thus, ministers had little reason to respect fellow deputies and for deputies there was no incentive to develop 'soviet power.' Career advancement and electoral success depended neither on collegiality within the parliamentary party group nor on the competent completion of parliamentary duties. Ministers answered to the central party leadership within a tightly controlled and closed system.

The New Electoral Law

Draft electoral legislation based on proposals made at the 19th Party Conference was published in October 1988 for public discussion. Despite the image cultivated in the press, the terms of debate, including a 'public discussion' of the law in the press in the fall of 1988 and its ratification at the final session of the old Supreme Soviet, were established and controlled by the central party apparatus. The formal process for discussing the draft legislation included the creation of a commission of legal experts attached to the Supreme Soviet's Presidium. The commission, charged with preparing materials for a deputies' subcommission of the legislative proposals commissions of the old Supreme Soviet, included academics as well as apparatchiks from the Central Committee and the Supreme Soviet's Presidium. It examined letters to the party and the government, the central and local press, and materials forwarded by the Presidia of republican Supreme Soviets, created a computerized data bank of suggested revisions, and sent a summary to the Supreme Soviet. The commission's principal role was to provide an academic air of legitimacy. The secrecy that surrounded the commission's work as well as subsequent complaints about the vagueness of the new electoral law suggest, however, that the professional skills of the commission's five doctors of juridical science were underemployed.[2]

The new electoral law included a number of significant innovations: (1) secret voting, (2) self-nomination, (3) an increased number of mandates (2,250 vs. 1500) to the state's highest representative institution, a Congress of People's Deputies (CPD) that would elect a full-time Supreme Soviet, (4) provision for nominations according to a geographic principle of representation, (5) elections from social organizations, a second new principle of representation, (6) the right for citizens to conduct electoral agitation for or against candidates, (7) a requirement that candidates operate under equal conditions, financially and otherwise, (8) a requirement that winners receive 50% plus one vote of all ballots cast, with provisions for a second-round ballot if no candidate won outright, and (9) the possibility of multi-candidate elections. While some of these innovations seemed to promise a move toward democracy, others appeared to be based on an attempt to maintain the status quo.

Secret voting was, in light of 70 years of Soviet practice, perhaps the most revolutionary concept in the new electoral law. Although citizens always formally had the right to step into a booth to vote in private, it was rarely done. People feared demonstrating their opinions publicly. The new law required that voters pass through a booth where they could draw a curtain and vote in private. Secret voting was a step toward instituting a new type of political accountability: concrete legitimation of the right to vote no—or not to vote at all—was an influential factor in many electoral districts during the 1989 campaign.

The right to self-nomination was a second key innovation in the new law. Although potential candidates were required to meet a number of conditions, including nominating themselves at a public meeting operated by local officials, this right weakened the ability of party committees to control the outcome by vetting all potential deputies. Concerned party officials could, of course, take action at many other steps along the way; nonetheless, self-nomination was an essential matter of principle. Alternatives to officially-sponsored candidates became a real possibility.

The increased number of mandates, 2,250, was a product of the creation of the Congress of People's Deputies: 750 deputies would be elected in territorial districts roughly equal in terms of population, 750 in national-territorial districts that would account for the USSR's multinational character, and 750 by social organizations. The old Supreme Soviet had only 1500 seats. The size of the new CPD suggested that it would never become a genuine working body and, in fact, provision was made for creating a smaller working body, a new Supreme Soviet. Mathematically, however, not all of the deputies of the CPD, even if rotated according to the mandated schedule, would be able to serve in the Supreme Soviet. This left questions of both accountability and representation. How could deputies represent their constituents adequately if they were denied full access and a working place in the Supreme Soviet? How could citizens hold their elected representatives accountable if they never had the opportunity to participate in the daily work of the Supreme Soviet? These questions were never adequately addressed.

The nomination of candidates at neighborhood caucuses introduced a new principle of representation. Electoral meetings of no fewer than 500 citizens from any district were given the right to nominate candidates. This not only established an alternative to nominations from industrial enterprises based on the 'reflection' principle of representation, it also had the potential to weaken the hold of local officials on the elections. Local party committees were experienced in old-style workplace nominations—the innovations might give independent newcomers a chance. Although, as we will see below, it was no simple task to gather 500 citizens, the creation of this nomination principle helped undermine the control exercised by the party apparat.

The introduction of elections by social organizations was significant for two reasons. First, the 750 seats assigned to these organizations strengthened the representation of conservative party members by guaranteeing that one-third of the CPD's seats would be held by groups easily controlled by the party. The party apparatus designed the formula that decided which social organizations would be given seats. Second, elections by social organizations was that it established a second new principle of representation.[3] The elections at the USSR Academy of Sciences, discussed in-detail below, suggested that this innovation made it possible for forces outside the conservative apparat to play a role in the elections and, ultimately, in the new legislative politics.

The requirement that candidates compete on equal footing presented a series of problems. Mandated equality was difficult to enforce, so candidates ended up in very unequal circumstances. This requirement also gave electoral commissions a control tool to limit the initiative of 'unofficial' candidates. Thus, having more than one candidate on the ballot did not ensure that voters were given a meaningful choice between candidates.

The draft law contained enough loopholes and ambiguities to ensure that local party leaders would be able to manipulate the elections to include only 'acceptable' candidates on the ballot. Moreover, because the elections were held on a non-party basis, it was difficult for voters to gather enough information to make an informed decision. Despite these shortcomings, competitive elections, at least in theory, became possible. Moreover, independent candidates sometimes managed to turn the double-edged sword of 'equality' against the party.

The right to conduct agitation for and against candidates created the possibility of genuine political campaigns and principled public debate. An important related change was the requirement that candidates receive 50% plus one vote of all ballots cast. This requirement virtually guaranteed that multiple-candidate elections would produce run-off elections between the two highest vote getters or, in certain circumstances prescribed by law (most commonly districts where only two candidates were registered) that elections where no one won outright would be invalid and have to be run again. The run-offs and repeat elections provided an opportunity for genuine political battles.

In sum, when the Supreme Soviet passed the new electoral law in December 1988, deputies ratified a party-controlled document that had been approved at the highest levels. Despite significant changes in the law that made competition possible for the first time at the national level, local party committees received an assortment of tools for managing the process and ensuring their own predominance in delegations to the CPD.[4]

The Campaign

The 1989 elections started formally in December 1988, when the all-union Central Electoral Commission and local electoral commissions were created, and ended late in May 1990 with a final round of runoff elections.

The Central Electoral Commission

The membership of the USSR's Central Electoral Commission was ratified by the old Supreme Soviet on 2 December 1988. The commission's membership was stacked in favor of the status quo: no public advocates of radical democratic change were included. Although respected scholars gave the CEC some intellectual weight, as a whole it was a creature of the central party apparatus. The CEC's chairman, Yurii Orlov, was elected by the Supreme Soviet and played the most visible role in the commission's work by acting as a spokesman.

Citizens tended to side-step local electoral commissions and apply directly to the center for relief. By early February, the CEC had received over 2,300 letters, more than 900 phone inquiries, and met with more than 500 visitors.[5] A staff headquartered in Moscow in the Central Hall of Unions, a convenient central location close to both the Kremlin and the Central Committee's headquarters, undoubtedly took care of the vast majority of the CEC's work. This staff monitored the campaign and played the most influential role in the day-to-day interpretation of the electoral law. The bias was almost always to the status quo. Indeed, the flood of inquiries and complaints—and the absence of adequate means of enforcement—made it impossible for the commission to pay attention to more than a fraction of the cases. The complexity, scale, and novelty of the electoral process encouraged mistakes, as well as fraud and abuse. Manipulation occurred at each stage of the campaign, both by local party officials and by the central party apparat. The unwritten message communicated by the action and inaction of the CEC might be paraphrased as follows: 'Do whatever you want and as long as you do not get caught in a public, flagrant, and fundamental violation of the law that cannot be swept under the carpet, we will leave you in peace.'[6]

Forming Electoral Districts

Electoral districts, in theory, were formed by local electoral commissions according to the demographic and geographical requirements outlined in the electoral law. Territorial districts should have been of roughly equal size throughout the country. National-territorial districts should have varied according to the population of the republic, autonomous oblast, or other geopolitical unit. In practice, party committees created districts using standards that allowed them to control outcomes with the least possible expenditure of energy.

Substantial variations in the size of electoral districts, attributable to two factors, occurred throughout the country. First, the law on elections allowed electoral districts to accommodate existing administrative subdivisions. In Moscow, for example, 26 territorial districts were formed in such a way as to minimize the administrative headaches involved in dividing Moscow's 33 regions among the electoral districts. Bureaucratic inertia alone made it unlikely that local party committees would bother going to the extra effort to change boundaries.

Gerrymandering was a second reason for variation in district size. At the first session of the CPD, Deputy V. Alksnis, a lieutenant colonel who later became well-known as a supporter of Russians living in other republics and proponent of authoritarian solutions to the problems of *demokratiza-*

tsiia, argued that gerrymandering in Latvia deprived "Russian-speaking citizens of their right to representation." An independent study later supported Alksnis's claims when it reported that in Latvia the variation in the number of voters among national-territorial districts was striking: "Because Latvians are the majority of the rural population and [Russians] are concentrated principally in the cities... This directly affected the representation of ethnic groups."[7] Given the depth of nationalities problems throughout the USSR, as well as the proven ability of the party apparat to manipulate the rules, it is reasonable to assume that gerrymandering occurred elsewhere.

Local Electoral Commissions

Local electoral commissions were formed in late 1988 in territorial and national-territorial districts as well as in those social organizations allotted mandates. This stage of the elections, perhaps the least publicized, was arguably the most important. Local party committees stacked the commissions by using a closed system of nominations. The organizational department of the corresponding local soviet called the principal state enterprises and social organizations in its district and asked for nominees. Only after the campaign was over, in attempts to analyze the 'lessons' of the elections, did the press complain that the commissions were formed "according to established canons."[8]

Commission members and chairmen were amateurs while workers from the soviets who staffed the commissions were professionals who, typically, had run old-style elections many times. Deference to the professional staff was only natural. Violations would not be punished as long as the principal violators (usually the local political leadership) controlled the interpretation of the rules through commission staff. A report to the executive committee of the Moscow City Soviet by its department for work with soviets, the organizational center of the capital's electoral campaign, pointed out that "many [of the commissions] were unable to cope... with the large and important volume of work that they had to complete." According to this report, the apparat often tried "to impose its own decisions," and worked "according to old, condemned stereotypes."[9]

Many—but not all—of the commissions' mistakes can be attributed to political manipulation. Some complaints were probably the result of inexperience and others the product of bureaucratic errors. The complex electoral law placed enormous new demands on a system that had been perfected, and petrified, for decades. Discussing the situation in Saratov, one analyst argued that the authorities pushed for single candidate elections because they wanted "to get by with a minimum of effort and worry" by making "the present campaign maximally resemble past experience."[10] Although many honest mistakes were made, it cannot be denied that the commissions were a political tool. Addressing the first session of the Congress of People's Deputies, Deputy I.P. Drutse declared that "although we stand here before you in nice suits, all of us are covered with scars and wounds. These were very difficult 'battles,' and, no, not 'battles' with the local population... We fought the apparat."[11]

Elections

Nomination. The first public stage of the campaign lasted from 26 December 1988 to 24 January 1989 when nomination meetings were held. In territorial and national-territorial districts 4,446 and 3,112 candidates, respectively, were nominated, or, on average, five candidates per seat. While in some districts the number of nominees exceeded 30, in almost 190 districts only one candidate was nominated.

Nomination meetings presented Soviet citizens with a new political opportunity, the chance to decide what type of individuals they wanted to become candidates. An article in *Literaturnaia gazeta* in early January outlined one non-traditional set of criteria: deputies should be prepared through both education and life experience to play a political role at the highest intellectual level and should have the personal courage to fight for both their beliefs and the interests of their electors. Adherents of this type of thinking rejected old stereotypes of deputorial behavior. One potential candidate, for example, refused nomination when he learned that it was expected that he would help find supplies for a local factory. "A USSR People's Deputy," he declared, "is first of all a political figure, not a supplier of a high rank."[12] Many local party officials clearly had different criteria: obedience, loyalty, and an unwillingness to rock the boat.

Nomination meetings were conducted both according to the traditional 'labor principle,' i.e. in the workplace, and a new 'geographic principle,' by the inhabitants of electoral districts. Nominations in the workplace were easily controllable by the local party organizations. Workers who wanted to nominate alternate candidates to oppose those supported by the relevant party committee would think twice, knowing that their jobs, housing, or other privileges could be threatened. There were, nonetheless, some exceptions to this rule.

Neighborhood caucuses held according to the 'geographic principle' were valid if they were attended by 500 voters. All candidates approved by more than half of those present were nominated. Local officials had several different tools at their disposal to influence these meetings.[13] First, representatives from the local electoral commission usually ran the meetings and were often able to produce the results they desired by orchestrating an inexperienced crowd. Second, they controlled access to all meeting rooms seating 500 people. It was impossible to hold a meeting without the knowledge and approval of the local electoral commission and, therefore, of the local party apparat. Often, approval for nomination caucuses was given at the last minute, which made it difficult to attract people. The local elite controlled access to the meeting room, either packing it with their own supporters, denying entry to people unable to prove residency, or, toward the end of a marathon session, announcing that enough people had left to disqualify the results. In sum, because of the control tools available to the apparat, nominations according to the 'geographic principle' were relatively uncommon. In Latvia, for example, 3,570 nomination meetings were held in workers' collectives but only 19 by neighborhood caucuses.[14]

Registration. The second stage of the electoral campaign took place from 26 January to 26 February, when electoral districts where more than two candidates were nominated were given the option of conducting registration meetings to decide which nominees would appear on the ballot.[15] In theory, the 832 registration meetings conducted nationwide promoted debate over the candidates by organizations that nominated them while widening participation for citizens who did not attend nomination meetings. In practice, local leaders often used these meetings to attain their own goals: as a rule, they reduced the number of candidates.[16]

Electoral commissions had two principal control levers during the registration stage. First, they had the power to control attendance at the registration meeting. The electoral law mandated no procedure to divide mandates among organizations that nominated candidates and residents of the district. Cooperation between the local electoral commission and the executive committee of the local soviet could ensure that the majority of delegates at the meeting were trustworthy.[17] In Moscow's Taganskii Electoral District, for example, the electoral commission put together a schedule for "meetings of the local population to nominate participants in the registration meeting." The schedule broke the region down by apartment block, set a date, time, and place for each meeting, and assigned an instructor from the local soviet and a member of the electoral commission to conduct the meeting.[18] By making a few phone calls to veterans' clubs and pensioners' organizations and failing to advertise the meetings the organizers could and did virtually guarantee the election of pliable delegates. In Moscow's Leninskii Electoral District, delegates were carefully chosen by the commission while other 'unoffical' delegates, freely elected at spontaneous meetings of citizens or by workers' collectives, were rejected.

A second weapon in the hands of the local authorities during registration meetings was the fact that procedures were undefined—delegates were supposed to establish their own procedures. This gave experienced apparatchiki from local electoral commissions the opportunity to orchestrate the meeting. Although there were some major exceptions to the control exercised by electoral commissions during the registration meetings—Yeltsin's success in the registration meeting for Moscow's national-territorial district No. 1 suggested that even handpicked delegates cannot be controlled once a meeting started—control over invitations was a powerful tool. Many citizens complained that the registration meetings were invalid and argued that voters should be allowed to choose among the candidates on election day. In Estonia, local electoral commissions decided to register all nominated candidates.[19]

In addition to the nomination and registration meetings, local officials used several other control levers. Party leaders or the electoral commission pressured candidates to decline nomination or drop out of the race.[20] In a system where the state controls employment, housing, health care, and other aspects of everyday life, this type of pressure was often quite effective. In some districts, candidates were 'imported' from Moscow or republican capitals. This was useful for the candidate, who received a safe seat, and local officials who hoped for support from their patron. For example, national-territorial electoral district No. 24 in Rostov 'hosted' A.V. Vlasov, chairman of the RSFSR's Council of Ministers and a candidate member of the Politburo. Although Vlasov lived and worked in Moscow, the local electoral commission registered him as the only candidate.[21] Another popular tactic was to place two identical candidates—tea pickers or milk maids for example—on the ballot.[22] In other districts, particularly where party secretaries were candidates, no opponents were tolerated. In sum, local officials manipulated the nomination and registration stages and thereby controlled who would appear on the ballot.

The Campaign. The third stage of the electoral process, the campaign of registered candidates, started on 26 February and stretched through election day on 26 March to second round elections and repeat elections that lasted until 9 May. To win, a candidate had to get more than 50% of the vote of registered voters. In districts where several candidates were registered, and no candidates won more than half the ballots, a run-off vote was held between the top two candidates. In districts where two candidates were registered and neither received a majority, repeat elections were held that included all the steps of the initial elections in a shortened time period.

Local electoral commissions distributed campaign posters with photographs of the candidates as well as a biographical sketch. Candidates were largely responsible for getting their programs to the voters. Discussing the techniques available to candidates during the campaign, chairman of the CEC V.P. Orlov called for, "a complete pluralism of opinions...After all, this is a battle!"[23]

In many areas, candidates creatively approached this battle and found novel solutions. I.I. Zaslavskii (Moscow's Oktiabrskii electoral district) was one good example of a candidate who worked to establish an appropriate image. Crippled by a childhood illness, Zaslavskii projected himself in the early stages of the campaign as a candidate who could and would fight for the rights of citizens unable to defend their own interests, particularly invalids and pensioners. His campaign literature stressed the determination and intelligence that enabled him to overcome a handicap, earn a degree, and become a successful scholar. One of his campaign posters had a photograph of him walking with a cane and holding the hand of a child. Later, Zaslavskii and his team became concerned that he would be attacked as a one-issue candidate. They fought this threat with a series of speeches and handouts. Zaslavskii won in the first round with 55% of the vote.

The 'Yeltsin affair,' for both the Soviet and worldwide audience, was probably the most interesting element of the 1989 Moscow elections. Boris Yeltsin, a long-time CPSU official who started his career in Sverdlovsk and moved to Moscow in 1986, was removed as chairman of the Moscow gorkom in November 1987 and relieved of his duties as a candidate member of the CPSU's Politburo in February 1988 after he sharply criticized Gorbachev at a Central Committee Plenum for the slow pace of perestroika.[24] In March 1989, a week before election day, the CPSU Central Committee announced its plans to investigate Yeltsin's political conduct during the campaign. Shortly after the anti-Yeltsin campaign started, a group of candidates led by S.B. Stankevich (a young research scholar and self-proclaimed 'progressive' involved in a tightly-contested race in one of Moscow's outlying districts) sent a collective protest telegram to the Central Committee. Both anecdotal and statistical evidence suggests that these candidates tried to ride on Yeltsin's coat tails. In short, a phenomenon that one might call the 'Yeltsin effect' strongly influenced the elections: Yeltsin candidates (those who signed the telegram) averaged about 46% of the vote in the March 26 election. Candidates who did not sign only averaged 26% of the vote.[25]

Deputies often made great efforts to avoid criticizing their opponents: this was viewed as dishonorable. Nonetheless, mudslinging was almost inevitable. In the Donbass, one correspondent used a police report that campaign teams were tearing down each other's posters as an excuse to make some broader comments about the elections. He noted that the campaign was proceeding in unprecedented circumstances: candidates had the right to agitate against their opponents. "But democracy is far from squabbling in the street...Slogans of doubtful quality...ring out from cars rigged with loudspeakers and slogans are appearing on walls and in shop windows that are on...the edge of good taste. And this is called democracy?"[26]

After a candidate was nominated and registered, it became more difficult for local officials to determine the outcome of the campaign. At this point, they ran the risk of creating martyrs. Nonetheless, interviews with candidates and campaign team members as well as frequent reports in the press suggest that several methods were used to harrass both unwanted candidates and their supporters.[27] The local police were used to bully supporters and rip down campaign posters. The electoral commission, responsible for finding places for candidates to meet with electors, sometimes refused to help. Pressure was placed on candidates at work. The provision of the electoral law that mandated equality of conditions was used to harass candidates who found novel ways to get their message across. When local party committees or industrial enterprises provided help for 'official' candidates, the equality clause was quietly overlooked. Party leaders found access to newspaper coverage simple to arrange—a phone call would elicit an interview or column trumpeting the candidate's merits.[28] Leaders of large industrial enterprises enjoyed many advantages, including transportation, printing help, and a large staffs.[29]

If all else failed, local authorities could cheat on election day. Moscow's Proletarskii electoral district, for example, was tightly controlled by the party apparat in favor of A.S. Samsonov, a local factory director. Samsonov was the object of a boycott campaign by citizens who viewed him as an 'official candidate,' i.e. a pawn of the local party organization. The boycott organizers hoped to force repeat elections by keeping turnout under 50% in runoff elections scheduled for 14 May 1989. Official results showed that barely over 54% of the district's eligible voters cast a ballot and Samsonov won. This slim margin almost certainly was the result of the apparat's efforts on Samsonov's behalf. I.V. Bogantseva, a leader of the boycott, reported that polling places throughout Samsonov's district were open until 10:00 p.m. instead of 8:00 p.m. as mandated by law. Despite a ban on agitation on election day, buses with loudspeakers attached summoned voters to the polls. At polling station No. 135, V.M. Sokhor, a representative of a local workers' collective, reported that the chairman of the local electoral commission allowed people to vote for others and gave a suspiciously-large number of ballots to representatives of the electoral commission who were responsible for a portable ballot box transported to voters who could not come to the station. The chairman prohibited Sokhor from observing the elections, declined to discuss the commission's procedures, and refused permission to observe the counting of the ballots.[30] Bogantseva argued in a complaint to the CEC that, "considering the low percentage of people who participated, [these violations] not only affected the results of the election, but in essence falsified it."[31]

Social Organizations and the 1989 Elections

The 1988 constitutional amendments mandated that 750 of the CPD's 2,250 deputies be elected from social organizations. Although each organization followed the three general stages of nomination, registration, and a campaign, each was allowed to devise its own procedures. For the most part, conservative party officials dominated the process.[32] Although the number of nominations usually exceeded the number of mandates (the CPSU, as a whole, nominated 31.5 thousand candidates for 100 spots), filtering at the regional, oblast and republican levels significantly reduced the number of candidates. Plenums of the social organizations had the final word. Here, the leadership of these organizations usually put together suggested lists of candidates. Thus, the January 1989 Central Committee Plenum ratified with no changes the list of 100 candidates for 100 mandates prepared by the Politburo.[33] In all, only 880 candidates were nominated to the 750 mandates allotted social organizations.

The elections to 25 seats for the CPD at the USSR's Academy of Sciences, a process that stretched from January through April 1989, provided an interesting counterpoint to the elections held by the CPSU. The electoral battles that rocked the Academy provided an excellent example of the battle between conservative and progressive forces. While the Presidium of the USSR's Academy of Sciences was one of the more conservative organizations in the country, the Academy's rank-and-file scientists and staff turned out to be among the most active fighters for free elections.

An electoral commission created by the Academy's Presidium was responsible for the campaign. Each Academy institute was allowed to nominate 'candidates for candidate' and elect representatives to an electoral conference that would vote on nominees. According to a decision of the Academy's Presidium, the conference consisted of all members and corresponding members of the Academy as well as delegates from the institutes elected according to a formula of one delegate per 150 workers. In all, 554 electors represented the 162,000 Academy workers. Each of the 903 Academicians had one vote.

The electoral commission compiled a list of 132 candidates. Some nominees were supported by many institutes while others were nominated by a handful. On 18 January, a meeting of the Presidium was scheduled to reduce the list to manageable numbers for a ballot. Proposals that all 132 nominees be included were rejected. Only 23 nominees received more than half of the votes of the Presidium and were thereby placed on the ballot. None of the progressive nominees, including Andrei Sakharov, made it to the final list. To create the impression of alternate candidates, the Presidium decided to give five places to scientific societies associated with the

Academy. This left 23 candidates for 20 spots.[34] The Academy exploded with displeasure at the lack of choice. "The rank-and-file scientists who did real research," as Sakharov later pointed out, "felt that the Plenum had disregarded its mandate..."[35] On 2 February, a demonstration organized by a group of Moscow researchers was held near the Presidium's building at the Academy. The organizers claimed that more than 3,000 participants from 50 institutes voted unanimously for five resolutions: (1) a vote of no confidence in the Academy's Presidium, (2) a call to members of the Academy to elect a new Presidium, (3) a summons to the 23 'official' candidates to drop out of the election, (4) a request to participants in the electoral conference not to vote and thereby force new elections, and (5) a summons to all of 'scientific society' to unite and organize on a democratic basis.[36]

A committee, 'For Democratic Elections From the USSR Academy of Sciences,' was formed to coordinate actions to influence the electoral conference scheduled for 21 March. The committee issued a summons for help from everyone connected with the Academy's institutes, met several times per week to coordinate strategy, and eventually demanded that the Presidium change its decision to allow the conference to vote on all 133 nominees. The Presidium declined, perhaps hoping that the conference would not fill all 20 spots on the first ballot and that a way could be found to end the scandal quietly.

On March 20th, the first day of the electoral conference, after none of the 23 nominees agreed to resign their candidacies, the protest committee asked all participants in the conference to cross off *all* names on the ballot. In this way, the committee hoped to achieve new elections. Because of the relative numbers of Academicians and delegates (903 vs. 554), the committee's strategy was to try to convince Academicians to vote against the Presidium's candidates. Out of 32 speakers at the meeting, 22 spoke against the Presidium's list. Voting took all day because of the long list and minimal technical help. Only eight candidates were elected. The committee set to work immediately to identify democratic candidates for the next round. On the third day of the conference, 77 candidates were nominated for the next round, including the unsuccessful candidates from the first round. In all, the list included 142 candidates. Next, the committee identified the nominees who had garnered the most support from the Academy institutes. Sakharov, for example, received 216 nominations. On 10 April, the Presidium met to create its own official list. In all, it contained 27 candidates, including the top twelve candidates on the committee's list. On 12 April, the Academy's second electoral conference met. All candidates supported by the committee were elected.

The Results: Accountability Reborn

In all, 2,895 candidates were included on the ballot in 1500 distrcits on 26 March. One district had 12 candidates, one had 11 candidates, one had 9 candidates, one had 7, four had 6 candidates, 12 had five candidates, 27 had four candidates, 109 districts had three candidates, 953 had two candidates, and 399 had one candidate. Members and candidate members of the CPSU made up 85.3% of the candidates, women 16%, workers more than 25%, and collective farm workers 12%. In the 399 single-candidate districts, 54% of those on the ballot were party or industrial officials.[37]

Nationwide, 89.5% of registered voters went to the polls. Out of 750 territorial districts, elections were held in 749. Candidates were elected in 590, runoff elections were scheduled in 46 districts, and in 115 other districts repeat elections were scheduled. Out of 750 national-territorial districts, elections were held in 748. Deputies were elected in 636 districts, runoffs were scheduled in 30 districts, and repeat elections in 82. Out of the 750 mandates assigned to social organizations, 732 were filled by election day. Runoffs or repeat elections were scheduled for 18 places.[38]

The elections demonstrated some clear differences among regions of the country. One Soviet study concluded that two zones stood out: (1) the Baltic, the central, north-western, and northern regions of Russsia, and (2) the southern section of the European portion of the USSR, Kazakhstan and the republics of Central Asia. If, in the USSR as a whole, there was an average of 1.9 candidates per territorial district, in the first region the average was higher: in Lithuania 3.5, in Moscow 3.1, in Kiev 3.0, in Leningrad 2.4. "This serves as circumstantial evidence that the politicization of the population began and [was] proceeding at a faster tempo in the capital and regions with many cities." The number of candidates in the second region was below the national average, which reflected the control exercised by the local party elite.

An analysis of levels of participation reinforced the results of the analysis of numbers of candidates. In the RSFSR and the Baltics, participation was lower "because of the activity of informal organizations and a sharply nihilistic attitude on the part of many voters...." The situation was different in the Ukraine, the Caucasus, and Central Asia, where participation levels were as high as 98.6% in contests that varied little from the past. This study also pointed to evidence that party workers were much more likely to run in single-member districts. "In other words, representatives of this group ran principally in rural districts and in cities where representatives of the intelligentsia were popular the share of [party workers] was low."

One of the most striking results of the election was the defeat of a high percentage of the party and soviet leadership that ran for office. "Leningrad voters," for example, "[refused to elect] all party and soviet leaders of the city and oblast including the chairmen of the executive committees if the oblast and city soviets and their deputies." In all, 29 oblast and *krai* first secretaries were defeated. Most of these ran in regions of the North and North-Western part of the European territory of Russia, in the Urals, in Siberia, or in the Far East. One should also note that

> in addition to this 'zonal' factor... the voters of many big cities, including the capitals of the union republics, voted against [their] *gorkom* first secretaries... All this was recognized by the party leaders. The overwhelming majority... preferred districts in the periphery to districts in oblast centers and rural to urban districts. And this [practice] justified itself: in isolated rural districts local leaders almost always ran without competition and won. Out of 90% of winning party leaders, 70% ran without competition, and among losers 70% competed with other candidates.[39]

The same factors were visible in the campaigns of members of the government structure, including the heads of governments of union and autonomous republics and republican and oblast soviets.

The electoral protest against the party was not only expressed in the defeat of specific party-backed candidates. Voters had at least three other options: vote against *all* candidates on the ballot; stay home; or cast an invalid ballot. In Moscow, in each district an average of 11% of voters crossed off the names of all candidates on their ballot. These ballots can be viewed either as a protest against the electoral system as a whole or as a protest against the candidates registered in a given electoral district. More than 32% of voters crossed all names off their ballots in both Liublinskii Electoral District, where the unpopular head of the Moscow City Soviet ran against a factory worker, and Sverdlovskii Electoral District, where three candidates combined failed to earn 50% of the vote. Such behavior suggests a significant amount of voter dissatisfaction and a desire to express that dissatisfaction actively. Several organizations, including a 'Confederation of Anarcho-Syndicalists,' encouraged Moscow's voters to cast protest ballots. By limiting turnout to less than 50% the confederation hoped to force new elections. The confederation's one concession to the elections was to ask people to vote for Yeltsin, the 'leader of the inner-party opposition.' Various 'initiative groups' called for boycotts of the election to protest manipulation by the party apparatus, or undemocratic elements of the law on elections.

Registered voters who did not cast their ballots may have been apathetic, may simply have forgotten, or may have been consciously protesting the elections. In Moscow, on average, 83.5% of voters in each district went to the polls. The totals ranged from a high of 86.7% in Tushinskii Electoral District, where a popular candidate faced pressure from the party apparat to a low of 78.4% in Medvedkovskii District, where a hockey coach ran against a school teacher. If even one third of those who failed to go to the polls were protesting, the total proportion of protest votes in some districts was quite high. Moreover, if any portion of ballots declared invalid were consciously invalidated by disgruntled voters, and not merely a result of unfamiliar procedures, the percentage of protest votes was even higher.

Notes

1. Protest voting in the form of non-participation or voting against the candidate was not unknown. Although some citizens used the elections to protest living conditions or demonstrate dissatisfaction with society, this is a far cry from accountability through competitive elections. See, for example, D. Bahry and B. Silver, 'Soviet Participation on the Eve of Democratization,' *APSR*, Vol. 84, No. 3, 1990.; Rasma Karklins, "Soviet Elections Revisited: Voter Abstention in Non-competitive Balloting," *APSR*, Vol. 80, No. 3, pp. 449–470.; Werner G. Hahn, "Electoral Choice in the Soviet Bloc," *Problems of Communism*, No. 36, 1987, pp. 29–39.

2. My account of this process is based on discussions in the fall of 1988 with G.V. Barabashev, a participant in the process. For an account of the group's work see, "Zakonotvorchestvo." *Pravda*, 7 November 1989, p. 3. Michael Urban offers a more detailed description of this process, also partially based on discussions with Barabashev, in *More Power to the Soviets*, pp. 35–57.

3. On this point see A. Sobchak, "Ot sezda k sezdu: stanovlenie novoi politicheskoi sistemy," *Cherez ternii*, Moscow: Progress, 1990, pp. 458–459.

4. Jerry F. Hough provides an excellent overview of the elections in "The Politics of Successful Economic Reform," *Soviet Economy*, Vol. 5, No. 1, 1989, pp. 3–46. See also Vladimir N. Brovkin, "The Making of Elections to the Congress of People's Deputies (CPD) in March 1989," *The Russian Review*, Vol. 49, 1990, pp. 441–442.

5. For a discussion of the CEC's work see "Prezumptsiia spravedlivosti," *Pravda*, 7 February 1989, p. 3.

6. This may not be unusual: it is difficult to prove electoral fraud. See, for example, Chopra's discussion of the Indian national electoral commission in *Electoral Reform in India*, New Delhi: 1988. For a discussion of manipulative tactics used in 1989 see V. Brovkin, "The Making of Elections..."

7. *Izvestiia*, 3 June 1989, p. 5. See also V.A. Kolosov and E.V. Sidorova, "Geografiia vyborov v SSSR: Osnovnye cherty i spetsifika krupnykh gorodov (na premere Moskvy)," *Politicheskaia Geografiia: sovremennoe sostoianie i puti razvitiia*, edited by V.A. Kolosov and A.V. Novikov, Moscow: Moskovskii filial geograficheskogo obshchestva SSSR, 1989.

8. Interviews in several regional soviets in the spring and summer of 1989 confirm this point. See, for example, "Voskhozhdenie k demokratii," *Pravda*, 4 April 1989, p. 3.

9. *Moskvichi vybiraiut narodnykh deputatov, O nekotorykh itogakh vyborov narodnykh deputatov SSSR v g. Moskve v marte-mae 1989, Ispolnitelnyi komitet Moskovskogo Gorodskogo Soveta Narodnykh Deputatov, Otdel po rabote sovetov*, Moscow: 1989, p. 22. Only after the elections did V.P. Orlov, head of the Central Electoral Commission, complain about the weakness of local electoral commissions caused by the presence of amateur commission members. See "Demokratiia nabiraet silu," *Sovetskaia Rossiia*, 14 March 1989, p. 1.

10. "Luchshego—iz odnogo?," *Izvestiia*, 14 January 1989, p. 2.

11. *Izvestiia*, 2 June 1989, p. 7. Another deputy complained that he had faced the "might, strength, perfidy, cruelty, and treachery" of the apparat. See *Izvestiia*, 27 May 1989, p. 3.

12. "Vydvizhenie kandidatov: uroki i vyvody," *Pravda*, 28 January 1989, p. 3.

13. For a discussion of some of these difficulties see "Golos na vyborakh," *Literaturnaia gazeta*, 24 May 1989.

14. See, for example, "Kandidaty nazvany—borba vperedi," *Izvestiia*, 25 January 1989, p. 2.

15. Procedures for the registration meeting are discussed in "Vtoroi etap izbiratelnoi kampanii," *Izvestiia*, 23 January 1989, p. 2. For a discussion of the registration stage with G.V. Barabashev, a member of the CEC, see "Volna i krugi," *Izvestiia*, 9 February 1989, p. 2.

16. For a discussion of the role played by local leaders see "Demokratiia nabiraet silu," *Sovetskaia Rossiia*, 14 March 1989, p. 1.

17. For a review of this process see "Nadezhnye liudi v zale," *Izvestiia*, 6 February 1989, p. 2. See also "Golos na vyborakh," *Literaturnaia gazeta*, 24 May 1989, p. 10.

18. *Grafik provedeniia sobranii naseleniia po vydvizheniiu uchastnikov okruzhnogo predvybornogo sobraniia*. For a report on Yeltsin's registration meeting see "Dvoe kandidatov iz desiati," *Izvestiia*, 22 February 1989.

19. "Bez okruzhnykh sobranii," *Izvestiia*, 10 February 1989, p. 1.

20. See, for example, "Kak menia otgovarivali," *Izvestiia*, 22 February 1989, p. 2.

21. It is unclear how much the central CPSU apparat and local party bosses cooperated on this type of question. Most of the members of the highest level of the party elite were elected to the CPD through the safe mechanism of the CPSU's quota as a social organization. See "Zaregistrirovan kandidatom," *Trud*, 8 February 1989, p. 3. "Vremia aktivnykh deistvii," *Trud*, 15 February 1989, p. 1.

22. Discussing the results of the election in one oblast, a Soviet correspondent noted that "in the first electoral district a collective farm worker and a factory foreman competed, in a second—a foreman and a tractor driver, in a third—a mechanic and a foreman, and there was still one more district with only one candidate, the *obkom* secretary...My conclusion is most simple: the depths of the country have not awoken..." For an empirical, comparative analysis of the elections in several oblasts see V.A. Lavanskii, A.V. Obolonskii, and G.D. Tokarovskii, "Izbiratelnaia kampaniia po vyboram narodnykh deputatov SSSR 1989 (opyt sotsiologicheskogo issledovaniia)," *Sovetskoe gosudarstvo i pravo*, No. 7, 1989, pp. 12-25.

23. Orlov argues that the battle should be conducted within the framework of 'socialist morality.' See "Demokratiia nabiraet silu," *Sovetskaia Rossiia*, 14 March 1989, p. 1.

24. For Yeltsin's interpretation of the campaign see his biography, *Against the Grain*, New York: Summit, 1990.

25. For a discussion of the 'Yeltsin phenomenon' see Brendan Kiernan and Joseph Aistrup, "Moscow's 1989 Elections to the Congress of People's Deputies," *Soviet Studies*, Vol. 43, No. 6. 1991, pp. 1049-1064.

26. "Pod pokrovom temnoty," *Sotsialisticheskii Donbass*, 3 March 1989, p. 1.

27. I interviewed numerous campaign team members in Moscow in the summer of 1989. For a representative Soviet newspaper report see "Kompromat na kandidata," *Izvestiia*, 14 April 1989, p. 3. Candidates' campaign teams are discussed in "Doverie doverennomu litsu," *Izvestiia*, 4 March 1989, p. 1 and "Agitatsiia bez agitpunktov," *Izvestiia*, 4 February 1989, p. 2.

28. V.T. Saikin, the mayor of Moscow and a candidate for people's deputy, discussed his work in a half-page interview published in *Pravda* on 19 March 1989. See also "Milliony liudei, milliony problem," *Pravda*, 19 March 1989, p. 3.

29. For a report from the CEC on the difficulties of guaranteeing equality of conditions see, "Nakal borby," *Sovetskaia Rossiia*, 17 February 1989. A report from Perm on differences in the campaigns of two workers and a factory director see "V ravnykh li usloviiakh?," *Zvezda*, 3 March 1989.

30. *Zaiavlenie v tsentralnuiu izbiratelnuiu kommissiiu*, V.M. Sokhor, 15 May 1989.

31. Interview of I.V. Bogantseva, summer 1989. I.V. Bogantseva, *Protest v Tsentralnuiu izbiratelnuiu komissiiu po vyboram narodnykh deputatov SSSR*, 17 May 1989.

32. On this point, and for a broader discussion of the elections, see Michael Urban, *More Power to the Soviets*, pp. 93–98.

33. The results of the elections in the Central Committee can be considered a type of political barometer. Politburo members Egor Ligachev (78) and Alexander Yakovlev (59) received the most negative votes, a measure of the relative unpopularity of the conservative and liberal wings of the leadership. Gorbachev received 12 negative votes. See *Izvestiia*, 19 March 1989, p. 1.

34. See "Strasti po-akademicheskii," *Izvestiia*, 1 February 1989, p. 3 and "Deputaty ot Akademii nauk SSSR," *Izvestiia*, 21 April 1989, p. 3. This discussion of the inside maneuvering in the Academy is based on interviews with RSFSR deputy A. Shabad and K. Kuranov as well as "Kak prokhodili vybory na Sezd narodnykh deputatov SSSR ot Akademii Nauk SSSR," an unpublished interview of V.L. Sheinis, a principal figure in the protest against the Academy's Presidium.

35. A.D. Sakharov, *Moscow and Beyond: 1986 to 1989*, translated by Antonina Boius, New York: Knopf, 1991.

36. "Informatsiia o mitinge," undated leaflet.

37. "Demokratiia nabiraet silu," p. 1.

38. "Soobshchenie tsentralnoi izbiratelnoi komissii ob itogakh vyborov narodnykh deputatov SSSR v 1989 godu," *Izvestiia*, 5 April 1989, p. 1. An excellent summary of the results is presented by Stephen White in "The Elections to the USSR Congress of People's Deputies in March 1989," *Electoral Studies*, Vol. 9, No. 1, 1990, pp. 59–66. See also "Parliamentary Elections in the USSR: Voters Stun Officialdom," *FBIS Analysis Report*, 16 June 1989.

39. V.A. Kolosov and E.V. Sidorova, "Geografiia vyborov v SSSR: Osnovnye cherty i spetsifika krupnykh gorodov (na premere Moskvy)," *Politicheskaia Geografiia: sovremennoe sostoianie i puti razvitiia*, V.A. Kolosov and A.V. Novikov, eds., Moscow: Moskovskii filial geograficheskogo obshchestva SSSR, 1989. National representation is discussed by V. Tishkov in "Etnologicheskii analiz sovetskogo parlamenta," *Narodnyi deputat*, No. 7, 1990, pp. 6–16. For a general look at the composition of the newly-elected CPD see, "V zerkale tsifr i faktov," *Narodnyi deputat*, No. 1, 1990, pp. 24–25.

Chapter 5

The Congress of People's Deputies

Few Western tourists leave Moscow without a souvenir. Many purchase a *matryoshka*, a wooden doll with a series of smaller dolls nested inside. When trade moved into the streets after trade restrictions were loosened in 1988-89, the figures painted on the dolls changed dramatically. The dour but profitable faces of politicians replaced cherubic peasants. In 1990, one of the most popular new *matryoshka* dolls depicted Gorbachev with Brezhnev, Khrushchev, Stalin, and a tiny Lenin nested inside. Gorbachev, however, was not only the subject of *matryoshka* art—he tried it himself, if only in a figurative sense. The new Congress of People's Deputies and the Supreme Soviet can be considered a type of *matryoshka*: a clever set of nested institutions that reflect changes in the political climate, were fun to look at, but served little practical purpose.

Preparing the Congress

In December 1988, the final session of the old Supreme Soviet ratified constitutional amendments that radically altered the institutional structure of the USSR's central government.[1] A Congress of People's Deputies, a popularly-elected, unicameral, representative institution empowered to resolve any question within the competence of the USSR, became the highest organ of state power. In theory, the CPD set the USSR's political agenda and monitored the implementation of its directives by the Supreme Soviet, a smaller, standing body elected from among the CPD's members. The CPD consisted of 2250 deputies elected according to the following formula: 750 deputies from territorial districts, 750 from national-territorial districts, and 750 deputies from social organizations. The first meeting of a newly elected CPD was called by the Supreme Soviet not later than two months after the elections. Thereafter, the CPD was supposed to be called into session by the Supreme Soviet at least once a year.

As Chairman of the Presidium of the old Supreme Soviet, Gorbachev was responsible for organizing the work of the new Congress. He used a variety of methods, constitutional and extra-constitutional, to accomplish this task. Work done by Anatolii Lukianov and the Secretariat of the Presidium of the old Supreme Soviet, the Central Committee and its apparatus, republican deputy groups, and the CPD's party group was intended to encourage the smooth flow of the CPD's first session. That is, like any shrewd politician, Gorbachev did everything possible to shape the decisionmaking process in his favor.

Lukianov, the Central Committee, and the Secretariat of the Supreme Soviet's Presidium

Anatolii Lukianov, at the time a candidate member of the Politburo and Gorbachev's ally in the Secretariat of the Presidium of the old Supreme Soviet, managed the preparations of the first session of the CPD.[2] Lukianov started his political career at Moscow State University in the 1950s, where he was responsible for Komsomol activities through which he met Gorbachev for the first time. He rose through the party ranks, serving in a wide variety of posts while earning a doctorate in law. Between 1977 and 1983, Lukianov was head of the Secretariat of the Presidium of the old Supreme Soviet. In 1988, Gorbachev returned Lukianov to the Presidium's Secretariat, probably because his first six-year tour there qualified him as an expert in the preparation of political spectacles.

Preparations for the first session of the CPD were conducted in a manner consistent with past practice for the Supreme Soviet. Gorbachev and the party apparatus controlled the process through the Presidium of the Supreme Soviet. Lukianov outlined for the Congress the mechanism at work in the preparatory period. After the date for the convocation of the Congress was announced "packet of proposals prepared by the Presidium [of the Supreme Soviet] was sent to the Presidiums of the republican Supreme Soviets."[3] Decisions made by the central party apparat were implemented by local party organizations under cover of the corresponding soviets.

The CPSU Central Committee met on the eve of the session to approve the CPD's agenda. Although a stenogram of the plenum was not published, remarks made by deputies at the session of the CPD suggest that the Central Committee reviewed and approved all major issues connected with the Congress and the first session of the Supreme Soviet. Boris Yeltsin, for example, maintained that "the agenda of the Congress was established [at the plenum] without the participation of deputies..."[4] Deputy Iu.D. Chernichenko claimed that "even the leaders of parliamentary commissions were confirmed at the plenum of the Central Committee...Manipulations behind the scenes—what an anachronism!"[5]

The Party Group

References were made by deputies throughout the session to the role played by the 'party group,' a meeting of all Communist deputies held prior to the opening of the Congress. The party group had been one of the principal control instruments in the old Supreme Soviet. Article 63 of the party statute declared that "The corresponding party organ leads the work of party groups in non-party organizations..."[6] In the case of the CPD, the corresponding party organ was the CPSU Central Committee.

Unfortunately, no stenographic records of the party group's meeting were published, so it is difficult to evaluate the role that it played. Nonetheless, there is evidence that the Central Committee's list of candidates for government posts did not receive its unanimous support. This suggests that the group served both as a forum for discussion and a filter. Deputy Sobchak reported, for example, that the party group rejected a few candidacies recommended by the Central Committee for government posts.[7] Gorbachev summarized the main elements of an argument that took place in the party group over the nomination for the chairmanship of the Supreme Court: some members of the party group were dissatisfied with his qualifications and, consequently, his candidacy was withdrawn.[8] In sum, it seems, the party group discussed all major questions that would arise at the CPD, probably so that less time needed to be spent during the session.[9] Whether the group allowed rank-and-file members a vote equal to the leadership's is an open question. Deputy Chernichenko summarized one view of the situation when he argued that, although the Supreme Soviet had the right to confirm ministers, this right did not change the ministers' subordination to the central party apparatus.[10]

Deputy Groups

Republican, oblast, and other deputy groups also helped resolve a series of questions prior to the opening of the session. For instance, the deputy groups confirmed leadership decisions about who would serve in the Supreme Soviet. Deputy Afanasev described this process.

In most cases membership lists for the Supreme Soviet were made up by the party leadership of corresponding oblasts and republics *before the CPD*, on a non-alternative basis, and with non-secret voting. First Secretary Mesiats gathered us, the deputies from the Moscow region, and conducted this preliminary appointment to the Supreme Soviet, even though he is just a simple deputy like us, and in the RSFSR [Politburo member] Vorotnikov did the same thing.[11]

Meetings of republican groups served as rubber stamps for membership lists prepared in advance, and thereby gave party leaders the ability to influence the Supreme Soviet's membership.[12]

Any discussion of the preparations for the Congress should note that conservative elements had a strong say in most republican party and deputy groups, but that the central party apparatus was unable to control the process as it had in the past. Discussing proposals sent to the republics by the old Supreme Soviet's Presidium, Lukianov pointed out: "I will say frankly that [these proposals] were not always and everywhere given to the deputies..." That is, some republics and areas, Lithuania for example, refused to follow instructions. Moreover, after the preliminary 'appointments' were made to the Supreme Soviet, and after the start of the session, some additional changes were made.[13]

The Assembly of Representatives

On 24 May, Gorbachev conducted a meeting of representatives from republican deputy groups: 446 representatives met for nine hours to discuss the CPD's agenda, the membership of the Supreme Soviet's committees, nominees to government posts, and other organizational questions.[14] Deputies referred to this meeting throughout the session. V.A. Statuliavichius, for example, noted that the Assembly helped select nominees for elections to the Supreme Soviet.[15] Deputy Gavriil Popov noted that a group of deputies from Moscow proposed an alternative procedure for elections to the Supreme Soviet that was rejected.[16] The CPD's weekly bulletin stated that the Assembly was created "for the preparatory review of questions decided at the Congress of People's Deputies."[17] No such 'working organ' was defined in the Soviet constitution. That is, Gorbachev worked around the law to create a mechanism to control legislative outcomes.

The Moscow Deputies Group

One of the most revolutionary developments prior to the first session of the CPD was the creation of a group that offered an alternative agenda to the one proposed by the Communist Party. During the late winter and spring of 1989, a group of Moscow's self-described 'progressive' deputies met to prepare independent proposals for the CPD. These discussions were open to any elected deputy.[18] Deputies Popov, A.D. Sakharov, and others prepared a number of documents, including an alternate agenda, constitutional amendments on several aspects of the work of the CPD and Supreme Soviet, a new committee structure for the Supreme Soviet, and a list of economic reforms. The group submitted its proposals to the Supreme Soviet's Secretariat for distribution to the deputies before the start of the session. The Secretariat, however, refused to take action.[19]

Infrastructure

During the first session, Gorbachev's attitude toward political leadership and the participation of the 'party group' was revealed in infrastructural questions. One of Lukianov's principal responsibilities was to create the CPD's working environment. The stenogram of the entire first session is peppered with complaints about the inadequacy of the measures taken. Perhaps the clearest example of the infrastructural problems that plagued the session was the sound system. The CPD's 2,250 members conducted their business in the Kremlin's Great Hall of Congresses, an enormous auditorium that, in traditional Soviet style, dwarfs the individual. Microphones were placed on stands at strategic points around the hall. Deputies were required to stand on line to wait their turn to speak. The CPD's voting procedures also were inadequate: no technical means were installed to tally votes or keep track of voting records. The manual counting of 2,250 raised hands was time consuming; moreover, there was no way to hold deputies accountable to the public for their votes. Gorbachev was at times forced into the ludicrous position of counting votes out loud. Lukianov's attitude toward the problems of infrastructure suggest that Gorbachev was using this factor to help control the Congress.[20]

The First Session of the CPD

The first session of the Congress of People's Deputies met from 25 May until 9 June 1989 in the Great Hall of Congresses in the Kremlin. The agenda was published on the eve of the opening day. Gorbachev and the party apparatus expected to be able to march through it in three days.[21] They failed to anticipate the political spectacle that awaited them. Diversion from the agenda became a rule, not an exception.

The CPD's potential for political drama was demonstrated shortly before the opening of the first day when, just after the television cameras had been turned on and the broadcast had started, a Georgian deputy jumped to the podium, seized the microphone, and asked his fellow deputies to rise in a moment of silence in honor of people killed in Tbilisi on 9 April 1989 by Soviet troops. Television screens briefly went blank but returned almost immediately to the Congress.

Electing the Chairman of the Supreme Soviet

Andrei Sakharov was the first deputy officially to address the Congress officially. He spoke in the name of the Moscow Deputies' Group when he proposed that the CPD rearrange its agenda to force Gorbachev and Ryzhkov to make their reports *before* they could be nominated and elected to their respective posts of Chairman of the Supreme Soviet and Chairman of the Council of Ministers. Sakharov challenged the CPSU's right to power and leadership and proposed that the Congress pass a Decree on Power stating that it, not the CPSU, was the USSR's highest political institution. Other deputies, perhaps fearing that Gorbachev might not be elected, spoke in favor of the original agenda. It was not revised.

Deputy Chingiz Aitmatov nominated Gorbachev for Chairman of the Supreme Soviet in a lengthy speech given in the name of the representatives of the republican delegations and with the unanimous support of the CPD's party group. An unprecedented question and answer period followed. Perhaps the most controversial issue discussed was the advisability of allowing one person to hold the posts of General Secretary of the Communist Party and Chairman of the Supreme Soviet. Some deputies claimed that one man would have too much power if he held both posts and would be a virtual dictator. Others argued that the only way to transfer power from the Central Committee apparat to the CPD and the Supreme Soviet was for Gorbachev to manage the process through a dual appointment. Gorbachev was asked some pointed questions about his personal responsibility for several political decisions as well as inquiries about his lifestyle. Some deputies seemed to pin their support for Gorbachev, or the support of their delegations, on his response to their questions. Deputy M.I. Lauristin, for example, spoke in the name of the 'national-democratic movement of the Baltic' when she asked Gorbachev to answer three questions: What constitutional guarantees should be given for national and republican sovereignty?; What did he think of the use of the army against Soviet citizens?; and, Which Politburo members knew in advance that force would be used against demonstrators in Tbilisi on 9 April? Several deputies argued that it was undemocratic for Gorbachev to run unopposed: in this view, the essence of democracy is alternative candidacies. Deputy A.M. Obolenskii nominated himself for the position and was given time, at Gorbachev's urging, to present his ideas to the CPD.[22] The deputies decided, however, not to include Obolenskii on the ballot. Gorbachev was elected in a secret ballot with only 87 negative votes.

Electing the Supreme Soviet

The second day of the session was devoted almost exclusively to electing the Supreme Soviet. In the name of the Assembly of Representatives, Deputy E.S. Stroev, an *obkom* first secretary, presented the CPD with a list of 542 candidates for the Supreme Soviet, 271 for the Soviet of the Union and 271 for the Soviet of the Nationalities. Although republican and oblast delegations played the most important role in deciding who would be on the ballot, procedures and opinions on the elections to the Supreme Soviet varied. While Deputy I.O. Bisher pointed out that the Latvian delegation decided all questions by an open vote, Deputy Minzhurenko reported another procedure in his oblast. "It turns out that to get into the Supreme Soviet by bypassing the *obkom* first secretary, as in the past, in our delegation is impossible... This is undemocratic, comrades."

The most debated question during the elections to the Supreme Soviet, indeed throughout the session, was that of alternative candidacies. The Moscow delegation voted to include 55 nominees for the 29 places allotted to it in the Supreme Soviet. Some deputies interpreted this as an attempt to seize more places than would have been demographically correct, a type of egoism exhibited by the capital's representatives. The Moscow deputies claimed that democracy demanded a choice and that, if republican delegations decided everything, it would not be necessary to gather to vote as a whole legislature.[23] The Baltic deputies, fearing outside interference in their affairs, argued that Moscow's deputies should not ask other delegations to choose for them because there was no information available on the candidates. Deputy B.F. Pylin pointed out that the deputies had not even been given a list of their colleagues or information about republican delegations. Consequently, he argued, it would then be necessary to listen to the platforms of all the candidates.[24] In the end, the Moscow delegation refused to withdraw its 'extra' nominations, which led to the defeat of many of its more radical members.

Deputies also discussed whether they would leave their former jobs to work full time in the Supreme Soviet, a prerequisite for creating a professional parliament. Deputy F.M. Burlatskii pointed out what he considered the essence of the problem of part-time deputies: "We will end up with exactly the same situation that we had in the old parliament." Deputy R.Z. Sagdeev noted that 25 oblast and republican first secretaries were included in the list of nominees for the Supreme Soviet, hinting that they were hardly likely to leave these positions to work in Moscow. In the end, the CPD decided to leave a loophole: deputies 'as a rule' would leave their former jobs to work full time in the Supreme Soviet.[25]

A Stalinist-Brezhnevite Majority?

The third day of the session opened with a report by Deputy Iu.A. Osipian, the head of the CPD's electoral commission, on the results of the elections to the Soviet of the Nationalitiess. The Congress ratified the results and then conducted a debate over procedures while the electoral commission finished compiling results for the Soviet of the Union. Two of the most controversial issues of the session appeared during this debate. First, Deputy Afanasev charged Gorbachev with manipulating the Congress to create "an aggressively-obedient majority" in the Supreme Soviet. The voting lists compiled by republican and oblast delegations, he claimed, gave the apparat the tool it needed to create a compliant legislature. Second, Deputy Popov announced that the Moscow Deputies' Group would form a parliamentary group within the CPD. This announcement elicited a storm of rhetoric, both positive and negative. Finally, Osipian returned, reported, and the CPD ratified the results. After electing the Supreme Soviet, the CPD moved on to the next point in the agenda, electing the Supreme Soviet's vice chairman. Gorbachev nominated Lukianov, gave a brief nomination speech, and opened discussion. After a lengthy debate, the CPD adjourned without a decision.

On its fourth working day, the Congress continued its discussion of Lukianov's candidacy. He was questioned aggressively by deputies concerned with his participation in a number of political decisions. Perhaps the best indicator of the quality of the discussion was provided by the questions put to Lukianov by Deputies T.Kh. Gdlian and N.V. Ivanov. These two deputies had worked together as investigators for the USSR procurator and had uncovered evidence that, they claimed, demonstrated high level political corruption. They hammered Lukianov with a series of detailed questions. His answers were a political masterpiece of evasion and abstraction. In the end, issues of competence and integrity raised by the two prosecutors were brushed aside and Lukianov was elected.

The session's fourth day included debate over procedure, an issue that would return to haunt the CPD and Supreme Soviet again and again. First, after Deputies Shchelkanov and Konovalov questioned the process employed to elect Lukianov, and the CPD rejected their accusations, Gorbachev decided to head off further procedural questioning with a thinly veiled threat: "I have received information," he noted, "that there are certain people who want to... constantly poke a stick in the wheel of the Congress by means of procedural questions..." He declared that such actions would be a mistake and that "in such a serious situation it is the type of mistake that would be worthwhile for the Congress to evaluate."[26] Second, the question of alternative candidacies, a central issue in Gorbachev's election, was also raised in connection with Lukianov's nomination. For example, Deputy I.N. Shundeev asked, "Why is the Congress moving away from electoral democracy? Why was there no alternative candidacy to...Lukianov?"[27]

Although the CPD had decided to devote the afternoon session on May 29th to procedural questions, the discussion took an unexpected turn when Deputy Popov proposed a way to resolve the 'Yeltsin question.' Boris Yeltsin was elected by an overwhelming majority of millions of Muscovites to the CPD but had not been elected to the Supreme Soviet. A lawyer from Siberia who *had* been elected, Deputy Iurii Kazannik, announced that he was willing to resign his position in favor of Yeltsin. Popov and Kazannik outlined their plan to the CPD and a number of deputies took the floor to support or attack it. After a good deal of debate, no opposition from Gorbachev, and some procedural posturing, the proposal passed and a vote was taken. Yeltsin became a member of the Soviet of the Nationalities.

Gorbachev's Report

On May 30th, the CPD listened to Gorbachev's report, 'Concerning the principal directions of the USSR's domestic and foreign policy.' The first section of the speech, by far the longest, was devoted to the economy, to "turning the economy in favor of the people" by producing more and better consumer goods and improving the service sector. Gorbachev devoted the second section of the speech to political reform. Repeating a series of old arguments, he claimed that the roots of the changes could be traced directly to the April 1985 Central Committee Plenum, argued that the rebirth of the soviets was an important step, and claimed that further development depended on "a clear division of functions between party and state organs." The soviets should not only be given legislative responsibilities, but should exercise "real levers of power."

Gorbachev's speech was a success if for no other reason than it gave deputies who had started to complain about the debate over procedure something else to attack. The discussion was an unprecedented political spectacle, a series of speeches that touched on almost every aspect of Soviet life. However, aside from an opportunity to express individual opinions and present grievances, it was unclear what the goal of the discussion was: Gorbachev had already been elected. Representatives of each of the union republics, autonomous republics, and principal social groups were given the floor. Discussion had hardly gotten started, however, when the tragedy in Tbilisi that had been commemorated on the first day of the session once again commanded attention. Deputy T.V. Gamkrelidze sidetracked discussion of Gorbachev's speech by questioning the appropriateness of the fact that General I.N. Rodionov, a principal figure in the tragic events, was elected a deputy to the CPD and was sitting in the hall. General Rodionov rose to defend himself and the armed forces. A long debate ensued: deputies demanded to know who knew what, when they knew, and what actions were approved at the highest level.

Over the next several days, discussion of Gorbachev's report touched on a wide range of questions of interest to voters. Deputies V.A. Starodubtsev and V.A. Gontar, kolkhoz chairmen, spoke for a 417-member group of deputies from agricultural districts. Starodubtsev pointed out that, unless Soviet citizens were fed, perestroika would fail. He outlined many of the problems facing Soviet agriculture and called for a number of specific reforms, including "measures for limiting the monopoly powers of [the centralized agricultural administration] and giant factories," giving "electricity and gas to rural homes on a level with the conditions in the city and at the same price," and creating "in the Supreme Soviet...a committee for agricultural questions for the defense of the interests of the Soviet peasantry..."[28] Deputy B.S. Mitin, elected by the trade unions, spoke in the name of a group of "more than 200 deputies who are representatives of the sphere of education." The group had distributed a brief memo outlining the condition of the USSR's educational system. Mitin summarized the memo's contents and added some thoughts of his own.

Deputy Gorbunov, the Chairman of the Presidium of the Latvian Supreme Soviet, discussed one of the principal issues facing the USSR: the relationship between the republics and the federal government. He proposed a series of constitutional amendments intended to revive republican sovereignty.[29] Deputy Kolesnikov represented his constituents in Rostov by questioning the safety of a local nuclear power plant.[30] He noted that his delegation had forwarded to the Congress's Presidium "tens of thousands of letters" on this question.

Nationalities pressed their interests at the CPD. Deputy V.I. Belov, a well-known writer on Russian pastoral themes, Russian nationalist, and a deputy to the CPD elected by the Communist party, devoted his time to two subjects. First, he defended Russia and the Russians against 'Russophobia,' which, he claimed, was a result of the political oppression of Russia, not a sign of its dominance. He touched on many of the other favorite issues of the Russian nationalist movement, including cultural, ecological and economic questions. Deputy Amonashvili discussed the problem of teaching history in Georgian schools and insisted on speaking a few words in Georgian as a way of supporting the use of languages other than Russian. Deputy V.G

Ardzinba spoke for the people of Abkhazia regarding their conflict with Georgia and the Georgians. She claimed that the CPSU Central Committee and USSR Council of Ministers had refused to answer petitions sent by the Abkhazians, and therefore proposed the creation of a commission to investigate the problem.

Ryzhkov's Report

The Supreme Soviet confirmed Gorbachev's appointment of Ryzhkov as Chairman of the Council of Ministers. That afternoon, the Congress listened to and discussed Ryzhkov's report, 'Concerning the Program for Future Activities by the Government of the USSR,' a detailed review of the government's reform program divided into nine parts, including topics such as, "Perestroika of relations of production—a most important direction of the government's activities," and "Problems of the acceleration of scientific-technical progress and the establishment of a healthy environment for human development." Ryzhkov closed his speech with assurances that the Council of Ministers and its executive organs would cooperate with the revitalized Congress to further perestroika.

Ryzhkov's report, like Gorbachev's, served as a starting point for deputorial eloquence. After Deputy G.V. Bykov, a worker, reported on the "problems that worry the workers of Leningrad," economist N.P. Shmelev, a deputy from the USSR Academy of Sciences, took the floor. Shmelev offered a series of radical proposals aimed at undercutting Ryzhkov's ideas and saving the country from "economic failure." Shmelev's suggestions included returning to state control over the production and sale of alcohol, normalizing the domestic market for consumer goods by importing deficit items from abroad, paying for the goods in dollars, and destroying the rubles received from consumers, and removing the central bank from the control of the Council of Ministers.

Deputy A.M. Emelianov made one of the most interesting speeches of the entire first session. Emelianov, an agronomist and a Communist, was elected in one of Moscow's 26 territorial districts. He argued that the creation of genuine representative institutions that embody the power of the people, "changes the position of the party in our social and political system..." "Our Congress is higher than the Party Congress. The Supreme Soviet is higher than the Central Committee, and the constitution is higher than the party rules... First of all we are all deputies and only then are we party members."[31]

At the afternoon session on 8 June, the CPD discussed and ratified the Supreme Soviet's choices for chairman of the Council of Ministers, the Constitutional Review Committee, chairman of the People's Control Committee, chairman of the Supreme Court, Chief State Arbitrator, and Procurator General. Although the discussion was pointed and contained some of the most interesting debate of the session, the confirmations were made in short order. Discussion of A.Ia. Sukharev's candidacy for Procurator General was the most heated. Deputies Gdlian and Ivanov rose to make spirited and well-informed attacks on the candidate. Sukharev, nonetheless, was confirmed with little dissension. Once again, as with Lukianov's election, fundamental matters of principle were swept under the carpet.

Final Day of the Session

Discussion of Gorbachev's and Ryzhkov's reports concluded on the final day of the session, but were overshadowed by closing remarks by both chairmen. Ryzhkov's speech was most remarkable for the attention he paid to ecological issues. Clearly, he had heard the concerns voiced by deputies during the course of the session. He concluded with a promise to cooperate with the new legislatures.[32]

Gorbachev's closing speech included a political assessment of the session. "I am convinced," he declared, "that this Congress will lead us to a new stage of the development of democracy, glasnost, and perestroika itself." He argued that the range of opinions expressed at the Congress gave "a unique opportunity to ... understand our real situation..."

> It is in just such an atmosphere that the principle of a pluralism of opinions can be realized...I [decided] to stress this because certain people have suggested the idea of a constructive opposition, of political pluralism. I think that this Congress, all of its work, is a convincing argument that within the framework of the soviet political system... the widest possible comparison of views, disagreement, and the creation of arbitrated decisions... are possible.

Gorbachev also said a few words about the roots of these differences of opinion, representation, and the new political openness.

> Deputies brought... a multitude of views and experience behind which stand different interests, social, national, professional, generational, and regional... Differences of opinion, arguments, and discussions are unavoidable... I see nothing wrong with this. On the contrary, a pluralism of opinions widens the spectrum of possible decisions and [gives] a fuller conception of subjects under review... [We can have] different opinions, but our policy should be one, perestroika.[33]

Next, Gorbachev turned to the CPSU, arguing that it was invalid to identify the party apparat with the administrative command system and that attacks on the latter should not be made at the expense of the former. Without a competent managerial apparatus in the center and at the local level it would be impossible "to achieve anything sensible." He declared that the deputies faced

> a task uniquely important because of its scale and innovativeness, i.e. to organically unify the efforts of a renewed Soviet power and the political work of a renewed party in such a way that the enormous potential contained in the soviet social order be revealed. The party will fulfill its historic mission of renewing socialism by working out policy and presenting it to society. I am convinced that the system of soviets now being reborn will make its own decisive contribution, on the basis of popular power, to the realization of perestroika.[34]

The CPD and Political Leadership

Gorbachev's closing words to the Congress expressed a good deal of hope concerning the working relationship between the soviets and the CPSU. Clearly, the CPD had played the role of an arena—it was an unprecedented political spectacle. But could the Congress provide the political leadership needed to reform the country? The spectrum of opinions expressed at the session was enormous and the general closing statements of principle that it ratified could be interpreted in many different ways. One good way to go behind the facade of Gorbachev's rhetoric is to explore, concretely, the relationship between the Communist Party and the Supreme Soviet, the institution designed to turn the CPD's strategic leadership decisions into legislative reality. That is the goal of the following chapter.

Notes

1. Section Five of the constitution, "Higher organs of state power and management of the USSR," contained the amendments.

2. For a review of Lukianov's political career see Iu. Bychkov, "Slishkom 'seryi kardinal dlia perestroiki," *Stolitsa*, No. 2, January 1991, pp. 9–12. Lukianov's political biography is given in *Izvestiia TsK KPSS*, No. 7, 1990, pp. 107–108. Lukianov's views on the development of the soviets

before he moved to the top of the political hierarchy can be found in *Razvitie zakonodatelstva o sovetskikh predstavitelnikh organakh vlasti*, Moscow: Iuridicheskaia literatura, 1978.

3. *Izvestiia*, 30 May 1989, p. 2.

4. Even if the Central Committee Plenum did approve all major decisions, it is not certain that it was a rubber stamp for decisions made in the central party apparatus. Some sharp and principled proposals were made. Yeltsin pointed out to the CPD, for example, that "at the Central Committee Plenum that met on the [eve of the Congress] my proposal concerning the transfer...of power from the party to the soviets did not receive any support."

5. *Izvestiia*, 2 June 1989, p. 9.

6. For an announcement of the party group's meeting see *Pravda*, 24 May 1989, p. 1. See also *Materialy XXVII sezda kommunisticheskoi partii sovetskogo soiuza*, Moscow: Politizdat, 1986, p. 205.

7. *Nedelia*, 21 July 1989. For an extended discussion of this question see A. Sobchak, *For a New Russia: The Mayor of St. Petersburg's own Story of the Struggle for Justice and Democracy*, New York: The Free Press, 1992, pp. 20–26.

8. *Izvestiia*, 9 June 1989, p. 7.

9. *Izvestiia*, 27 May 1990, p. 2. See also A. Sobchak, "Ot sezda k sezdu: stanovlenie novoi politicheskoi sistemy," *Cherez ternii*, Moscow: Progress, 1990, p. 462.

10. Iu.D. Chernichenko, lecture at Aeroflot's Palace of Culture, 31 July 1989, Moscow. Remarks made by Gorbachev about the election of the Constitutional Oversight Committee suggest that non-Communists also were allowed to attend the meeting of the party group. It is unclear how many actually participated or what their status was. See *Izvestiia*, 10 June 1989, p. 6.

11. Iu.N. Afanasev, "Partiia i gosudarstvo," *Znamia kommunizma*, 24 June 1989, p. 3. For confirmation that this process occurred in Armenia see *Izvestiia*, 1 June 1989, p. 4.

12. During the session, republican groups also played a role. Attempting to resolve a dispute over the order of speakers, Gorbachev noted the importance of republican groups in deciding procedural questions. "They have decided all questions up to this point and introduced collective proposals," he argued. "Let the deputy groups decide [who will speak]. Let proposals from the groups be given to the Secretariat." See *Izvestiia*, 31 May 1989, p. 4.

13. Deputy A.E. Karpov discussed the approach taken by the Moscow delegation to the elections to the Supreme Soviet. "There are 195 of us and we were given 29 places in the Soviet of the Union...we needed only to

pick the best of the best and give them our blessing. But we chose another way. We conducted a survey [to find out] who wanted to and was able to work in the Supreme Soviet...To be there is one thing but to work is another thing entirely. Many of us have interesting jobs that we love and [cannot] abandon...In short, 55 people expressed such a desire...We asked the Congress to choose from among them." See *Izvestiia*, 3 June 1989, p. 4.

14. *Moskovskaia Pravda*, 26 May 1989, p. 1.
15. *Izvestiia*, 27 May 1989, p. 5.
16. *Sezd narodnykh deputatov SSSR, Stenograficheskii otchet*, Vol. 1, Moscow: 1989, p. 11.
17. *Vedomosti sezda narodnykh deputatov SSSR i verkhovnogo soveta SSSR*, No. 1, 14 June 1989, p. 87.
18. For a description of the group's work see, *Sezd narodnykh deputatov SSSR. Stenograficheskii otchet*, Vol. 1, Moscow: 1989, p. 225. See also Iu. Chernichenko's sarcastic attack on the group's opponents at the first session of the Congress of People's Deputies, *Sezd narodnykh deputatov SSSR, Stenograficheskii otchet*, Moscow: 1989.
19. Deputy I.I. Zaslavskii complained that this violation of procedure had narrowed the options available to the Congress. See *Izvestiia*, 31 May 1989, p. 5.
20. On this point see Iu. Bychkov, "Slishkom 'seryi kardinal dlia perestroiki," *Stolitsa*, No. 2, January 1991, pp. 9–12.
21. *Vedomosti sezda narodnykh deputatov SSSR i verkhovnogo soveta SSSR*, No. 1, Art. 2. A. Sobchak, "Ot sezda k sezdu: stanovlenie novoi politicheskoi sistemy," *Cherez ternii*, Moscow: Progress, 1990, p. 462.
22. *Izvestiia*, 27 May 1989, p. 4.
23. Ibid., 28 May 1989, p. 2.
24. Ibid.
25. Ibid., p. 4.
26. Ibid., 30 May 1989, p. 2.
27. Ibid.
28. Deputy Gontar outlined similar complaints and asked that his proposals be considered a draft for a decision by the Congress on the agricultural sector. See *Izvestiia*, 1 June 1989, p. 9.
29. *Izvestiia*, 1 June 1989, p. 9.
30. Ibid.
31. Ibid., p. 4.
32. Ibid., 10 June 1989, p. 3.
33. Ibid., 31 May 1989, p. 3.
34. Ibid., 10 June 1989, pp. 1–2.

Chapter 6

Creation of the New Supreme Soviet's Committees

The first session of the new Supreme Soviet, like the first session of the new Congress of People's Deputies, was a spectacular political show. Deputies interrogated candidates for ministerial posts, made emotional appeals to the public, the government, and each other, and, in sum, were the center of national attention for much of the summer. As the institutional cornerstone of the legislative reform program, the Supreme Soviet was an important source of information about the transformation of Soviet politics. This chapter investigates the nature of the new Supreme Soviet by taking a look at the birth of its committee system.

The 1988 Constitutional Amendments

The 1988 constitutional amendments created a new Supreme Soviet, a standing legislature whose 542 members were subordinate to the Congress of People's Deputies and elected from and by its deputies. The Supreme Soviet had two chambers with equal powers and equal numbers of deputies, the Soviet of the Union and the Soviet of the Nationalities. The chambers had the right to examine any question within the competency of the USSR; however, as a rule, the Soviet of the Union was intended to study questions of an all-union character while the Soviet of the Nationalities examined questions related to culture, language, and the development of the USSR's national and ethnic groups (Art. 116). Laws could be passed by a majority vote of both chambers (Art. 115). Each year, the CPD was to replace up to one fifth of the deputies in each chamber. Supreme Soviet sessions were to be convoked twice per year by its Presidium. Sessions, planned to last 3-4 months, consisted of separate and joint meetings of the chambers as well as meetings of the committees and commissions during and between sessions (Art. 112).

The 1988 constitutional amendments (later significantly revised to include a Soviet presidency) made the Chairman of the Supreme Soviet the highest state official, responsible for organizing the work of the CPD and the Supreme Soviet and representing the USSR in international relations. The Chairman was to be elected in a secret ballot by the CPD for not more than two terms of five years each, and was subordinate to both the CPD and the Supreme Soviet (Art. 120). The Supreme Soviet's Presidium was headed by the Chairman of the Supreme Soviet.[1] The Presidium organized the work of the CPD and the Supreme Soviet, and was subordinate to the Supreme Soviet. The Presidium's membership, according to the 1988 amendments, was composed of the Chairman of the Supreme Soviet, his first deputy, fifteen vice-deputies (the chairmen of union republic Supreme Soviets), the chairmen of the Soviet of the Union and the Soviet of the Nationalities, the chairman of the People's Control Commission, and the chairmen of the Supreme Soviet's committees and the chambers' commissions (Art. 118)

The constitution required the Soviet of the Union and the Soviet of the Nations to establish standing commissions for

> conducting legislative work, the preparatory review and preparation of questions within the competence of the... Supreme Soviet and also for assisting in the implementation of ... laws and other decisions made by the... Congress of People's Deputies and the... Supreme Soviet, and for monitoring the activities of state organs and organizations. (Art. 122)

The Supreme Soviet also had the right to form joint committees from both chambers on an equal basis. The constitution did not, however, dictate the procedures or principles to be applied in the formation of the committee system. Moreover, the Supreme Soviet's standing rules and the legislation that outlined the commissions' rights and responsibilities in the old Supreme Soviet offered few guidelines beyond the requirement that they represent both all-union and local interests. Whether this representation should be ensured structurally, or through membership composition, was an open question. The committees' constitutional responsibilities to review legislation, confirm executive appointments, and monitor the implementation of public policy (Art. 123) dictated no particular structure or membership composition, although they did suggest that specialization was desirable.

Commissions and Committees

Basic Principles. The committee system provided a measure of the type of content that Gorbachev planned to include in his new Soviet socialist democracy. This chapter focuses on how the committees were created during the first days of the new Supreme Soviet's first session. Although it was too early in this initial period to pass final judgement on the committee system, the attitudes and ideas of Gorbachev and his allies are appropriate evidence of their attitude toward reform. (Henceforth, except where clarity demands otherwise, the words committee or committee system will be used to denote both commitees and commissions.)

Gorbachev, as Chairman of the Supreme Soviet, was responsible for organizing, through the Presidium, the committee system (Art. 121). Anatolii Lukianov, Gorbachev's first deputy in the Presidium, supervised preparation of a proposal for the structure of the committee system. On 5 May 1989, at the CPD, Lukianov distributed a working draft with a list of committees.[2] A survey attached to the list asked deputies to indicate their first three assignment preferences and solicited comments.[3] He outlined four principles on which this proposal was based. First, he declared, the number of committees and commissions should be kept to a minimum because of the limited number of deputies (271) in each chamber. Unwilling to reduce the number of deputies in each committee, he argued that a larger number of committees would make it impossible to guarantee equal numbers of Supreme Soviet members and deputies from the CPD on each committee. Second, Lukianov argued that the committee structure should not reflect too closely the ministerial structure because this would disturb their "parliamentary profile and functions." Third, he pointed out that subcommissions would be formed to address "narrower" questions, so it was not necessary to form many separate committees. Fourth, he declared that the revitalization of the functional specialization of the chambers, defined in the constitution, dictated differences in the commissions in each chamber.

Although the committee system's auxiliary nature was stated clearly in the constitution, the Supreme Soviet's standing rules, and other legislation, both Gorbachev and Lukianov repeatedly emphasized the political implications of this point. They argued that the committees should consist of "specialists" who discuss and analyze public policy but that they did not make political decisions. Similar arguments concerning the division of functions between the CPSU and the Supreme Soviet and the separability of political decisionmaking and policy formulation were advanced throughout the course of the session. For instance, Gorbachev and Lukianov teamed up to argue with one unidentified deputy who questioned the absence of the word 'policy' in proposed committee titles. Lukianov declared that "as a scholar who studies the state, I do not think that we are talking about policy, but about concrete decisions." Gorbachev immediately added, "About the law, about legislative activity." Lukianov repeated, "About legislative activity..." The deputy gave up without pressing the point.[4]

One unidentified deputy summarized the ideas implicit in Gorbachev's attempt to separate policy formulation and political decisionmaking. "We are not the party," he argued, "we are parliament. Political questions are the party's business. We, the majority of us who are Communists, will work on politics in the party, but here we should occupy ourselves with laws."[5] Gorbachev's formulation of the interaction between policy and politics was also summarized in a statement made by the legal scholar S.S. Alekseev (later in the session elected chairman of the Supreme Soviet's legislation committee and subsequently head of the USSR's Constitutional Oversight Committee). Alekseev claimed that his committee would turn the party's political decisions into law.

> Our interrelationships are defined by the decisions of the 27th Party Congress and the 19th Party Conference and are based on the party's vanguard role in society. The Central Committee's [commission on legal policy] works out legal policy, and political conceptions of the most important legislative acts. The legislation itself, which professionals should work on, is the function of [our] parliamentary committee. We are convinced that there should be the closest contact between the Supreme Soviet's committee and the Central Committee commission. [Our] committee should take into account the strategic directions worked out by the [commission, and the commission] will base itself on [reality], including laws passed by parliament.[6]

In short, Alekseev suggested that legal scholars could translate political decisions made in the Central Committee's apparatus into public policy; moreover, he expressed alarm at the possibility that laws carefully worked out by specialists ("a sufficiently narrow group of like-minded individuals") might be amended in the Supreme Soviet. He declared that he would strive to perfect draft legislation and minimize open discussion.

Gorbachev's approach can be highlighted by comparing it to that of Boris Yeltsin, chairman of the Committee for questions of construction and architecture, who expressed a contradictory opinion. He emphasized his committee's responsibility to provide specialized analysis in both its legislative and oversight roles, but also argued that it should "work out the general strategic line in construction." Although he acknowledged the need to invite specialists to participate, unlike Gorbachev and Lukianov, Yeltsin posited no separation between politics and policy.[7] He declared that his committee would "decide whether it makes sense to finance a given project... The committee is a political organ and ought to formulate an investment policy."[8]

A second fundamental principle of operation of the committee system was the extent to which committees would operate as professional legislative organs. That is, if the Supreme Soviet wanted to develop committees capable of rendering expert opinions to help it monitor and control the executive, i.e. create a 'socialist system of checks and balances,' it needed to give deputies a chance to gain experience and sharpen their expertise. Despite these considerations, discussing whether deputies would be freed from their full-time jobs for committee work, Lukianov argued that "if we establish professional committees, not connected to practice, to the earth, we will take the life out of them."[9] Thus, the Supreme Soviet decided that only the chairman, vice-chairman and secretary of each committee would be freed from other responsibilities to work full time in the Supreme Soviet. Other deputies would participate only when the legislature was in session or when they were summoned by the chairman.[10]

Formation. The procedure used to establish the new Supreme Soviet's committees and its chambers' commissions significantly differed from past practice. That is, it no longer consisted of the unanimous ratification of a proposal made in the name of the Supreme Soviet's Councils of Elders. Although the central party apparatus and the Supreme Soviet's Presidium played the most influential parts in the early discussion stages by making proposals that set the broad parameters of the debate, they did not completely control the process.

According to Lukianov, the committee structure was composed in a manner that accounted for a wide range of opinions. First, deputies' wishes were accounted for in the survey mentioned above. Second, discussions were held at the meeting of the CPD's party group.[11] A third set of pre-sessional discussions of the committee system occurred on 24 May, when Gorbachev led a meeting of representatives from republican deputy groups. Meetings held by republican deputy groups before the general meeting of representatives were a fourth mechanism used during the pre-session discussions. A fifth control mechanism, a meeting of the Councils of Elders chaired by Gorbachev on 3 June, discussed the establishment of the committee system, including chairmen, vice chairmen, secretaries, committee membership, and subcommittees.[12] The Councils of Elders served as an arena for resolving conflicts and building consensus, and a partial filter to eliminate ideas unacceptable to the party leadership.[13] Lukianov declared that "in the Council of Elders we very carefully reviewed the [system of] commissions and committees." He argued that it was important to recognize the complexity of the problems involved in establishing the committee system, and suggested that the meeting of the Councils of Elders was an appropriate way to meet this goal. "That is why at the meeting...we carefully reviewed...the whole package of proposals concerning the committees."[14] Commenting on differences between the original survey list and the list proposed for ratification, Lukianov noted that "at the meeting of the Councils of Elders...certain changes were introduced into the project."[15] The Councils of Elders were not, however, a perfect filter. Several deputies whose ideas were rejected by the Councils renewed their proposals at sessions of the Supreme Soviet or its chambers.[16] For example, Deputy V.A. Shekhovtsov's proposal to revise the name of the Committee for questions of legislation was rejected, but he brought this issue to the attention of the Soviet of the Union.[17]

In sum, the procedures used in the formation of the committee system suggested a new willingness of party leaders to discuss their proposals but also demonstrated that the CPSU's political machine functioned efficiently. Gorbachev used the Councils of Elders, the party group, and the republican delegations to insure that as little time as possible was lost in the Supreme Soviet passing the Presidium's proposal with as few changes as possible. Apparently, the control machinery was also used to ensure that alternate proposals would stand little chance of gaining support. Deputy Stankevich submitted an independent proposal for the structure of the committee system that, except for a passing reference by Lukianov, was ignored.[18]

At the first session of the Soviet of the Union on 5 June, Lukianov, in the name of the Councils of Elders, presented a revised list of commissions and committees to the assembled deputies.[19] In the Supreme Soviet itself, the discussion of the formation of the committee system lasted three days. Debates in separate and joint sessions seldom focussed on matters of principle, although discussions of terminology often had political undertones. When one unidentified deputy argued that information technology is a basic part of communication and proposed adding these two words to the committee's title, Lukianov immediately agreed. On the other hand, there was a fierce discussion over where to monitor glasnost or whether it deserved separate attention at all.[20]

The Soviet of the Nationalities met on 6 June to establish its own commissions and discuss the proposed list of Supreme Soviet committees. Lukianov reminded the chamber that the Soviet of the Union had already revised the proposed list of committees, and argued that these changes were not mere formalities, but an attempt "to more exactly define the all-union nature of...[the committee system's] work, to concentrate a powerful block of problems whose resolution is beyond the competence of union republics...and should be decided by the Union as a whole."[21] The principles for deciding which policy areas would be covered by Supreme Soviet joint committees and which by commissions of the Soviet of the Union or the Soviet of the Nationalities were unclear. Moreover, during debates deputies did not seem to be aware of alterations in committee titles, which suggests that they were not given copies of the proposed changes.

In a joint session on 8 June, after a long and spirited debate over confirmation of Sukharev as USSR Procurator, the Supreme Soviet concluded business for the day by ratifying a final revised list of committees proposed by Gorbachev. There was no discussion of the changes before Gorbachev summed up the argument for ratifying the proposed list by arguing that "I do not think that we, just now, will ratify a perfect, ideal document. But we probably ought to do this..."[22]

Standing Rules and Procedures

Any committee system requires clearly defined and generally recognized operating rules and procedures to function effectively; nonetheless, neither the CPD nor the Supreme Soviet debated legislative regulation of the committees' powers. The *new* Supreme Soviet simply borrowed the *old* Supreme Soviet's standing rules without revising them to account for the December 1988 constitutional amendments.[23] Lukianov did not even announce that the Supreme Soviet's standing rules and the committee system's operational procedures were borrowed until 10 June.[24] Although there is little essentially undemocratic about the old rules, deputies were not instructed on how they would be applied or interpreted under the new conditions. The decision not to debate or draft new editions of these documents apparently was made in order to avoid discussions that would delay what Lukianov and others often referred to as the Supreme Soviet's 'real work.'[25] Gorbachev's refusal to resolve the committee system's existential questions signalled his desire to control them. Commenting on this situation, Deputy V.D. Iudin noted on 30 June that

> we do not know our own functions...Who are we? What are we? What should we be doing? What rights de we have? And what [rights] do we lack? We are returning time and again to procedural questions...We forever will be coming back to this if we do not devote one or two...meetings to the question of our rights and duties.[26]

Both the stenographic record and the similarity of complaints by other deputies corroborate Iudin's statements.

The Presidium's reluctance to discuss procedural questions included the scheduling of committee meetings. On 16 June, Deputy K.D. Lubenchenko tried to convince the Soviet of the Union that work in committee was more productive than sessions of the chambers or joint sessions of the Supreme Soviet and asked his colleagues to consider revising their work schedule. Primakov, chairman of the Soviet of the Union, responded to Lubenchenko with a typically evasive answer, "There already is a proposal in connection with this. That is, we devote one day, Friday, [to committee work]. If this one day is not enough, let's decide as we work along... Let's get to work, comrades." This response was quite effective politically. Millions of Soviet citizens, and many deputies as well, were unfamiliar with the importance of procedural questions, expressed their shock during the session of the Congress of People's Deputies to see so much 'empty talk' and so little 'work.' Deputy S. Khadzhiev, for example, argued that "...in the next two or three months we must pass a series of important, fundamental laws. People are waiting for this from us. *Procedure is irrelevant here.*"[27]

In addition to failing to discuss and define the committees' powers, the committee system was weakened through several constitutional loopholes. The USSR's constitution assigned the Supreme Soviet's committee system three principal tasks: (1) discuss drafts of legislation, (2) conduct hearings on nominees to government posts, and (3) monitor the implementation of public policy. However, the committee system only 'as a rule' discussed legislation passed by the Congress and the Supreme Soviet. No indication was given of the circumstances under which legislation should or should not be sent to the committees. Committees did not confirm or reject government appointees but only offered a non-binding recommendation to the Supreme Soviet. This meant that when the Supreme Soviet confirmed appointments and the CPD ratified these decisions they could ignore the committees' opinions. The committees' monitoring tasks were limited to assisting in the implementation of public policy. Although committees had the right to demand information from the government on any topic, their recommendations were non-binding. Government bodies were required to submit a review of committee recommendations, but could choose not to fulfill them if they were willing to gamble that the Supreme Soviet would not support the committee's recommendations. Finally, Lukianov declared that the Supreme Soviet would exercise its right to form *ad hoc* commissions outside the formal committee structure. In late July, for instance, the Supreme Soviet established a commission to investigate "privileges enjoyed by various categories of citizens."[28] In early September, the Soviet of the Nationalities established a temporary commission to study "the socio-political situation in Moldavia."[29] These commissions addressed politically sensitive topics that seemed to be in the bailiwicks, respectively, of the committee for questions of glasnost and citizens' rights and petitions, and the Soviet of the Nationalities' commission for nationalities policy. The right to establish ad hoc commissions gave party leaders the power to avoid potentially embarrassing discussion in the committee system.

Chairmen and Members

Gorbachev nominated candidates for committee and commission chairmen at separate and joint sessions of the chambers. There was little debate over personalities or procedures. Some nomineees answered questions from the floor while others were ignored, but all were confirmed. The only procedural debate over the election of chairmen concerned, not surpisingly, the question of alternate candidacies. Nonetheless, several deputies argued that they did not want to be reduced to 'voting machines' like their counterparts in the old Supreme Soviet. Deputy Bocharov, for example, complained that committee chairmen were chosen by the Presidium and that there was no preparatory discussion with regional or republican deputy groups.[30]

If Gorbachev wanted to create specialist committees, the professional competence of chairmen would seem to have been a key prerequisite. Reasonable people often disagree over professional qualifications, especially for positions as difficult to define as these; however, some chairmen appeared to be grossly unqualified for their jobs. For example, budget committee chairman V.G. Kucherenko, before his election to the Supreme Soviet, was head of the executive committee of the Donetsk oblast soviet, where he produced a R70 million budget deficit. Addressing the joint session that ratified committee chairman nominations, Deputy Emelianov argued that Kucherenko was unqualified, and suggested that the party's desire to keep tight control over the Supreme Soviet was behind the nomination:

> Out of all the committees, finance is [probably] the most specialized... I am an economist... I have worked in this field my whole life... [but] if they offered me a similar position, I would feel out of place... isn't the financial crisis of our system a result of the fact that a man, maybe an honorable person and loyal to the party, was put in a position where he didn't really know what was going on? Haven't we put [Kucherenko] in the same spot?[31]

Kucherenko is not the only chairman whose credentials have been questioned. Deputy Iu.E. Andreev, a construction engineer from the railroad industry, argued that V.A. Tetenov, chairman of the Soviet of the Union's transport committee and deputy director of a local railway division, was not a 'serious' figure.[32] Deputy K. Salykov, an *obkom* secretary nominated for head of the ecological committee, elicited an explosion of unrest when he found it difficult to define 'ecology.' Nonetheless, the session confirmed him.

Committee membership was, of course, another important influence on the 'specialist' nature of committee work. Before looking at the details of the selection process, it makes sense to discuss briefly the quality of the pool from which committee members were selected, i.e. the Congress of People's Deputies. Any discussion of the deputies must start with an analysis of the elections. Simply put, in many districts the elections were rigged: deputies from such areas owe their seats to the support and patronage of local political leaders, and this dependence influenced their conduct in the CPD and the Supreme Soviet. A number of observers commented on the voting behavior of republican delegations in the CPD: deputies looked to see how the delegation's leader voted, and followed suit. One might expect deputies to start exercising independence as they mature politically; nonetheless, when one considers the power that local party and state leaders have over deputies' lives and the lives of family members and friends, it is clear that they were subject to outside pressure.

The membership selection process for the committee system was divided into four stages. First, the Presidium distributed tentative committee membership lists based on the survey that was taken at the CPD and encouraged discussion in the Council of Elders and other pre-session meetings. Second, Gorbachev asked Primakov and Nishanov, the chairmen of the chambers, to help settle conflicts in consultation with deputies, committee chairmen, and republican delegations.[33] Third, committee chairmen were allowed to make additions and subtractions.[34] Fourth, the chambers debated and voted individually on commission membership, and, in a joint session, for committee membership. Deputy Alekseev expressed satisfaction at the membership composition of his committee, which includes three corresponding members of the USSR Academy of Sciences, two doctors of jurisprudence, and several experienced lawyers. He argued that, "they never would have come here if they did not sense the possibility of genuine professional work with an effect on practical decisions."[35] Yeltsin, unlike Alekseev, was unhappy with the membership composition of his committee. He argued that there were neither enough architects nor economists on his committee.[36]

Professional qualifications were not the only standards used by deputies during the formation process. The membership battle often was fought over questions of national representation. For instance, one unidentified deputy argued that "in the planning and budget-finance committee there are no representatives from certain republics, including Latvia. I am now beginning to wonder what we have in mind when we talk about the interests of the Union."[37]

Some committees were more popular than others.[38] Lukianov noted that many deputies wanted to join the ecology committee while other committees were not filled through preliminary enrollment. In fact, the enormous difference between supply and demand meant that the Presidium had a convenient excuse to include deputies it found desirable and exclude those it found undesirable. Lukianov, Primakov, and Nishanov often mentioned the yearly rotation of one-fifth of the committee system's members mandated by the constitution as a cure to the problem of excess demand for a limited supply of seats. Nonetheless, the competitive aspect of the membership selection process helped fuel mistrust between the Supreme Soviet's leadership and its rank-and-file members. One deputy argued that deputies should establish a committee with, "the power of appointing deputies to the commissions and committees and to conduct rotation in the next five years so that [membership] questions depended on us and not on technical personnel."[39]

Staff and Infrastructure

Staffing, infrastructure, and budget questions are part of the foundation of any committee system. Even before the opening session of the CPD, many deputies called for the establishment of independent committee and deputorial staffs as well as an information service. In a roundtable discussion published in mid-May, Deputies Murashev, Poltoranin, Stankevich, and Tretiakov supported financing the development of an infrastructure that would give deputies and committees a degree of independence from the Presidium.[40] Despite deputies' requests, the support given to the committee system during its first month of existence was insufficient to guarantee effective professional operation.

In the summer of 1989, each committee was given temporarily a two-room suite with a small entrance hall in the Moscow Hotel across the street from the Kremlin.[41] Committees also were assigned meeting rooms that seat approximately 30 people in the Presidium's building at No. 4 Kalinin Prospect.[42] Not until the final day of the session was it decided that deputies would be paid 500 rubles per month and given a small monthly allowance to hire a secretary. Deputies from outside the capital stayed in the Moscow Hotel, where conditions, apparently, are far from ideal.[43] On 4 July, Lukianov announced that an information service had been established within the Supreme Soviet to handle deputies' requests. He also pointed out that deputies could use both the nearby Lenin Library and the Secretariat's library.[44] Despite the efforts made by the Presidium, Deputy S.B. Stankevich claimed that the Supreme Soviet leadership's monopoly on information was complete. "We get what they give us, and this information is not always reliable or complete."[45]

Each committee was assigned a consultant from the Presidium's Secretariat.[46] The relationship between the committees, the consultants and the consultants' corresponding sectors in the Presidium's Secretariat evolved slowly. For example, Deputy A.F. Veprev, chairman of the agricultural committee, claimed the Secretariat and its consultants were deaf to his committee's needs.[47] Many other deputies were unhappy with what they viewed as poor conditions. Deputy Bocharov complained about the committees' staff and infrastructure and maintained that the construction committee had relied on volunteers to handle its workload. He outlined a number of problems and asked what steps had been taken to resolve them.

> Today...we know nothing. We have practically no staff, and cannot resolve even a single question. Each committee has, we might say, one 'representative' from the [Secretariat]. I repeat, one. And what's the result? We do not know our own salary...We do not even have simple items, like an identification card... *What* are we waiting for?[48]

In early July, Veprev declared that "we still do not even have typists to produce documents, and there is no secretary" and complained that deputies were forced to waste time on routine work that they should not have to worry about. Deputy Iaroshenko reported that the committees had no individual budgets and could not afford to hire independent expertise.[49]

In addition to information and staffing problems, the committees were plagued by poor communication. One consultant complained that it was almost impossible to find deputies when they were needed, and suggested that giving them all offices nearby would greatly simplify matters. The deputies have been assigned a large office building on Kalinin Prospect, but the ten-minute walk required to reach the Kremlin from this location made it inconvenient.[50] Stenographic records of committee meetings were not published consistently, even for the use of deputies. The torrent of words overwhelmed 18 stenographers, who struggled to cope with the demands placed on them. If telephone service, another element of the committee system's communication infrastructure, is an appropriate indicator of professionalism and competence, their staffs worked poorly all summer long. Some committees' phones were constantly busy, some committees answered their phones sporadically, other committees never answered their phones.[51]

Procedure and Debate

Gorbachev's refusal to discuss procedural questions during the formation process, as well as the hurried approach to the Supreme Soviet's work seemed to be a tactical approach to control the course of the session. Discussing the schedule for the first few days of the session, Deputy Emelianov complained that the deputies were rushed. "An enormous number of candidacies to discuss, a multitude of questions. Three days would have been needed to work normally. We fit it all into one. This did not help the strengthening of democracy."[52]

Although a majority of deputies proved willing to accept without question the leadership's proposals, others asserted their independence. Deputy N.S. Sazonov, for instance, reacted negatively to the survey taken at the CPD and the hurried way that the committees were formed. He proposed

> first, to halt enrollment in the committees...; second, to establish a working group consisting of deputies—one from each union republic and from Moscow and Leningrad, to work out a proposal for the Supreme Soviet's structure; third, to discuss [this proposal], ratify it, and only then renew enrollment. Why? We already made a serious mistake in the formation of the Supreme Soviet, whose membership consists [in part] of 231 workers from among the leaders of party, soviet and economic organs who as a rule will be absent, and [therefore] our parliament will not be [a genuine standing institution].[53]

E.M. Primakov and R.N. Nishanov, the chairmen of the Soviet of the Union and the Soviet of Nationalities respectively, often cut short discussion by the repetition of phrases like 'let's get to work.' At the first working session of the Soviet of the Union, for example, Primakov cut off debate over the committee system when he declared that, "after we start work it will be possible to make corrections... this system will be modernized. But for now, let's get to work, and work for a while, and let's not start by tearing apart the [proposed list]."[54] The chairmen also tried to tone down politically pointed discussions. Nishanov repeatedly requested deputies "not to draw political conclusions" from one or another aspect of the formation process. One related rhetorical tactic employed by the chairmen was to accuse deputies of playing politics. Primakov pointed out to one deputy that, "in parliaments in certain countries there is a practice whereby a speaker may talk as long as he wants," but argued that "if you want to borrow... everything from the bourgeois [parliamentary model], I don't think it will suit us." He urged the deputy to "work as productively as possible, work in a businesslike way, and not for the microphones or the television."[55] Perhaps the best example of the disregard for procedure in the desire to ratify the Presidium's proposals as quickly as possible was when Lukianov rushed the deputies to complete the formation of the committee system before returning home for a week of consultations and rest. One might argue that this is not unlike behavior in the US Congress or other legislatures at the end of a session; nevertheless, important considerations at a critical moment were brushed aside in a general rush to the airport.[56]

Formation of the Defense Committee

The debate over the establishment of the committee for questions of defense and state security presented a number of useful examples of the issues involved in the formation of the Supreme Soviet's committee system. The very existence of this committee suggested a desire on the part of the party leadership to change at least the appearance of the relationship between executive and representative institutions. That is, the principle of the subordination of the executive to the Supreme Soviet was highlighted by potential interactions between the committee and the armed forces. Perhaps the most commonly used example was the argument that popular control through the committee and the Supreme Soviet would prevent future 'Afghanistans.'

The personal and professional qualities of chairmen and members influenced the effectiveness of the committee system. V.L. Lapygin's election as chairman of the defense committee suggested that Gorbachev wanted to maintain control over its work. Instead of choosing a world-class scientist like E.P. Velikhov, whom fellow deputies proposed as an alternate candidate, Gorbachev nominated and the Supreme Soviet elected a relatively unknown defense industrialist. Lapygin, a long-time member of the military-industrial complex, knew the rules of the game in the defense industry and all of the key players and therefore was unlikely to do or say anything that might accidentally upset the status quo. Based on discussions with insiders, Robert C. Kaiser argues that Velikhov concluded that "officials of the Central Committee and Ministry of Defense had managed to block his appointment precisely because it threatened to create an independent power center that might limit their influence..."[57]

The debate over the defense committee's membership offers insight into the viability of the system's specialist role. Discussing the formation of the defense committee, Primakov argued that the 'dialectical unity' of two problems, the need to reduce defense expenditures and the need to maintain national security, dictated its membership composition. Despite this argument, however, the actual selection process did not suggest that the party leadership was interested in 'objective' specialists. One deputy discussed the leadership's telephone tactics to control committee membership. "They called me and said, in part, that [too] many deputies had applied for the [security committee]... But I just learned that deputies were included... who did not even agree to work there... Why are they deceiving [us]?[58] In short, the excess supply of deputies surely helped the party apparat find acceptable members. Primakov's 'dialectical unity' argument does not obscure the leadership's ability to favor specialists with acceptable opinions.[59]

The debates held over the formation of the defense committee highlighted three other political weaknesses of the attempt to establish a specialist role for the committees: the artificial separation of political decisionmaking and policy formulation; a problem that one might call the 'goat guarding the cabbage patch' issue; and the question of national representation. Gorbachev's attempt to artificially separate politics and policy was clearly visible in the formation of a 'specialist' military committee. Introducing Lapygin to the Supreme Soviet, Primakov argued that, besides Lapygin himself, the committee would include "a whole series of serious scholars, people who... absolutely objectively... will analyze all these questions."[60] Whether or not Primakov actually believed this argument, few political analysts would agree that 'objectivity' is desirable or possible when making national security decisions.

The debate over the formation of the defense committee also touched on the 'goat guarding the cabbage patch' issue. That is, deputies questioned the independence of committee members with close ties to the military, including both officers and defense industrialists. Deputy B.V. Miroshin pointed out that a deputy minister of defense, someone "who should report to the committee, but not be a member,"[61] was included on the preliminary membership list. One deputy expressed the membership problem succinctly when he suggested that, "it turns out that the military-industrial complex will [be responsible for] controlling itself..."[62] Another unidentified speaker noted that "24 out of 40 people on the proposed list represent military enterprises or the military-industrial complex. That is,... [their] interests will dominate the committee, even if only formally... It is difficult to imagine the possibility of public, political control by this [committee]."[63]

The question of national representation, better than all other aspects of the committee formation process, demonstrated the futility of Gorbachev's attempt to cloud political decisions with technical arguments. For example, deputies from the Baltic and elswhere demanded to know why none of their representatives had been included on the defense committee, expressed indignation at perceived "mistrust," and successfully pressed for changes. Steps were taken to resolve this "mistake."[64]

One final aspect of the debate over the establishment of the defense committee was related to the long-term institutionalization of the committee system. An exchange between Lapygin and Gorbachev demonstrated both the sensitivity of shifting power relations and the fact that the definition of committee functions will be a long-term process. At a joint session on 28 June, the Supreme Soviet discussed the candidacy of I.S. Belousov for chairmanship of the Council of Ministers' military-industrial commission. Lapygin spoke in favor of Belousov, and made a few additional remarks about the role of the Supreme Soviet's committees in the formulation of military-industrial policy. At this point, Gorbachev interrupted Lapygin and interjected that the committee and the Supreme Soviet should stick to legislative work. "Here, you know, it would be possible to get confused and take upon ourselves the functions of the [executive]. If we...duplicate [the executive's] functions...we will hinder [its] work."[65] Suggesting that Lapygin should take care not to overstep his rights, Gorbachev argued that each relevant part of the political system, the executive, the Supreme Soviet, the committees, and the Defense Council should fulfill its own role.

The Interregional Deputies' Group

Political activity organized outside the party was anathema to the old Supreme Soviet. In the new Supreme Soviet, several different groups organized independent political activity. The most controversial and best organized new political organization at the first sessions of the CPD and the Supreme Soviet was the Interregional Deputies' Group (IRDG).[66] Analysis of the IRDG's political organization provides an interesting counterpoint to activity organized by the CPSU in the Supreme Soviet's committee system.

The IRDG's roots were formed during the spring of 1989 prior to the opening of the CPD, when a group of Moscow's self-proclaimed 'progressive' deputies met to prepare a common proposal for the CPD's agenda. This nucleus grew, attracting deputies from outside Moscow. At the first session of the CPD, Deputy Popov, a radical Moscow economist, announced the formation of the IRDG. On 7 June, at the IRDG's first meeting, 388 deputies expressed a desire to join, including 90 members of the Supreme Soviet, 210 members of the Supreme Soviet's committees, and three committee chairmen. On 10 June, the IRDG elected a coordinating committee of five deputies, Afanasev, Yeltsin, Palm, Popov, and the late Andrei Sakharov. On 24 June, the group drafted a note to Gorbachev announcing the establishment of a news bulletin, *People's Deputy*, and on 8 July, published the number of a bank account that had been established to hold funds donated by citizens who wanted to support deputorial initiatives.[67]

On 29 July, in an auditorium provided by a Moscow film society, Popov outlined the IRDG's goals.[68] He argued that by preparing alternative legislative proposals the group hoped to encourage political and economic reforms that would not even be considered by the conservative government and party bureaucracies. One of the IRDG's principal goals was to give members of the Congress who had not been elected to the Supreme Soviet the opportunity to participate more actively in its work. Perhaps the best-reasoned argument for the IRDG's existence was made by Deputy Stankevich. He claimed that the only way to build a working parliament was through organized group activity.

> If we admit that serious and often conflicting interests, positions, and views exist within society, and if we accept the fact that these views are represented in parliament, then we have nowhere to hide from group conflict. Parliaments exist in order to resolve social conflicts.
>
> It is no accident that in the overwhelming majority of parliaments around the world there are rules for the formation and registration of deputorial groups. Such groups guarantee [deputies] everything needed for normal [parliamentary] activity, and play a highly constructive role in the legislative process.[69]

Stankevich argued that the Supreme Soviet's committee system might work as a net to eliminate radical proposals and that the IRDG would widen the spectrum of available ideas. The IRDG did, in fact, present several legislative proposals during the first session. On 29 July, it asked the Supreme Soviet to convene a session of the CPD to discuss amendments to the all-union law on elections. The group offered amendments to the law on state enterprises, and proposed a law that would reinstate citizenship for people deprived of it during the Brezhnev period.

Gorbachev did not condemn the IRDG outright, but expressed his dissatisfaction in both word and deed. He sent Primakov to one of its first meetings to try to convince deputies that there was no reason for its existence. "I'm not against the deputies clubbing together to work out alternative bills," Primakov declared. "Yet I see no point in organizing for organizing's sake."[70] Addressing the Supreme Soviet's final session, Gorbachev argued that the IRDG was "an attempt to give organizational form to a natural difference in views and approaches to problems of social development." Suggesting that nothing could be gained from the IRDG, he asked, "Will not such an artificial demarcation lead to conflict on concrete questions that the Supreme Soviet must resolve, will it not complicate the fulfillment of tasks that electors and Soviet society are waiting for us to resolve?" He exhorted deputies to "unite, and not divide up into groups," arguing that their common goal should be to uncover the "rich potential" of socialism through perestroika. If deputies could unite behind this goal, he claimed, they "always will agree."[71]

Politics, Policy, and Leadership

At the Supreme Soviet's first session the CPSU created a committee system based on the premise that 'specialist' committees could translate the party's strategic political decisions into public policy. Gorbachev posited an artificial split between 'political decisionmaking' and 'policy formulation' that put the committees and their members, and therefore the Supreme Soviet as well, in a subordinate position. In its drive to establish control, the Presidium weakened committee membership, chairmen, and committee infrastructure. The close attention given by the Presidium to establishing a committee structure was not, however, matched by a desire to outline committee functions, or to discuss the potentials of committee power or deputies' rights. The new Supreme Soviet's standing rules, the rules that guided the committee's work, and a number of other regulatory acts were borrowed from the old Supreme Soviet; moreover, they were given no new interpretation and no effort was made to explain them to the deputies.[72] By avoiding debate over procedural questions, the Presidium guarded the time at its disposal, helped guarantee the swift passage of its proposals, short-circuited any attempt to expand either the Supreme Soviet's or the committees' power, and kept deputies in check by increasing uncertainty. Gorbachev's 'party leadership' was imposed from outside the legislature rather than arising as an organic part of the political process. The next chapter discusses how this control was used in the legislative process.

Notes

1. The old title was Chairman of the Presidium of the Supreme Soviet.
2. A deputy gave me copy of this document.
3. *Izvestiia*, 5 June 1989, p. 2.
4. *Izvestiia*, 8 June 1989, p. 11. For a similar argument by Lukianov on the agricultural commission see his remarks in, *Pervaia Sessiia Verkhovnogo Soveta SSSR: Stenograficheskii otchet*, Moscow: 1989, Vol. 1, p. 72.
5. *Pervaia Sessiia Verkhovnogo Soveta SSSR: Stenograficheskii otchet*, Moscow: 1989, Vol. 1, pp. 30–31.
6. *Izvestiia*, 30 July 1989, p. 2.
7. *Izvestiia*, 20 July 1989, p. 3.

8. *Literaturnaia gazeta*, 28 July 1989, p. 10.
9. *Izvestiia*, 5 June 1989, p. 2.
10. For an interesting analysis of this question see comments by Iu.A. Ryzhov, chairman of the science committee, in *Informatsionnyi biulleten', Izdanie mezhregionalnoi gruppy narodnykh deputatov SSSR*, 15 September 1989, p. 15.
11. For the announcement of the party group's meeting, see *Pravda*, 24 May 1989, p. 1.
12. *Vedomosti sezda narodnykh deputatov SSSR i verkhovnogo soveta SSSR*, No. 1, 14 June 1989, p. 87. See also *Izvestiia*, 12 June 1989, p. 4.
13. Republican and regional groups appointed deputies to the Council of Elders. This maintains the direct tie of local elites to the central power structure that existed in the old Supreme Soviet. In at least some oblasts, the local party committee selected delegates to the Council of Elders. Both Lukianov and Primakov confirmed the Council's role in creating the agricultural commission. See *Pervaia Sessiia Verkhovnogo Soveta SSSR: Stenograficheskii otchet*, Moscow: 1989, Vol. 1, pp. 9, 72.
14. *Izvestiia*, 8 June 1989, p. 10.
15. *Izvestiia*, 5 June 1989, p. 3.
16. Ibid.
17. Ibid.
18. *Izvestiia*, 2 June 1989, p. 7.
19. *Vedomosti sezda narodnykh deputatov SSSR i verkhovnogo soveta SSSR*, No. 1, 14 June 1989, pp. 80, 82-85.
20. *Literaturnaia gazeta*, 28 July 1989, p. 10.
21. *Izvestiia*, 8 June 1989, p. 10.
22. *Izvestiia*, 9 June 1989, p. 9.
23. *Vedomosti sezda narodnykh deputatov SSSR i verkhovnogo soveta SSSR*, No. 1, 14 June 1989, p. 75. The problems presented by this are discussed by T. Dudko, chairman of one of the committees, in "Predely polnomochii," *Narodnyi deputat*, No. 7, 1990, pp. 16-23.
24. See *Pervaia Sessiia Verkhovnogo Soveta SSSR: Stenograficheskii otchet*, Moscow: 1989, Vol. 2, pp. 49.
25. I asked Lukianov (anonomously through a written question at a scholarly conference at Moscow State University in December 1988) when the new drafts would be published and what would be the essential differences between the old and new rules. He avoided the question by labeling me a 'juridical maximalist' and argued that the constitutional issues then under debate were more important.
26. *Izvestiia*, 30 June 1989, pp. 37-38.
27. For Primakov's remarks see *Pervaia Sessiia Verkhovnogo Soveta SSSR: Stenograficheskii Otchet*, Moscow, 1989, Vol. 2, p. 206. Khadzhiev

is quoted in A. Romanov, "Vlast na doroge ne valiaetsia," *Moscow News*, No. 28, 9 July 1989, p. 13.

28. *Vedomosti sezda narodnykh deputatov SSSR i verkhovnogo soveta SSSR*, No. 8, 2 August 1989, p. 285.

29. *Vedomosti sezda narodnykh deputatov SSSR i verkhovogo soveta SSSR*, No. 14, 13 September 1989, p. 426.

30. *Pervaia Sessiia Verkhovnogo Soveta SSSR: Stenograficheskii otchet*, Moscow: 1989, Vol. 2, p. 26.

31. *Izvestiia*, 11 June 1989, p. 11. For further discussion of this candidacy see *Pervaia Sessiia Verkhovnogo Soveta SSSR: Stenograficheskii otchet*, Moscow: 1989, Vol. 2, pp. 29, 31.

32. Interview of Iu.E. Andreev, 14 September 1989, Moscow. For E.P. Velikhov's arguments against Tetenov's candidacy see, *Pervaia Sessiia Verkhovnogo Soveta SSSR: Stenograficheskii otchet*, Moscow: 1989, Vol. 2, pp. 39–40.

33. *Izvestiia*, 11 June 1989, p. 11. *Pervaia sessiia Verkhovnogo Soveta SSSR, Biulleten No. 3, Zasedanie Soveta Natsionalnostei*, 26 June 1989, p. 37. For evidence that republican delegations played a role in this process see *Pervaia Sessiia Verkhovnogo Soveta SSSR: Stenograficheskii otchet*, Moscow: 1989, Vol. 2, p. 109.

34. Ibid., p. 54.

35. *Izvestiia*, 30 June 1989, p. 2.

36. *Literaturnaia gazeta*, 28 June 1989, p. 10. For a discussion of the effect of membership on the Supreme Soviet's foreign affairs committee see "Shevarnadze acknowledges Supreme Soviet Foreign Policy Role," *FBIS Trends*, 17 October 1990, pp. 15–20.

37. *Izvestiia*, 11 June 1989, p. 11. The stenogram is peppered with announcements and appeals by various groups. For example, see *Pervaia Sessiia Verkhovnogo Soveta SSSR: Stenograficheskii otchet*, Moscow: 1989, Vol. 1, p. 52, for an appeal by the autonomous republics.

38. Several technical considerations affected the formation of the committees. First, 50% of each committee's members were Supreme Soviet members (25% from each chamber), 50% were people's deputies not elected to the Supreme Soviet. In sum, about one third of the Congress's total membership of 2250 could become committee members.

39. *Izvestiia*, 12 June 1989, p. 2. For one example of Lukianov's reliance on the rotation argument see, *Pervaia Sessiia Verkhovnogo Soveta SSSR: Stenograficheskii otchet*, Moscow: 1989, Vol. 1, p. 24.

40. "Peoples' Deputies Congress: Round One," *Moscow News*, No. 20, 14 May 1989, p. 9. At the first session of the Soviet of the Union, Deputy A.I. Chabanov called for the creation of an economics institute to serve the Supreme Soviet. See *Izvestiia*, 5 June 1989, p. 2.

41. *Izvestiia*, 20 July 1989, p. 3. See *Nedelia*, 31 July 1989 for confirmation of the modest environment in committee chambers.

42. *Izvestiia*, 20 July 1989, p. 3.

43. One day in the middle of the summer of 1989, I noticed a large truck filled with cartons of new televisions parked outside the hotel entrance principally used by deputies. Clearly, someone in the 'administrative-command system' was making an effort to keep the deputies comfortable. For a description of deputorial life in the Moscow Hotel, see "V Kreml, na rabotu," *Pravda*, 18 July 1989, p. 6. For a debate during the session over the existence and meaning of privileges see an exchange between Deputies Boldyrev and Korshunov in *Pervaia Sessiia Verkhovnogo Soveta SSSR: Stenograficheskii otchet*, Moscow: 1989, Vol. 7, p. 26.

44. "Na pervoi sessii verkhovnogo soveta SSSR," *Pravda*, 5 July 1989, p. 1. Only 13 deputies not registered as readers at the Lenin Library before the start of the session enrolled during the summer. See O. Svistunova. "Informatsionnyi tsentr dlia parlamenta," *Izvestiia*, 29 August 1989, p. 2.

45. Interview of S.B. Stankevich, summer 1989, Moscow.

46. Consultants had one-room offices in the Moscow Hotel and additional office space somewhere in the Kremlin.

47. *Izvestiia*, 6 July 1989, p. 4. For complaints during the formation process on this point see remarks by Deputy Dubko, *Pervaia Sessiia Verkhovnogo Soveta SSSR: Stenograficheskii otchet*, Moscow: 1989, Vol. 1, p. 87.

48. M.A. Bocharov, *Pervaia sessiia Verkhovnogo Soveta SSSR, Biulleten No. 3, Zasedanie Soveta Soiuza*, pp. 45–46.

49. Interview of Iaroshenko, 9 September 1989, Pan American flight 31, Moscow-New York.

50. Deputy Bocharov questioned the Presidium when it decided to move the deputies so far away. *Moscow News* correspondent A. Romanov dismissively suggested that Bocharov was merely worried about the symbols of power. This is probably true, but one should not forget the practical considerations of time and distance. See A. Romanov, *Moscow News*, 9 July 1989, p. 13.

51. A stenographer I observed in the committee meeting I attended arrived late with a rudimentary tape recorder. One day in committee chambers I discussed with a deputy and a consultant the principle of accountability involved in publishing and distributing the stenogram. Both claimed that this conversation was the first time they thought of the issue in such terms. I phoned the committee for questions of glasnost and citizens' rights and petitions many times over the course of several weeks in the summer of 1989 but, ironically, no one ever answered.

52. A.M. Emelianov, "Pozitiv, negativ, i nashi deputaty," *Moskovskii Universitet*, 1 September 1989, p. 3.

53. *Izvestiia*, 2 June 1989, p. 7.

54. *Izvestiia*, 5 June 1989, p. 3. Gorbachev and Lukianov shared in this effort. For remarks by Gorbachev see, *Pervaia Sessiia Verkhovnogo Soveta SSSR: Stenograficheskii otchet*, Moscow: 1989, Vol. 6, p. 47.

55. *Izvestiia*, 11 June 1989, p. 11.

56. Lukianov reminded the deputies that many of them were sitting with "tickets in their pockets." See *Izvestiia*, 12 June 1989, p. 2.

57. Kaiser's argument can be found in *Why Gorbachev Happened: His Triumphs and his Failure*, New York: Simon and Schuster, 1991, p. 291. For interviews of Lapygin see, "Glasnost i gosudarstvennaia bezopasnost'," *Izvestiia*, 26 June 1989 and "S pozitsii novogo myshleniia," *Krasnaia Zvezda*, 22 June 1989. Lapygin's program for the March 1989 elections to the CPD can be found in *Tuvinskaia Pravda*, 5 March 1989, p. 2. See also *The New Soviet Legislature: Committee on Defense and State Security*, Report of the Committee on Armed Services, House of Representatives, One Hundred First Congress, Second Session, 11 April 1990, Washington: U.S. Government Printing Office, 1990.

58. *Pervaia Sessiia Verkhovnogo Soveta SSSR: Stenograficheskii otchet*, Moscow: 1989, Vol. 2, p. 107.

59. E.M. Primakov, *Pervaia sessiia Verkhovnogo Soveta SSSR, Biulleten No. 3, Zasedanie Soveta Soiuza*, 26 June 1989, p. 75.

60. *Izvestiia*, 12 June 1989, p. 2.

61. Ibid.

62. See *Pervaia sessiia Verkhovnogo Soveta SSSR, Biulleten No. 3, Zasedanie Soveta Soiuza*, 26 June 1989, p. 65.

63. Ibid., pp. 44–45. Almost a year later, Deputy V.N. Lopatin, an army major, made similar charges. See *Verkhovnyi Sovet SSSR, Tretia Sessiia, Biulleten No. 76 Sovmestnogo Zasedaniia Soveta Soiuza i Soveta Natsionalostei*, 14 June 1990, p. 39. Perhaps the best evidence of the defense committee's stacked membership and poor performance is that it was one of the first to be dissolved after the coup. See a proposal by S.S. Alekseev, *Verkhovnyi Sovet SSSR, Vneocherednaia Sessiia, Biulleten No. 9 Sovmestnogo Zasedaniia Soveta Soiuza i Soveta Natsionalnostei*, 28 August 1991, p. 7.

64. See remarks by Lithuanian Deputy V.V. Antanaitas, *Pervaia Sessiia Verkhovnogo Soveta SSSR: Stenograficheskii otchet*, Moscow: 1989, Vol. 2, p. 210.

65. *Pervaia sessiia Verkhovnogo Soveta SSSR, Biulleten No. 5, Sovmestnogo Zasedaniia Soveta Soiuza i Soveta Natsionalnostei*, 28 June 1989, p. 36.

66. For a summary of the IRDG's work during the first session from a conservative point of view see S. Karkhanin, "Kak poniat' pozitsiiu?," *Sovetskaia Rossiia*, 5 August 1989, p. 2.

67. *Sovetskii fizik, Spetsialnyi vypusk*, No. 34, 28 July 1989, p. 1. "Sotsiologicheskii portret MDG," *Informatsionnyi biulleten', Izdanie mezhregionalnoi gruppy narodnykh deputatov SSSR*, 15 September 1989, p. 32.

68. Popov questioned the strength of Gorbachev's commitment to a 'socialist pluralism of opinions' by pointing out that the Presidium had refused to provide a room for the meeting or duplication services to produce invitations.

69. S.B. Stankevich, *Sovetskii fizik*, 28 July 1989, p. 4.

70. *Moscow News*, 20 August 1989, p. 4. Not all deputies agreed on the usefulness of the IRDG. See, for example, "Why should the deputies split?," *Moscow News*, 9 August 1989, p. 9. For one Moscow deputy's arguments against the group see "Gotov k otkrytomu sporu," *Sovetskaia rossiia*, 22 July 1989, p. 3.

71. *Pravda*, 5 August 1989, p. 1.

72. See *Vedomosti sezda narodnykh deputatov SSSR i verkhovnogo soveta SSSR*, No. 1, 14 June 1989, p. 75.

Chapter 7

The Committees at Work

Analyses of the new Supreme Soviet by its deputies, not surprisingly, were contradictory. Prime Minister and Politburo member Nikolai Ryzhkov faced a barrage of deputorial ire during confirmation hearings for his ministerial colleagues and, not coincidentally, argued in July 1989 that the party needed to find "new approaches, new methods, new principles" to control the Supreme Soviet. He complained that the legislature was starting to exercise rights that formerly belonged to the Politburo and Central Committee, and that the party "may lose its influence in state management."[1] Deputy Gavriil Popov, a leader of the IRDG, implied the opposite when he asked, "What can voters think about the Supreme Soviet when they see that its members do not have the text [of bills], but allow discussion to continue anyway...that [it] meekly takes up discussion of [bills] received the day before?"[2] One way to resolve the contradictory opinions expressed by Ryzhkov and Popov concerning the Supreme Soviet—and thereby get a better look at the development of the new institutions—is to take a closer look at its committee system.

Committee Responsibilities

Committees performed three functions during the Supreme Soviet's first month of operation: they conducted confirmation hearings for nominees to government posts; they discussed and recommended legislation to the Supreme Soviet and worked on ideas for future laws; they monitored the implementation of public policy. The Supreme Soviet's Presidium organized the committee system's work.[3] Lukianov, as Gorbachev's first deputy, played the major role in the daily organizational process. Individual committees did, however, have the freedom to draft their own work plans, undoubtedly with a good deal of help from the Supreme Soviet's Secretariat. Deputy V.M. Vologzhin, chairman of the economic reforms committee, explained that his members set up a work plan at their first meeting and also had drafted a set of goals. Another chairman stated that his committee had drafted a plan to cover its schedule until the end of the year and that its work would be directed toward discussing laws that were on the Supreme Soviet's agenda.[4]

Confirmation Hearings

During the summer of 1989, millions of Soviet citizens tuned in every evening to watch deputies grill the Supreme Soviet's latest executive 'victims,' nominees to ministerial posts, for past, present, and possible future mismanagement. Unfortunately for the beleagured nominees, this was, in fact, a second round: they had been questioned earlier in private by the committees. Confirmation hearings were a significant symbolic element of the first session because they demonstrated the new Supreme Soviet's right to monitor the executive's activities. Later, by publicly upholding negative committee evaluations and refusing to confirm nominees for eight government posts, the Supreme Soviet showed that it at least had the potential to be a demanding partner. In fact, Premier Ryzhkov withdrew several candidates before they were considered by the Supreme Soviet because they received negative evaluations in committee hearings.[5]

The meeting of the CPSU party group before the opening of the CPD shaped but did not dictate decisions of the committee system. In hearings, heated discussions were common and several nominees were rejected. Confirmation votes were not subject to party discipline. The agriculture committee was the first to give a nominee a negative recommendation. Chairman Veprev stated that V. Kalashnikov, a nominee for the first deputy for agriculture position in the Council of Ministers, did not present a concrete program of policy initiatives and that he was concerned only about trying to protect his budget and staff. Committee members questioned Kalashnikov's role in eliminating an innovative agricultural program under the pretense of fighting unearned income. Veprev reported that the committee did not see a commitment to change and innovation in his remarks.[6] Committees gave some nominees conditional recommendations and required them to return at some future date with a solution to a problem, or a program of action in a given policy field. The construction committee recommended V. Chirskov as minister for construction enterprises in the oil and gas industry, but instructed him to return in two days with recommendations for ecological problems in the industry.[7]

Both the meeting of the party group and the confirmation hearings suggest that the CPSU's monopolistic approach to cadres policy was changing. Although the Central Committee's *nomenklatura* system undoubtedly had veto power over nominees, it no longer completely controlled who worked where. That is, Central Committee support was a necessary but not sufficient condition for a candidate to any post.[8] The Supreme Soviet's new status in the confirmation process was illustrated by the fact that after several nominees had been turned down, and potential nominees started to refuse consideration, Ryzhkov began consulting with the committees on the acceptability of people whom he was thinking about nominating. For example, filling the chairmanship of the state committee for ecology was especially difficult. Three members of the Academy of Sciences declined consideration. Perhaps wishing to avoid future conflict, or trying to give committees a further stake in the process, Ryzhkov asked them to help identify suitable nominees.[9]

Candidates for government posts were expected to present a 'program' for action in their new positions. The relationship between individual ministerial programs and overall party policy is unclear. A front-page article in *Pravda* declared that a minister's program "is the fruit of collective thought. It is based on the decisions of the CPSU Central Committee, and the first [CPD]. It is worked out not by the minister alone, but by the [ministry's leading officials]...But the final word belongs to the Supreme Soviet."[10] Despite this neat model, it appeared that candidates were allowed to 'campaign' with little coordination from the top.

One of the most important aspects of the relationship between the Presidium and the committee system was coordination of committee work. The question that needs to be answered in regard to the confirmation process might be phrased: Which committees listened to which candidates, when, and under what circumstances? When Yeltsin suggested that it was necessary to draft a schedule of which committees would listen to which candidates, Lukianov said that he would give the proposal to committee chairmen and the chairmen of the two chambers so that appropriate agreements could be reached, "if this is necessary."[11] The Supreme Soviet decree that instructed "corresponding committees" to examine the Council of Ministers' structure offered no guidance on which committees should be included. Apparently, this was left to the Presidium's discretion, which led to problems.[12] Deputy Shapovalenko suggested that political considerations played a role in what he perceived as scheduling irregularities.

> If [Lukianov] says that there is no apparat, then who assigned the discussion of candidates to [various] commissions? How did it turn out that the minister of the biological products industry,

> comrade Bykov, suddenly disappeared [from the schedule] of the ecology committee?[13]

Shapovalenko recited a list of deficiencies of the Presidium's work, including scheduling problems and the failure to distribute necessary information. Often, several committees met simultaneously so that it was difficult or impossible for interested deputies to participate in all of them. Other deputies complained that biographical data and additional information needed to make competent decisions about nominees was unavailable. They complained that hearing schedules were not posted, and that the schedules were poorly organized. Deputy Murashev reported that in the absence of better data his colleagues sometimes relied on 'accidental' information about the nominees.[14] One unidentified deputy argued that the committees suffered from poor support.

> We have no staff to get to the bottom of [these questions]. How did we select ministers? Either we like them or not, if they answered glibly, good, clumsily—they're not fit. Did we have any kind of materials? Did we have any kind of dossiers? Did we have a summary of the press about every ministry? We had nothing.[15]

This deputy went on to suggest that, if these problems were not addressed, they would adversely affect the legislative process. Deputy V.D. Iudin argued that discussions at joint sessions of the Supreme Soviet often could not rely on the committee's opinions because they were not made available.

> I am not prepared to make decisions on ministerial candidates without receiving on time the results of the committees' discussion. I would like to know which proposals, which principal positions of the ministers' programs received the approval of the commissions, what principal remarks were made to the ministers, and why certain ministers made it through, as they say, 'with a cheer,' and others were rejected.[16]

Even at committee meetings, the deputies were given only biographical summaries of the candidates, and did not have written information on the performance of the ministry or the candidate's plans for the future.[17]

Changes in voting procedure designed to ease attendance requirements at committee meetings suggested that the leadership was more interested in appearances than the actual quality of the committees' work. Lukianov proposed changing voting procedures so that committee meetings would be empowered to make decisons on most questions as long as more than 50% of their membership was present. A simple majority of deputies in attendance would decide any vote. Apparently, this rule was stretched even farther. Addressing a joint session, one unidentified deputy asked, "why weren't deputies given [the full conclusions] of commissions, with voting results, where the candidacies of comrades Lemaev, Kolpakov, Gusev, and Busygin did not even receive 50% of the votes of those present, not to mention the [full membership]?"[18] Committee chairmen were not above bending, or even breaking, the voting rules. I.O. Bisher, deputy chairman of the Soviet of Nationalities, noted at a joint session of the Supreme Soviet that positive recommendations were given to two ministerial candidates, despite the fact that less than half of the deputies participating in the discussion voted accordingly. There is no indication in that day's stenographic record that Bisher's question was answered.[19]

Committee chairmen reported to the Supreme Soviet on the results of the confirmation hearings and the merits of the nominees. These reports sometimes seemed more like campaign speeches than reasoned summaries based on professional analyses of the nominees' strengths and weaknesses by objective specialist committees. Often, the Supreme Soviet's leaders supported nominees against deputy attacks. The clearest example of this phenomenon was the renomination of Ministers Konarev and Kamentsev after both had already been denied posts by the Supreme Soviet. Gorbachev and Ryzhkov lobbied extensively for both candidates. Criticizing such pressure from above, Deputy Iudin argued that deputies should reach their own conclusions by starting

> from another point of view. [Ryzhkov] looks at the problem, if you will, from above, but we look at it from below, [from the point of view] of the voters. It is in just this unity of points of view in which the truth we are seeking is born. Otherwise we will return to [the system] that we left behind... Trust does not mean the unthinking acceptance, without discussion, of a decision.[20]

The confirmation process demonstrated that the committee's role was auxiliary to the Supreme Soviet. The Supreme Soviet did not always accept the committees' opinions; in fact, many nominees were grilled extensively *after* facing the committees.[21] In the case of V. V. Geraschenko, nominated to a position in the state bank, the Supreme Soviet "relied completely on the conclusions of the committees and commissions that had discussed his candidacy" because "the overwhelming majority of deputies were unable to conduct a dialogue with him on equal terms."[22] In some cases, where two or more committees gave conflicting recommendations, the Supreme Soviet listened to all opinions before making its own decision.[23] In sum, however, the difficulties that deputies faced during the confirmation process turned the committees' specialist function into a fiction: competence in relevant fields was often irrelevant to the final decision.

Monitoring Implementation

During the summer of 1989, the committee system took only its first steps in exercising its power to control the Council of Ministers. First, as pointed out above, the committees discussed the implementation of public policy during the confirmation process. Second, the committees planned a number of projects, both independent and cooperative, to analyze various policy questions and problems. Third, the committees took part in the annual budget process. However, before discussing the ways that the committees started to exercise their monitoring powers, it is appropriate to ask whether it is possible for *any* legislative committee to fulfill the monitoring role outlined in the Soviet constitution? The information problems that plague all bureaucracies were multiplied in the USSR, where a centrally planned economy distorted performance indicators. How, for example, could anyone decide if investment policies were sound if input prices did not reflect relative scarcities or in the absence of genuine capital markets? Deputy Alekseev argued that without economic decentralization the commissions would be unable to monitor the executive successfully. Condemning 'instructions,' 'rules,' and other intra-ministerial guidelines or trying to revise them would not be enough: the need for such regulations, he asserted, must be reduced by market-type reforms.[24]

The committees began the monitoring process when grilling ministerial candidates during confirmation hearings. Indeed, when discussing the candidacies of incumbent ministers and veteran officials it would have been impossible to avoid discussing present and past performance. For example, reporting to a joint session on June 27, Deputy F.M. Burlatskii summarized the results of confirmation hearings held for positions in the foreign trade organs by the committee for international affairs. Burlatskii and his colleagues encouraged the foreign trade committee to increase purchases of consumer goods overseas.[25]

Some committees actively cultivated working relationships with executive organs that promised to facilitate the monitoring process. On the last day of the session, the chairman of the Soviet of the Union's commission for questions of labor, prices, and social policy called in representatives from the ministry of finance, the state committee on pricing, and the state committee on labor to discuss future cooperation. In an exchange of opinions, the chairman told them what questions interested the commission. The representatives from executive organs had expected a confrontation, and were happy to see that a working relationship was possible. A second example of relationship building was provided by N.N. Gritsenko, chairman of the Soviet of the Union's commission for questions of labor, prices, and social policy, who outlined some of the first steps taken to start the monitoring process. Together with the USSR People's Control Commission, his commission planned to examine the work of the State Pricing Committee and report its findings to the Supreme Soviet. With *Gosplan*, the State Labor Committee, and union republic governments, the commission planned to work out measures for full employment in regions with high population growth.[26]

The committee system's review of the plan and budget was one of the principal elements of its monitoring function; however, during the first session little effort was made to develop the rules and procedures needed to make the review a genuine instrument of legislative control. Chairman of the Soviet of the Union E.M. Primakov declared that the Supreme Soviet's control over the executive "should and can be realized... through a very serious discussion of the budget. Separate and joint sessions of the chambers, as well as committee... meetings should be devoted to this question."[27] Primakov argued that the Supreme Soviet should not ratify the budget "mechanically," and that "the structure of the budget and concrete sums assigned to one or another goal" should be professionally reviewed in the Supreme Soviet's committees, "like, for example... the commissions in the US Congress."[28] Primakov's proposals regarding the budget process were undermined by the fact that, as Deputy Iu.Iu. Boldyrev pointed out, there was no legal regulation of the process. Despite Primakov's seemingly firm support for strong Supreme Soviet participation in the budget process, actual practice turned out differently. On 26 June, Deputy Velikhov expressed concern that the Supreme Soviet would miss its chance to participate in the budget process. He argued that it should be allowed to work on the budget immediately because, he felt, time was slipping by, and the legislature would once again be reduced to playing a formal role. In the end, nothing got done.

The Legislative Process

Attempts by deputies to establish formal regulation of the legislative process, like attempts to discuss the committees' standing rules, were defeated. On 26 June, at a meeting of the Soviet of the Union, Deputy Velikhov proposed discussing the legislative process and offered to share with the chamber materials he had gathered concerning the operation of the US Congress. Later that day, Velikhov forced his way to the microphone to ask why his proposals had been ignored. After initially refusing to give him the floor, Primakov employed two tactics that he used throughout the summer. First, he accused Velikhov of wanting to rush through discussion of legislative procedures, a serious topic. Next, he reminded the deputies how much 'real work' awaited them, thereby suggesting that procedural questions could wait.[29]

Application of the 'as a rule' clause in the constitutional article that defines the committees' responsibilities means that they had no right to discuss draft legislation unless they were asked to do so. During the first session, this clause was used several times. The committee system did not review a number of decrees passed by the Presidium and ratified by the Supreme Soviet, nor did it review treaties with Cuba and India.[30] When a number of deputies from Central Asian republics asked for revisions in indicators of local economic performance, the Supreme Soviet, at the Presidium's suggestion, instructed the Council of Ministers to examine the question but did not ask any of its committees to participate.[31] Deputy B.V. Miroshin complained that the committee for questions of the work of soviets of people's deputies and the development of management and self-management had not reviewed draft laws in its bailiwick.

Discussing problems associated with bypassing the committees, Miroshin argued that every bill should go through a preparatory stage and that deputies should have time to consult with voters; otherwise, the process would produce "completely unprepared decisions."[32] Deputy Bocharov argued that legislation should be prepared "exclusively by the Supreme Soviet's commissions and committees. Today," he continued, "projects under review are prepared by [executive organs]...or by the apparat of the Supreme Soviet's Presidium."[33] Even when the executive did not draft bills independently, it still had significant influence in the process. Deputy Vologzhin reported, for example, that the USSR state commission for economic reform and deputy chairman of the Council of Ministers L.I. Abalkin had provided a great deal of support in drafting the law on economic self-management in the Baltic.[34]

Legislative practice in the first few weeks of the Supreme Soviet's operation demonstrated that the influence of executive institutions or the party apparat were not the only ways that politics impinged on 'specialist' committees. Deputies sometimes pursued private political goals. Deputy Andreev, a member of the construction committee, reported that deputies defended local interests in committee meetings by trying to protect construction projects in their home districts.[35] Deputy Bocharov criticized his colleagues by arguing that "more than two months after the opening of the Congress, deputies pose many questions from the [point of view] of local interests. We were not elected...to [represent] only our own district."[36]

Despite Andreev and Bocharov's charges, however, the battle to defend local interests may not have extended to all the committees. Agricultural committee chairman Veprev declared that "for now, no one has tried to drag the blanket over to his side of the bed by standing up for the interests of only his union republic."[37]

A Committee Meeting

On 5 August 1989, the Committee for questions of the work of soviets of people's deputies discussed a draft of its recommendations for a proposed law on local economic self-management. The discussion held at this meeting demonstrated several aspects of the legislative process: (1) the inseparability of political decisionmaking and policy formulation, (2) relations between the Supreme Soviet and the ministerial apparatus, and (3) the importance of procedural questions.[38] Out of 40 committee members only approximately 20 attended, probably because the Supreme Soviet's session officially closed on 4 August.

"According to tradition," Chairman N.D. Pivovarov started the meeting on time. Following a brief discussion of the agenda, N.N. Daniliuk, chairman of the executive committee of the Khabarovsk soviet, and A.P. Rubiks, chairman of the executive committee of a Latvian city soviet, two members charged with drafting the committee's recommendations, summarized their analysis.[39] Daniliuk argued that three aspects of the law needed further work. First, the unclear division of powers between locally elected soviets and executive organs responsible to central ministries raised the question of how local soviets should derive their income. Daniliuk argued for revisions that would state that the main income producer for local budgets should be an income tax. The second principal weakness that Daniliuk identified was that the bill did not state clearly the responsibilities of each layer of government. Third, he argued that local soviets should be given more power, including the right to review ministries' construction projects on their territory. Daniliuk concluded that, if the proposed changes were included, the bill under discussion could be recommended for a first reading.

The legislation discussed at this meeting provided several examples of the dilemmas faced by party leaders and members during a legislative process in 'specialist' committees. First, no consistent party strategy can be created for all deputies on matters of policy when concrete issues demand that decisions be based on local and, in an immense federal system, often contradictory interests. Deputies from Uzbekistan and Estonia, for example, were likely to reach different conclusions about the needs and rights of local government. Second, a number of issues are tied together in this legislation, and deputies might come to different conclusions about the overall bill depending on which aspect of party policy they emphasized. For example, Gorbachev often argued that a strong USSR requires "a strong center and strong republics." In this case, in the absence of clear and binding instructions from above, it was unclear whether deputies should emphasize a strong center or strong republics. How should party members have applied this inconsistent strategic message from the party leadership as it relates to local government? 'Strategy' can become so vague that it is meaningless. A third dilemma illustrated by this example is the temporal dimension to the formulation of public policy that traditional party leadership was too inflexible to cope with. As committees monitor the implementation of public policy, needs and strategies change; moreover, policies are formulated and monitored simultaneously in more than one issue area.

The discussion of taxation and fiscal policy offered some additional insights into the committees' specialist role and their ability to monitor the Council of Ministers and its executive organs. Although Pivovarov's committee contained a number of members who work in soviets at various levels, it was far from obvious that such people were the best analysts of problems faced by local government. Moreover, except for Deputy Boldyrev, none of the members seemed prepared to counter or discuss the working group's conclusions. Although handwritten notes were visible around the table, deputies did not demonstrate that they were prepared to conduct a specialized discussion. Rubiks argued that his colleagues need to look more carefully at the press and at scholarly articles, which suggests that even their general knowledge of relevant problems was minimal.

The committee meeting offered insight into the relationship between the Supreme Soviet, the committee system, and executive organs, especially the Council of Ministers. First, the committee had no clear idea of whom it should be communicating with in the Council of Ministers. Deputies argued that the committee needed to find out who in the Council of Ministers, especially *Gosplan* and the state statistics committee, would be working on the law. Not surprisingly, this meeting also suggested that the executive is reluctant to give up power. When one deputy suggested that enterprises subordinated to central ministries should contribute to local budgets, either through taxation or rent, another countered that the Ministry of Finance constantly fought this idea and that similar language had been removed from an earlier draft received through the Council of Ministers. Finally, the discussion also suggested the inertia and power of the executive. One deputy asked Daniliuk to identify the government organs that ultimately would decide local soviets' budget sources. He replied that the republican Council of Ministers would play the most important role in this question. The deputy who asked the question retorted sarcastically that the traditional command of the executive still reigned at the local level. This line of discussion was not pursued. In short, a matter of fundamental principle was ignored.

At the end of the meeting, Pivovarov explained to the deputies that Lukianov would write a letter asking the Council of Ministers to review the committee's suggestions. This underlines the principal weakness in the committees' relationship with the executive—their recommendations were non-binding. Although, in this case, the committee's recomendations were substantial and would have significantly altered the proposed legislation if included, the Council of Ministers could ignore committee advice as long as it thought that the Presidium and the Supreme Soviet would not suppport the committee's position. Pivovarov adamantly summed up the committee's position when he declared that, "We should not work for them." "Them," in this case, meant the Council of Ministers.

'Specialist' Committees and Political Leadership

Both the confirmation hearings and the monitoring process suggested that the committees would not be allowed to play their 'specialist' role. The Presidium played a decisive role in political control by coordinating the committee system's work.[40] Deputorial dissatisfaction with the Presidium boiled over late in June. Representatives of the IRDG, Deputy N.D. Tutov in the Soviet of the Union and Deputy V.N. Zubkov in the Soviet of Nationalities, read indictments of the Presidium's work. Tutov maintained that deputies who were not members of the Supreme Soviet and its organs "did not receive any information concerning the discussion of candidates nominated to government posts," and that hearings were scheduled so that deputies could not participate in discussions in which they wanted to take part.[41] Tutov claimed that ministerial candidates were rushed through hearings to increase their chances, and that deputies did not receive necessary information. R.N. Nishanov, chairman of the Soviet of Nationalities, avoided discussing and voting on the proposal.[42] Later the same day, Deputy Bocharov expressed angry confusion over the Presidium's work.

> We have [no information]...Is [the Supreme Soviet] here to serve the apparat or is the apparat here to serve us? That is, what are the essential elements of the relationships between the committees...and the apparat, [including] the distribution of necessary documents to Supreme Soviet members and the possibility of effectively resolving those questions addressed by

> a committee?...Why should the...[Presidium's] apparat be located in the Supreme Soviet's buildings [located close to the Kremlin]? Why shouldn't *they* move to the 20-story building [all the way out] on Kalinin Prospect?[43]

Deputy Podziruk pointed out that deputies were notified of a new organizational structure planned for the Council of Ministers only fifteen minutes before they were expected to vote. Deputy Bogdanov argued along similar lines.

> They are playing cat and mouse with us. Allegedly, the Presidium...is a powerful organization, yet it is unable to prepare information for us. We lived for a week [in the deputies' hotel] and did not see a single information stand. No matter where you call, no one can tell you anything sensible. No communication...As I was leaving one Saturday, I asked what the first order of business would be on Monday...For now, nothing is ready...That is, a forty-day Supreme Soviet session is scheduled, and allegedly there is nothing ready in the Presidium...We agreed that we should receive documents two weeks in advance. But today we arrived, and literally ten minutes before the start of business they handed out a list. Take it, agree with, and vote for it.[44]

Bogdanov feared that deputies would be reduced to their old role as voting automatons, and that "comrades from the party's Central Committee again will soon forget that the Supreme Soviet exists."[45]

Faced with an explosion of dissatisfaction, Lukianov tried to explain the Presidium's organizational problems:

> Let's stay calm. Our powers and the order of our work are only just being worked out; therefore, of course, many questions are appearing. We discussed this in the Presidium...We need to arrange a few...lectures for deputies about our problems...It is impossible...to answer all questions at once...A new parliamentary structure with its own work rules is being born. The rules will crystalize gradually.[46]

Lukianov expressed disbelief at accusations that the apparat would try "to manipulate" deputies, claimed to be under orders from Gorbachev "to ensure that every effort was made to serve the deputies," but admitted that there were "operational" problems. He claimed that attempts to change the Supreme Soviet's agenda to resolve them would not be productive.[47]

Lukianov's argument that a new Supreme Soviet would "crystallize gradually" was probably one of the soundest arguments offered in the newborn legislature in the summer of 1989. Legislative institutionalization takes time in any political system, not to mention one that had abandoned parliamentary principles for seventy years. One essential ingredient for such development, however, is sound leadership. The following sessions of the Supreme Soviet would settle the question of whether Lukianov's 'mistakes' were due to inexperience or something else.

Notes

1. *Pravda*, 21 July 1989, p. 4.
2. *Informatsionnyi biulleten', Izdanie mezhregionalnoi gruppy narodnykh deputatov SSSR*, 15 September 1989, p. 3.
3. The legislative agenda for the Supreme Soviet's first session was published in a Presidium decree on 23 June. The agenda's 21 points included an ambitious number of legislative projects on a variety of questions of socioeconomic and political reform. See "O povestke dnia i poriadke raboty pervoi sessii verkhovnogo soveta SSSR," *Vedomosti sezda narodnykh deputatov SSSR i verkhovnogo soveta SSSR*, No. 3, p. 127 and "Ob organizatsii raboty po vypolneniiu poruchenii dannykh verkhovnomu sovetu SSSR sezdom narodnykh deputatov SSSR," *Vedomosti...*, No. 8, p. 275.
4. *Pravda*, 17 July 1989, p. 2.
5. Ryzhkov requested that the Supreme Soviet not review any candidates while he travelled to Hungary for a Warsaw Pact meeting. See *Pravda*, 7 July 1989, p. 1. See also, S. Karkhanin, "Reshaiushchii golos," *Sovetskaia rossiia*, 22 July 1989, p. 1.

Eugene Huskey, who pointed out that "one must be cautious...in using the parliamentary confirmation of the government in 1989 as evidence of a fundamental and permanent realignment of executive- legislative relations," presents an excellent overview of the confirmation prcess in his chapter in Robert T. Huber and Donald R. Kelley, eds., *Perestroika-Era Politics: The New Soviet Legislature and Gorbachev's Political Reforms*, New York: M.E. Sharpe, 1991.

6. *Izvestiia*, 6 July 1989, p. 4.
7. *Literaturnaia gazeta*, 28 July 1989, p. 10. For the construction commission's opinion on the candidate for minister of oil and gas see, *Pervaia Sessiia Verkhovnogo Soveta SSSR: Stenograficheskii otchet*, Moscow: 1989, Vol. 3, pp. 48–49. For Yeltsin's evaluation of the candidate see *Pervaia Sessiia Verkhovnogo Soveta SSSR: Stenograficheskii otchet*, Moscow: 1989, Vol. 5, pp. 65–66.

8. Iu. D. Chernichenko, lecture at Aeroflot's Palace of Culture, 31 July 1989, Moscow.

9. A. Fyodorov, *Moscow News*, No. 34, 1989. For a discussion of the first round of Kamentsev's confirmation battle see A. Guber, "Posle dramy," *Novoe Vremia*, No. 30, 1989, pp. 22-23.

10. "Programma ministra," *Pravda*, 14 July 1989, p. 1. For the unsuccessful program of a candidate for minister of the railways see, *Pervaia Sessiia Verkhovnogo Soveta SSSR: Stenograficheskii otchet*, Moscow: 1989, Vol. 5, p. 31.

11. *Izvestiia*, 12 June 1989, p. 2.

12. *Vedomosti sezda narodnykh deputatov SSSR i verkhovnogo soveta SSSR*, No. 1, 14 June 1989, p. 81.

13. *Pervaia sessiia Verkhovnogo Soveta SSSR, Biulleten No. 3, Zasedaniia Soveta Natsionalnostei*, 26 June 1989, p. 35.

14. Interview of A.N. Murashev, 15 August 1989, Moscow.

15. *Pervaia sessiia Verkhovnogo Soveta SSSR, Biulleten No. 3, Zasedaniia Soveta Soiuza*, 26 June 1989, pp. 27-28.

16. *Pervaia sessiia Verkhovnogo Soveta SSSR, Zasedaniia Soveta Soiuza*, 30 June 1989. pp. 37-38. For similar remarks by V. N. Zubkov see, *Pervaia Sessiia Verkhovnogo Soveta SSSR: Stenograficheskii otchet*, Moscow: 1989, Vol. 2, pp. 133-134.

17. E. Gongalez, V. Dolganov, and E. Zhbanov, "Khoroshee nachalo—poldela," *Izvestiia*, 20 June 1989, p. 1.

18. *Pervaia sessiia Verkhovnogo Soveta SSSR, Biulleten No. 3, Sovmestnogo Zasedaniia Soveta Soiuza i Soveta Natsionalnostei*, 27 June 1989, p. 37.

19. *Pervaia sessiia Verkhovnogo Soveta SSSR, Zasedaniia Soveta Soiuza*, pp. 37-38. For similar complaints concerning a number of other ministerial candidates see *Pervaia Sessiia Verkhovnogo Soveta SSSR: Stenograficheskii otchet*, Moscow: 1989, Vol. 3, p. 26.

20. *Pervaia sessiia Verkhovnogo Soveta SSSR, Biulleten No. 3, Sovmestnogo Zasedaniia Soveta Soiuza i Soveta Natsionalnostei*, pp. 20-21.

21. See, for example, "Segodnia v tsene kompetentnost'," *Izvestiia*, 12 July 1989, p. 1.

22. V. Kurasov and A. Davydov, "Vremia smelykh reshenii," *Izvestiia*, 4 August 1989, p. 2.

23. For example, the ecology and health care committees disagreed over the nomination of V.A. Bykov. See *Pervaia sessiia Verkhovnogo Soveta SSSR, Biulleten No. 3, Sovmestnogo Zasedaniia Soveta Soiuza i Soveta Natsionalnostei*, 27 June 1989, p. 9. Remarks by A.I. Iablokov are instructive on this point. See *Pervaia Sessiia Verkhovnogo Soveta SSSR: Stenograficheskii otchet*, Moscow: 1989, Vol. 5, p. 56.

24. Premier Ryzhkov often found himself the object of deputorial ire. Discussing Ryzhkov's role, Deputy Boldyrev pointed out a major problem in the monitoring process. When one commission questioned Ryzhkov about the construction of chemical plants he answered briefly, off the cuff, without any documentation. Boldyrev argued that deputies should not have accepted such an incomplete answer. See Iu.Iu. Boldyrev, "Osoboe mnenie," *Sobesednik*, No. 35, August 1989. For a discussion, from the government's point of view, about its relations with deputies after a year of development see "Deputat obratilsia v pravitelstvo," *Pravitelstvennyi vestnik*, No. 7, 1990, pp. 2–3.

25. *Pervaia sessiia Verkhovnogo Soveta SSSR, Sovmestnogo Zasedaniia Soveta Soiuza i Soveta Natsionalnostei*, 27 June 1989, pp. 3–4.

26. *Pervaia Sessiia Verkhovnogo Soveta SSSR: Stenograficheskii otchet*, Moscow: 1989, Vol. 5, p. 79.

27. *Literaturnaia gazeta*, 21 June 1989, p. 10.

28. *Izvestiia*, 5 June 1989, p. 2.

29. E.P. Velikhov, *Pervaia sessiia Verkhovnogo Soveta SSSR, Biulleten No. 3, Zasedaniia Soveta Natsionalnostei*, pp. 30–31.

30. For the treaty with Cuba, see *Vedomosti sezda narodnykh deputatov SSSR i verkhovnogo soveta SSSR*, No. 6, 19 July 1989, p. 231. For the treaty with India, see *Vedomosti...*, No. 8, 2 August 1989.

31. *Vedomosti...*, No. 6, 19 July 1989, p. 227.

32. B.V. Miroshin, *Pervaia sessiia Verkhovnogo Soveta SSSR, Biulleten No. 3, Zasedaniia Soveta Soiuza*, 26 June 1989, p. 42.

33. *Izvestiia*, 7 August 1989, p. 1. More than a year later this remained a problem. See remarks by Deputy S.V. Belozertsev in *Verkhovnyi Sovet SSSR, Chetvertaia Sessiia, Biulleten No. 1 Sovmestnogo Zasedaniia Soveta Soiuza i Soveta Natsionalnostei*, 10 September 1990, p. 19.

34. *Izvestiia*, 10 July 1989, p. 2. For a discussion of a similar working relationship in the veterans' affairs committee see an interview of V.N. Bosenko, "Prioritet miloserdiiu," *Izvestiia*, 23 July 1989, p. 2.

Vologzhin noted that scholars participate in the legislative process. "The main point was to recruit the country's leading scholarly forces..." *Izvestiia*, 15 August 1989, p. 1. Deputy Alekseev reported a similar situtation in the legislation committee. "Acting together with other committees and commissions," he declared, "we will attract the best specialists...to legislative work. *Komsomolskaia Pravda*, 11 July 1989, p. 2.

35. Interview of Iu.E. Andreev, 4 September 1989, Moscow.

36. V. Dalganov, "Sdelan vazhnyi shag," *Izvestiia*, 7 August 1989, p. 1.

37. *Izvestiia*, 6 July 1989, p. 4.

38. Uniformed guards stood at the entrance to prevent uninvited guests. A committee consultant met me at the door. Deputies were required to present identification cards.

39. Rubiks is interviewed in "Deputatam realnuiu vlast," *Izvestiia*, 28 June 1989, p. 3.

40. "Chem zaniaty sluzhby apparata," *Izvestiia*, 4 July 1989, p. 2. Stuart Goldman discusses the apparat's structure and role in his chapter in Hubert and Kelley, eds., *Perestroika-Era Politics...*

41. *Pervaia sessiia Verkhovnogo Soveta SSSR, Biulleten No. 3, Zasedaniia Soveta Soiuza*, 26 June 1989, pp. 22–23.

42. Ibid., pp. 33–34.

43. For Podziruk's remarks see *Pervaia Sessiia Verkhovnogo Soveta SSSR: Stenograficheskii otchet*, Moscow: 1989, Vol. 2, p. 136. This quotation of Bogdanov is taken from *Pervaia sessiia Verkhovnogo Soveta SSSR, Biulleten No. 3, Zasedaniia Soveta Soiuza*, 26 June 1989, pp. 45–46.

44. Ibid., pp. 23–24. The cat and mouse analogy was used often throughout the Supreme Soviet's existence. For example, see remarks by Deputy V.A. Shekhovtsov in *Verkhovnyi Sovet SSSR, Tretia Sessiia, Biulleten No. 53 Sovmestnogo Zasedaniia Soveta Soiuza i Soveta Natsionalnostei*, 25 May 1990, p. 49.

45. Ibid.

46. Lukianov's explanation as well as a series of other arguments can be found in *Pervaia sessiia Verkhovnogo Soveta SSSR, Biulleten No. 3, Zasedaniia Soveta Natsionalnostei*, 26 June 1989, p. 27.

47. Ibid., p. 37.

Chapter 8

Development of the Supreme Soviet

The Supreme Soviet's first session suggested that Gorbachev was unwilling to revise internal party competition in a way that could drive a liberalized decisionmaking process in the committee system. This chapter reviews subsequent development of party leadership in the Supreme Soviet, once again through the prism of the committee system. The discussion, however, is broadened to account for subsequent developments in both the Supreme Soviet and the Soviet political system: (1) the creation of the presidency, (2) intra-CPSU politics, including the Democratic Platform movement and the 28th Party Congress, (3) the strengthening of political groups in the Supreme Soviet, and (4) the drive toward republican sovereignty that culminated in the coup. The arument advanced here is *not* that the Supreme Soviet was toothless and passive: its refusal in June 1990 to raise bread prices, a major setback to Gorbachev's attempt to end subsidies, is clear evidence that the legislature (at times) had a mind of its own. Instead, this chapter suggests that the Supreme Soviet never developed the internal structures that would enable it to play a real role in controlling the executive.

The Supreme Soviet's First Year

On 3 June 1990, at the close of its third session, the Supreme Soviet celebrated its first anniversary. An official evaluation of the legislature's work was published in a pamphlet sent to deputies on 20 June 1990 over the signature of Anatolii Lukianov. He argued that the Supreme Soviet, as an "organic part" of the CPD, had "built up necessary parliamentary experience." A year of work showed that the Supreme Soviet was the "optimal variant of a standing [representative institution]" and was "not an obedient decorative forum but...a working corporation capable of deciding in a qualified manner any question within its competence."[1]

The most important legislation ratified by the Supreme Soviet during its first three sessions were, of course, the constitutional amendments that created the presidency. Other major bills ratified included laws on the press and land reform as well as a major overhaul of the country's pension system. The Supreme Soviet's first and second sessions ratified 10 laws (*zakony*) each and reviewed in their first reading 18 other drafts, 6 of which were published for national discussion. A foundation for further legislative activity was created through 148 decrees (*postanovlenie*) passed by the Supreme Soviet and 32 decrees passed by the Soviet of the Union and the Soviet of Nationalities. The Supreme Soviet's third session was interrupted by the third, extraordinary session of the CPD that ratified the creation of the Soviet presidency; nonetheless, changes were made in the agenda to account for lost time. In all, 76 joint meetings of the Supreme Soviet and 17 meetings of the chambers were held during the third session, 33 laws (*zakony*) were ratified, and 6 draft laws accepted for a first reading. The Supreme Soviet passed 90 decrees and the chambers passed 59.[2]

Lukianov discussed developments in legislative practice. The third session, he claimed, "significantly enriched the practice of the Soviet parliament. Thus, all draft laws were reviewed by the Supreme Soviet in two readings. One innovation...was the creation of conference committees when difference of opinion arose between the chambers...Characteristically,...in all cases a variant was found to produce consensus." In addition to smoothing out kinks in the legislative process, the Supreme Soviet made some personnel changes and solved many of the infrastructural and procedural problems that deputies had complained about in the summer of 1989. Lukianov replaced Gorbachev as chairman of the Supreme Soviet in March 1990 when the latter became USSR President. At the same time, I.D. Laptev replaced Evgenii Primakov, who left his position as chairman of the Soviet of the Union to accept a position in Gorbachev's Presidential Council.[3] Probably the most noticeable infrastructural development was the installation of an electronic voting system and scoreboard.[4]

The Supreme Soviet's Operating Budget

The Supreme Soviet's operating budget provides some useful clues to the evolving role of the new institution. Unfortunately, the Supreme Soviet's budget was not published for public scrutiny.[5] Nonetheless, Lukianov's report at the end of the third session offered some interesting evidence—not only because of what it included but also because of issues it was silent about. The most indicative aspect of the budget was not its size or subdivisions, but the fact that Lukianov did not cite the source of the Supreme Soviet's operating funds. Some deputies maintained that the Supreme Soviet's budget was controlled—unconstitutionally—by the CPSU Central Committee apparat and the Council of Ministers, institutions to which the legislature is formally superior. Even though, in a comparative context, the budgets of many of the major parliaments of the world are proposed by the executive, the new Supreme Soviet, as an institution trying to establish its independence, might have been expected to define quite demonstratively its own operating expenses.[6]

According to Lukianov's report, during its third session, the Supreme Soviet paid deputies a total of more than 2.1 million rubles for salary, per diem expenses, and travel, or an annual rate of close to 4 million rubles.[7] The report does not, however, mention the cost of the staff support provided by the Supreme Soviet's Secretariat, probably one of the most expensive elements in the budget. Lukianov touched on a series of other activities and services but, once again, failed to mention their cost. The Supreme Soviet paid for 59 parliamentary trips abroad and for hosting 45 foreign delegations. Hosting delegations in Moscow is probably relatively inexpensive compared to the hard currency demands of foreign trips. Operating in an economic system where convertible currencies are scarce, the Supreme Soviet earns none of its own; therefore, it would be interesting to know where and how the legislature acquires its foreign capital. Other non-quantified items in the Supreme Soviet's budget included personal benefits. More than 1,700 deputies and their families enrolled in the Supreme Soviet's medical clinic. Deputies took 124 trips to resorts, allegedly for medical reasons. Apartments were given to the families of 134 deputies. Traditional housing problems made it essential that non-Muscovite members of the Supreme Soviet be given special consideration.

Information published after the August 1991 coup fills in the misleading blank spots in Lukianov's report. The Supreme Soviet's operating budget for 1991 was more than 222 million rubles, including 22.5 million rubles for the support of the Secretariat, 65 million rubles for servicing sessions of the CPD, the Supreme Soviet, and committee meetings, and 50 million rubles for the support of deputies.[8] Even at these prices, significantly inflated from the figures outlined by Lukianov, one might consider the Supreme Soviet a bargain (if one is interested in economizing on democracy) compared to the United States Congress, which in fiscal year 1991 planned to spend more than $2.2 billion on the House of Representatives, the Senate, and their affiliated institutions, or approximately $4.4 million *per member*.[9]

Committees and the Secretariat

Lukianov reported that the Supreme Soviet's committee system became more goal-oriented during, "organizational and preparatory work on draft laws and other questions..."[10] He declared that they had "significantly strengthened work on problems within their competence. The number of questions worked out... on their own intiative increased and in a number of cases introduced significant changes in laws." This positive appraisal of the committee system was not shared by all of Lukianov's colleagues. Deputy Ryzhov, chairman of the Supreme Soviet's science committee and, therefore, a member of the Presidium and informed about organizational and political battles in the new legislature, summarized a negative, inside view of the committee system by declaring it a "decoration."[11]

The conflicting evaluations of the committee system offered by Ryzhov and Lukianov were based on a simple political fact: the latter was satisfied with the committee system because he controlled it. The Secretariat and Presidium continued to be principal control tools in the new Supreme Soviet. While strengthening its control, the Presidium's official view was that it merely "organized and coordinated" the work of the USSR Supreme Soviet, its committees, and the standing commissions of the Soviet of the Union and the Soviet of Nationalities. "[The Presidium] guaranteed the timely preparation of an agenda for the review of questions during the session. Deputies were regularly supplied with draft legislation and other materials. [The Presidium] took measures to guarantee that meetings of the chambers had the necessary quorum." In the official view, deputies were the principal actors. In reality, they played only a secondary role in working out legislation and little role in defining fundamental questions and setting the basic agenda.

Lukianov's review of the Supreme Soviet's first year offers little information on the Secretariat and no reason to think that it did much more than insure that the stenogram was published and distributed. By not drawing attention to the expenses involved in staff work, Lukianov probably hoped to avoid criticism of the way he used the Secretariat to control the Supreme Soviet and its committee system.[12] The Secretariat's organizational structure, which was complete in its principal form and personnel by March 1989, covered all of the main areas of the Supreme Soviet's work. The Supreme Soviet's committees and commissions were assigned to relevant sections of the Secretariat. Instructors and other staff members in each of the sections, recruited from the apparat of the old Supreme Soviet, the CPSU Central Committee apparat, the Komsomol, the central organs of other all-union organizations, and elsewhere controlled the committees.[13]

CPSU Central Committee commissions often supplied the text for laws and the Secretariat, through its consultants, ensured that legislation corresponded to these specifications.[14] Deputy Konstantin Lubenchenko, a Moscow State University law professor, argued that the Supreme Soviet's apparat was obedient to the Central Committee. "It is well known that the majority of the staff of the Supreme Soviet's Secretariat attended party schools and recognize party discipline. And those who have in their hands the organizational levers and the material means define politics." Lubenchenko supplied evidence to back this argument during debates in the CPD in early 1990 over the presidency. He had been assigned to draft an opinion for the Supreme Soviet's committee on legislation concerning the proposed law on the presidency. Not one of the committee's recommendations was included in the draft given for discussion to the Congress of People's Deputies. In short, consultants, in cooperation with their sector heads in the Secretariat and with the committee chairmen, organized the discussion, drafting, and distribution of legislation. Although there was a good deal of cooperation between the staff and the deputies, when outspoken deputies refused to cooperate on matters of basic political principle, or invited independent experts who offered 'unacceptable' opinions, the consultants' principal management method was not subtle: they altered draft legislation without the knowledge or participation of deputies. Consultants threatened independent experts by suggesting that they would not be invited back if they did not cooperate. Deputies often complained that the Secretariat failed to inform them of the schedule for committee meetings.[15]

In addition to amending draft legislation, the Presidium and Secretariat worked together to control the committees by manipulating their schedules and the Supreme Soviet's agenda. Although Lukianov's review of the Supreme Soviet's first year pointed out that its "agenda and a preliminary work schedule...began to play an important role," he offered no hint of how this schedule was put together.[16] The law on publishing, for example, was delayed many times over the course of several months by the Presidium. One deputy hypothesized that it finally was passed in the late spring of 1990 because Yeltsin announced that it would be one of the first laws passed in the new RSFSR Supreme Soviet and CPD.[17] Deputies claimed that the Presidium forced committees to spend too much time reviewing legislation irrelevant to their specialties. Some deputies contended that the Supreme Soviet spent too much time in plenary session, which sharply limited the amount of time that could be devoted to committee work.[18] Consequently, they were unable to concentrate on areas where they could have worked productively.[19] Indeed, at least one Soviet scholar has suggested that Gorbachev's and Lukianov's control over the committee system was less important than their ability to manipulate the Supreme Soviet's deputies while in session.[20]

Although the Supreme Soviet's information resources expanded rapidly during its first year, the key point to note is that all requests were handled through the Secretariat and its staff. The Secretariat controlled the committees by managing the flow of information. Lukianov outlined the development of the information resources available to the committees and the Supreme Soviet. More than 70 organizations and institutes, including the USSR State Committee on Statistics, the Ministry on Foreign Affairs, the Ministry of Internal Affairs, the Ministry of Justice, the Lenin Library, the Academy of Sciences' Institute for Scientific Information for the Social Sciences, and TASS were designated official support centers. The principal elements of an automated information system were installed and "a number of committees and commissions and departments of the Secretariat [have been equipped] with automated work stations." "The information service of the Secretariat ... during the third session registered more than 24 thousand inquiries by deputies, correspondents, ministry officials, organizations, and citizens, and more than 71 thousand answers were given." Lukianov also declared that steps were taken to guarantee the information supply for legislative work, including a practice of preparing special information packages for legislation under review. A pyramidal structure, where Lukianov sat at the top and committees requested data and reported vertically (stenograms of committee meetings were not readily available, if at all) guaranteed that information would be controlled in a manner acceptable to the Secetariat. Perhaps the most telling criticism of the Supreme Soviet's information system was provided by Deputy Ryzhov, who argued in an interview in the summer of 1990 that deputies could not intelligently discuss the federal plan and budget because they did not have access to relevant data.

Committees did not have independent budgets and therefore could not hire their own support services. All support for the committees, including infrastructure, was provided by the Secretariat. Lukianov pointed out steps that were taken to improve the situation: his optimistic report suggested that everything possible was being done to insure that deputies would be able to work effectively.[21] Nonetheless, many deputies argued that the Secretariat purposely handicapped them. Deputies were unsatisfied with their offices, their communication facilities, and even the building into which they had been placed.[22] Committee members did not even have access to photocopiers and had to ask consultants, sometimes unsuccessfully, to reproduce documents. This, of course, strengthened the Secretariat's control by limiting horizontal communication between deputies.[23]

The committee system was handicapped by poor attendance, which was probably a result of both the membership's preoccupation with their full-time jobs and frustration with the system. At the end of the third session,

Deputy Andreev reported that only five out of 46 members of his committee worked regularly. Deputy Ryzhov reported that he had seen some members of his committee only once or twice over the course of three sessions. These figures may be low in comparison to other committees or may have been exaggerated by liberal deputies trying to make a point; nonetheless, they suggest a trend that was confirmed by interviews with Secretariat staff, in Lukianov's report about the third session, and throughout the stenogram.[24]

One telling point to note about control over the committees is one area where the Secretariat *did not* play a role—questions of defense and state security. According to the organizational structure listed in the Supreme Soviet's internal telephone directory, unlike the well-developed structure of four sectors dedicated to social and economic questions, military and security questions are managed by a small 'section.' With no staff, interested deputies could do little. Discussing problems in the military and the work of the Supreme Soviet's defense commitee, Deputy V.N. Lopatin, a reform-minded major and member of the committee complained on the final day of the Supreme Soviet's third session that there had never been a real discussion in the committee of military reform. He suggested that this was the result of a do-nothing chairman and the committee membership's close association with the military-industrial complex. Speaking in the name of a group of reform-minded officer-deputies, he noted that neither the Supreme Soviet nor the defense committee had discussed their proposals. He pointed out that the defense committee was one of the few committees whose membership was not rotated, and proposed the immediate inclusion of younger officer-deputies who were genuinely interested in reform.[25]

The Secretariat's control methods were clearly and repeatedly demonstrated in the legislative process, for example during drafting and discussion of the law on the press and, in particular, in debates on the law on the press on 23 and 24 November 1989.[26] Although the final draft of the law was not ratified by the Supreme Soviet until 12 June 1990, this early debate was significant because it suggests how the Secretariat shaped the course of the debate. Deputy Ezhelev was one of the principal supporters of a free press and head of a working group in the Committee on questions of glasnost that wrote an independent, widely-accepted first draft of the bill. During debate over the law, Ezhelev informed his colleagues that the version that the Presidium distributed "was not reviewed, discussed, nor...ratified by either the committee on questions of glasnost or the committee on questions of legislation."[27] Deputy Fedorov, another member of the original working group, clarified the origin of the replacement text:

> In September, another draft was ready, once again agreed upon at the highest level. Subsequently, they invited us to [Central

Committee headquarters]. I must tell you that the final variant ...reflects thoughts laid out by Deputy Medvedev [Central Committee Secretary for Ideology] during an...unpleasant three-hour meeting...the corrections introduced [by Medvedev make it] a new piece of legislation, a new conception of the bill.[28]

Deputy Batynskaia complained about interference in the legislative process and commented ironically, "They told us that the typists were to blame. Of course, having such politically well-qualified typists [in the Secretariat] is a cause for joy, but [ratifying the original legislation] is, after all, more important."[29] During the law's second reading, the working group reviewed nearly two thousand proposed amendments and changes. The final project was discussed in almost all of the committees and commissions and their suggestions were included in the final draft. The joint meeting of the chambers that debated the law touched on more than 70 different questions.[30]

In sum, duirng its first year the Supreme Soviet's committees never developed into a significant political arena. One good indication of the limited significance of the committee system is that the IRDG and other deputy groups seldom tried to use the committee system to tactical advantage. Nor did Boris Yeltsin, a member of the IRDG's coordinating council, a committee chairman and ambitious politician, ever attempt to use his committee post as a political mechanism. Instead of working through the Supreme Soviet and its committee system to encourage change, liberal deputies began to leave the institution during the fall of 1989. As the electoral campaign for republican and local soviets moved into full swing, the deputies realized that they could accomplish more elsewhere and left.

The Soviet Presidency

Excluding the dissolution of the Communist Party in August 1991, the most important influence on the CPD and the Supreme Soviet during their brief existence was the simultaneous creation in February 1990 of the post of Soviet president and the constitutional revisions in Articles 6 and 7 that eliminated the CPSU's monopolistic 'leading and guiding role.' For the third time in less than a year, the Soviet political system fundamentally changed its form.[31] Most importantly, yet another open break with traditional soviet-style government (with its insistence on supreme legislative power) was made.

When the CPSU's Central Committee gathered on 5 February 1990 to discuss the party's platform for the 28th Party Congress, no one would have guessed that in a few short weeks its members would vote to create a presidency. Everything pointed to maintenance of the status quo. When the agenda for the third session of the USSR's Supreme Soviet was ratified by its Presidium on 16 January 1990, a presidential system was not among the 48 questions planned for discussion.[32] Indeed, at the second session of the CPD in December 1989, Gorbachev barely defeated attempts by the IRDG to include in the agenda debate over Articles 6 and 7.[33] Although several speakers at the February plenum touched on the issue of the presidency, it was not a focus of debate.[34] Boris Yeltsin, one of Gorbachev's principal opponents, did not mention the presidency and spent most of his time talking about perestroika in the party.[35] The account of the Central Committee's work for February 1990 published in *Izvestiia TsK KPSS* did not mention the possibility of creating a presidency.

The constitutional amendments creating the presidency were drafted by the Central Committee apparat in an old-fashioned manner closed to public scrutiny. The first public signal that Gorbachev would seek the presidency was given on 12 February 1990 when the Supreme Soviet's Presidium published the membership of a commission designed to prepare a proposal for the creation of a Soviet presidency.[36] The same day, a Presidium meeting conducted by Gorbachev "unanimously suppported the introduction of presidential power." Shortly thereafter, the Supreme Soviet ratified a resolution calling for a special session of the CPD to discuss the question.[37]

The third session of the Congress of People's Deputies opened on 12 March 1990. The agenda included three points (1) recognizing the credentials of new deputies, (2) changes in the constitution and creation of the post of president, and (3) election of the president.[38] Only after Gorbachev was safely elected president was the election of a new Supreme Soviet Chairman placed on the agenda. Anatolii Lukianov reported to the deputies on the proposed amendments. He called for the immediate discussion and institution of the presidency in the context of the changing role of the party, "when the party no longer plays the role of direct state and economic management and management itself is moving from party structures to structures of the state mechanism." He argued that even after the institution of the presidency the CPD would remain the highest organ of state power in the country and that neither the Supreme Soviet nor the Council of Ministers would lose power. The presidency would be an institution connecting legislative and executive activity.

A series of speakers supported the amendments. The first orator during the discussion of Lukianov's report was S.S. Alekseev, Chairman of the Constitutional Review Committee, who characterized the situation in the country as a paralysis of power. He argued that the party had lost its former power but that new structures had not yet taken over. He claimed that the decision was "connected with the most important changes in our political system," the introduction of a multi-party system. "Without a sufficiently civilized, strong [president]," he argued, "multipartism will lead to the further disintegration of our social system... moroever, the presidency in current conditions may be the only real way to transfer power from party structures to the state."[39] Deputy V.A. Medvedev, Politburo member and head of the Central Committee's ideological commission, declared that the simultaneous discussion at the CPD of the creation of the presidency and changes in Articles 6 and 7 of the constitution was in 'no way a coincidence.' On the one hand, he claimed, without a strong and effective president the change in the party's role could lead to anarchy. On the other hand, any decisions concerning the power of the president lose their sense if the leading role of the party remains in the constitution. "Our approach to political reform," he argued, "is based on the fact that in a law-based state the party cannot exist in its present form as the nucleus of the managerial structure."[40]

Iurii Afanasev presented the IRDG's argument against the amendments, the clearest formulation of opposition. He declared that the group did not support the creation of the presidency at the CPD and was decisively against the immediate election of a president. A presidency should be created only within the context of a new democratic constitution. The IRDG, he declared, proposed several conditions for the creation of the presidency: (1) a new union treaty of sovereign states; (2) the creation of a fully empowered Supreme Soviet capable of becoming a legislative counterweight to executive power; (3) election of the president after and on the basis of the new union treaty by direct, equal, and universal election; (4) a system of multi-party elections of the president; (5) the president should not combine presidential power with a place in the party nomenklatura; (6) freedom of the press. Afanasev argued that the hurried attempt to introduce the presidency was a "most crude and serious political mistake." "The reason for the paralysis of power," he argued, "is not the absence of power [in the government] but the lack of trust in it."

When discussion ended and the deputies turned to voting on the amendments, an argument broke out because many deputies felt that they had been deceived by a procedural trick. They first approved the package of amendments (including both the presidency and the revisions to Articles 6 and 7) as a whole, so any further editing would require a two-thirds majority. The most significant change proposed for Article 6 was the elimination of any mention of the CPSU. Some of the changes proposed in article seven were: (1) the elimination of political organizations in industrial enterprises, (2) depoliticizing military, police, and security institutions and forbidding military officers to belong to any party, (3) eliminating the word soviet from the articles in connection with the creation of a presidential system. Although the amendments were ratified, not one of the changes proposed for the two articles was accepted by the necessary two-thirds margin.

Nominations for president were made on 14 March. Deputy Ivashko, first secretary of the Communist Party of the Ukraine, spoke first and nominated Gorbachev in the name of the Central Committee. Deputy Alksnis, speaking for the deputy group Soiuz, nominated Bakatin, Gorbachev, and Ryzhkov. Agrarians, trade unions, veterans, and representatives of the Union Republics all supported Gorbachev. Discussion of the candidates proceeded in alphabetical order. The nominees did not speak.

During discussions of Gorbachev's candidacy, only three or four out of 17 speakers directly supported him—the others spoke about the general situation in the country and the tasks facing the new president. There were, however, several speeches *against* Gorbachev. Indeed, after Ryzhkov declined nomination, Deputy G.S. Igitian argued that a spectacle was being played out—it was clear from the start that Bakatin and Ryzhkov would not run. He also complained that the CPD was unable to nominate from its own members even one alternative candidate. Speaking from his place, one unidentified deputy argued that the CPD should take a break, think things over, and reconvene to nominate alternate candidacies. Otherwise, "It will be embarrassing to look our constituents in the eye."[41]

At the conclusion of the discussion, the deputies voted: 2,000 deputies received ballots; 1,878 ballots were found in the urns; 54 ballots were considered invalid; 1,824 ballots were considered valid; 1,329 voted for Gorbachev; 495 voted against. Gorbachev received 59.2% of the 2,245 deputies of the CPD, 66.45% of the 2,000 deputies that received ballots, and 70.76% of those who took part in the vote, and thus became president.

After the election, Gorbachev gave a brief address. Confronting allegations of slowness and indecision, he argued that, although there was a measure of truth in the accusation, deputies should understand that all change took time. "A preparatory stage was objectively unavoidable." Addressing deputies who wanted him to reject the combination of posts, he argued that it was dictated "by the interests of perestroika." One of the central questions of his speech was the relationship among various political currents in the country. He argued that one of the principal functions of the president and the organs founded to serve him was the consolidation of political currents and social movements. At the same time, however, he argued that "certain groups and actors" are trying to promote their own ideas through violence and the threat of civil war and revolution. Such actions are not acceptable for society, for perestroika, "or our young democracy."

Presidential Powers

The president became the USSR's head of state. The previous constitutional order included a collegial head of state, i.e. the Presidium of the Supreme Soviet. The chairman of the *new* Supreme Soviet acquired most but not all functions of the old Presidium. The new president had both the powers of the old Presidium and the Chairman of the Supreme Soviet and coordinated the legislative and executive branches, serving as a binding link between them. The competencies of the legislative and executive branches remained the same. The Soviet government continued to be formed by the Supreme Soviet. The CPD had the power to confirm the president's nominee for the chairman of the Council of Ministers. The president could ask the CPD to replace the Council of Ministers or its chairman. With the agreement of the chairman of the Council of Ministers, the president could appoint or fire members of the government with the right of confirmation of new candidates given to the Supreme Soviet. He could also stop the action of administrative orders of the Council of Ministers, although the constitution provided no basis for this power. The president could issue executive orders that the government had to fulfill. The Council of Ministers was required to regularly inform the president of its actions. The Supreme Soviet could vote no confidence in the government either at its own initiative or the initiative of the president. The President, as the commander-in-chief, made decisions about the armed forces; therefore, this question was no longer in the jurisdiction of the Council of Ministers.[42]

The Supreme Soviet's Second Year

The USSR Supreme Soviet's second and final year of existence witnessed a remarkable series of political events. Developments in the legislature were strongly conditioned by party politics, or, more to the point, the absence of strong and capable leadership by the CPSU and, simultaneously, the growth of deputy blocs. At the republican level, new legislatures began to challenge Moscow's freedom to infringe on what they considered to be their sovereign rights. Gorbachev's presidency began to seem more and more irrelevant as the republican legislatures became uncontrollable and the federal executive refused to follow his lead in questions of economic reform. Even as he received more and more formal powers, his fungible power declined. Moreover, the USSR Supreme Soviet, encroached on by both Gorbachev's presidency and the republican legislatures, began to question its own legitimacy.

Throughout the Supreme Soviet's second year, deputies complained that the committee system was plagued by familiar information and infrastructure problems. Perhaps the most telling criticism was that the Supreme Soviet never was able to adequately monitor the USSR's budget. "[The Supreme Soviet controls neither the country's budget nor the government's financial activity, " complained Deputy E.A. Pamfilova. Deputy A.K. Miloserdnyi asked why the government had printed more than twice as much money as the Supreme Soviet had agreed to and was "flooding the country with money not backed by goods." Deputy V.I. Voskoboinikov pointed out that without the "power of the purse" the Supreme Soviet could not defend the interests of the people. It had become a rubber stamp ratifying decisions taken elsewhere.[43]

The deputies' disdain for the committees was suggested by difficulties encountered during the rotation of deputies at the end of 1990. The 1988 constitutional amendments declared that one-fifth of the committees' membership would be renewed every year. This article was amended to allow for rotation of "up to one-fifth" of the members, apparently because it was difficult to attract deputies to Moscow to work full time.[44]

Party and Bloc Politics

Any discussion of the Supreme Soviet would be incomplete without a discussion of bloc politics. Deputies started uniting in blocs in the spring of 1989, when the IRDG first announced its existence. At the CPD's first session a number of other less-organized blocs formed, including groups of farmers, teachers, and doctors. On the eve of the CPD's second session in December 1989, a social democratic group was formed whose main goal was "the unification of all democratic forces in a whole, unified organization united by theory and fighting for democracy."[45]

Official recognition of deputorial organizations was not given until 25 December 1990, when 18 groups were registered—18 months after the birth of the CPD. The largest group was the Communists, with 730 members, or about one third of the total membership. Others included Soiuz, a bloc of conservative deputies (561 members), farmers (431), workers (400), ecologists (220), women (216), centrists (153), young deputies (125) and veterans of the war in Afghanistan (52). The IRDG registered 229 members, a significant decrease from the 400 members it claimed in June 1989. In the Supreme Soviet, 365 deputies were registered in 12 groups, including 110 in Soiuz, 104 in a group called Constructive Interaction, 94 in the Communist group, 71 in a group called Justice, and 59 in the IRDG.[46]

The CPSU. The Communist group was the third largest in the Supreme Soviet. Gorbachev chose Genadii Yanaev, the parliamentary leader of the Communist bloc in the CPD and a Central Committee Secretary, to become his vice-president. To get Yanaev confirmed, Gorbachev was willing to suffer the indignity of nominating him twice (he was defeated in a first attempt) as well as embarrassing accusations of cheating to achieve a majority. Why was Gorbachev so intent on Yanaev? Since Yanaev was not forced to give up his deputorial responsibilities, one could argue that one motive was that Gorbachev wanted to reward the leader of the Communist bloc or keep him close at hand.[47]

Despite the appearance of bloc politics in the CPD and Supreme Soviet, and although intra-party politics took an unprecedented pluralist turn in 1990, the CPSU never altered its internal structure and operating principles to account for the legislative and electoral environments that challenged its existence. In short, although it formed blocs (with far more potential than actual members) in the CPD and Supreme Soviet, the CPSU never became a parliamentary party and never developed the type of party discipline used to run legislatures in the West. This section suggests why by briefly describing two key developments during this period, the birth of Democratic Platform, a reform movement inside the CPSU, and the 28th Party Congress.[48]

At the same time that the discussion of the presidency was taking place in the CPSU's Central Committee and the Supreme Soviet in Moscow, changes were rocking the party at the grassroots level. A conference of 750 delegates, representatives of the more than 35,000 communists in Leningrad and Leningrad oblast who were members of a nationwide movement called 'Democratic Platform in the CPSU,' decided to form a group within the Leningrad party organization. Resolutions ratified by the congress stated that the split between the party leadership and its rank-and-file members was growing. Delegates argued that the political line of the Leningrad *obkom* and *gorkom* was expressed in its close relations with the United Workers Front, a movement created by conservative forces in the CPSU, and by nonstop conflicts with the democratic forces.[49] The resolutions also condemned attempts by party leaders to avoid responsibility for the horrible condition of Leningrad by shifting the blame onto Moscow or onto the old Leningrad party leadership, which was relieved of command by Gorbachev in the summer of 1989. The resolutions noted with discontent that the Leningrad party organization had become a stronghold of the conservative movement within the party.[50]

The conference held in Leningrad was just one part of a much larger movement. The founding of an organization called the 'Democratic Platform in the CPSU' was the result of months of discussion and development. V. Lysenko, a founder of the movement, offered a short history:

> The first horizontal structures in the CPSU began to arise in the spring [of 1989] on the wave of the elections and the

dissatisfaction of Communists with the decision of the CPSU Central Committee Plenum that created a commission [to investigate] 'the Yeltsin affair.' Even then it was clear that within the framework of the CPSU's vertical, hierarchical structure it was impossible to change anything. In May 1989, a Moscow party club was founded that included Communists from many party organizations in Moscow and Moscow oblast. The club managed to work out, with the direct participation of leading social scientists, a conception for the radical reform of the CPSU...and succeeded in making contact with Communists in more than 100 cities, in many of which party clubs had already been founded.

The strength of the democratic movement in the party was shown by 455 delegates from 102 cities and 13 republics were represented at the All-Union Conference of Party Clubs that took place in Moscow on January 20-21. Among them were representatives of large factories, strike committees, and the national-democratic movement. The main goal of the Communists of the Democratic Platform [was] the dismantling...of the CPSU...and a change to a parliamentary-type party acting within a multi-party system.[51]

The Moscow conference of the Democratic Platform pointed out the crisis in the CPSU and posed the questions of splitting with "conservatives and Stalinists" and creating "a new party within a new multi-party system." The principal slogan of the declaration was "From a totalitarian party to a party of parliamentary type!" The main short-term goals planned by the group were regional conferences and preparations for elections of representatives to the 28th Party Congress.[52] The Moscow Higher Party School and its rector Shostakovskii became a principal supporter of the group and offered logistical assistance. The Democratic Platform elected a Coordinating Council that included USSR People's Deputies Afanasev, Yeltsin, Popov, Gdlian, Ivanov, Burbulis, Sulakshin, Borodin, and Travkin.[53]

The Democratic Platform movement threatened conservative interests, which fought along a wide fron, including old-fashioned attacks in the party press. Addressing the question of 'Leninism and Perestroika' at a meeting of the CPSU Central Committee's ideological commission in late March, G.L. Smirnov, director of the Central Committee's Institute of Marxism-Leninism, pointed to the meeting of the Democratic Platform 'party' and argued that its goal was to unite members of the party on an anti-Leninist position. This meant, he argued, that there were two parties battling for power inside the framework of the CPSU. E.E. Antonovich, an assistant rector of the Central Committee's Academy of Social Sciences, suggested that the Democratic Platform consisted of "well-organized forces acting against socialism, forces so evil and fanatical that the result of the battle is not yet clear."[54]

Members of the Democratic Platform movement wanted to participate in the CPSU Central Committee's preparations for the 28th Party Congress, including, of course, working on the party platform and the party statute. The question was raised as early as January 1990 at the first all-union Conference of Party Clubs, when a letter was sent from the group's coordinating council to the Central Committee. No answer was forthcoming.[55] The group finally got a positive answer when N.I. Travkin, a member of its coordinating council, spoke with Gorbachev on March 11th at the third session of the USSR CPD. Although Travkin himself did not receive an invitation, V. Lysenko and V.S. Shakhnovskii did. Lysenko reported that neither he nor his colleague were allowed to address the plenum during the time allotted for discussion. Lysenko did, however, fight his way to the microphone to defend the Democratic Platform when Boris Gidaspov, first secretary of the Leningrad *gorkom*, suggested that the movement wanted to form a separate party. Later, Lysenko assessed the plenum.

> Now I understand why they so stubbornly refuse to televise Central Committee Plenums. One single telecast would destroy completely the remnants of the myth of the highest party organ. By its composition, by its political position, and by the [level of] democracy of the session, the [Central Committee] is the rearguard of the party. [It consists of] people who by an overwhelming majority represent no one and express no one's interests except the nomenklatura's. It is a kingdom of shadows, political mummies left to us from bygone days.[56]

The 28th Party Congress was held in July 1990. Gorbachev weakened his rivals and strengthened his own position by making the office of party leader dependent on the Party Congress and not the Central Committee and by making a series of changes in the central party organs, including widening the Politburo to include the heads of the Communist Parties from each of the union republics. More importantly, however, the Congress gave him another opportunity to revise the party from within. Nonetheless, the delegates produced little more than vague generalities: one side-effect was numerous defections from party ranks, including Boris Yeltsin's dramatic demarche on the last day of the session. Anatolii Sobchak and Gavriil Popov, well-known USSR People's Deputies and the chairmen of the city soviets of Leningrad and Moscow, issued a statement shortly after the conclusion of the Congress that reflected the feeling of a large number of liberal party members and some of its most active political figures.

> The 28th Party Congress, in which the party and the people had so much hope, demonstrated the complete inability of the party to present the country with a real program for transition to a new society.
>
> The majority of the delegates of the Congress refused to support ideas already supported by all of [our] people: a rejection of class antagonism, the priority of universal human values, the transition to a market economy and to various forms of property including private property, decisive intra-party democratization, rejection of the CPSU's monopoly on the means of mass communication, the transfer of all power to the soviets, the transfer of the majority of state and party property to private citizens. The Congress rejected fractions and preserved within the party the principle of democratic centralism.
>
> In such conditions, only democratically elected soviets can become the organizers of a real perestroika. Leaders of the new soviets have a special responsibility.
>
> Recognizing the full measure of the responsibility before the people and before history, we decided... to leave the CPSU in order to encourage the creation of a multi-party system and have the possibility to more effectively lead the soviets we head.
>
> We call upon the leaders of soviets of all levels not to belong to any party.

The IRDG. The IRDG's failure in the second year of the Supreme Soviet's existence was probably foreordained by a dismal performance in the legislature's first year. Despite some successes, like the group's attempt to weaken the Soviet presidency, in March 1990, after nine months of work, the IRDG's Secretariat published a summary of the group's work motivated by a survey that showed that 79% of the IRDG's members considered its activities unsatisfactory. "There is no doubt about what elicited this dissatisfaction—the IRDG's work in parliament is not effective." In fact, the IRDG's Secretariat maintained that the group's parliamentary activity was almost non-existent. Members worked in the Supreme Soviet's committees and commissions and at its general sessions as independent deputies with no unified strategies or tactics. No alternative legislative projects were drafted and "even for those key questions for which a nationwide political strike was called, the IRDG was unable to take any measures in the Supreme Soviet." Concerned with this situation, the IRDG's Secretariat analyzed the group's platform, inner structure, staff support, and goals.[57]

The IRDG's platform was prepared in the summer of 1989 and ratified, in the face of some fundamental splits, at the IRDG's second general meeting. Although new sections were added to the platform, no one bothered with a full-scale revision. An attempt to ratify a new platform was frustrated at the third general meeting by the lack of a quorum. Although a survey of the meeting's participants showed that a majority thought that all divisions of the platform needed revision, no one took on the job. As a result of all this activity, the Secretariat declared, "the IRDG in fact has no program."

The Secretariat concluded that the IRDG's structure, co-chairmen, a coordinating council, and a general assembly, was unable to work effectively and that the principal organizational problem was the absence of standing rules to control interaction within the group. Attempts to discuss organizational questions in the fall of 1989 were pushed off the agenda by debates over a general strike and the upcoming republican elections. As a result, no one was given a standing right to speak in the name of the IRDG to the Supreme Soviet or the press. The group could not speak as a united whole—any declarations were really only joint statements signed by separate groups of deputies. The Secretariat declared that "none of the members of the coordinating council considered the work of the IRDG sufficiently important: as a result, no more than half of the members attended sessions of the coordinating council or general assembly.

The IRDG's staffing problems arose primarily from the absence of any standing rules, but also could be traced to financing. In principle, the deputies had decided to pay 200 rubles per year in dues, which would have meant approximately 60 thousand rubles, at the time a firm financial base. In practice, they received only a little more than 6 thousand rubles from 102 members: "apparently, deputies have no long-range plans to be connected to the IRDG." The social fund established by the IRDG was also unable to gather any significant amount of money. The group was unable to convince any of its members to work seriously on a newspaper.

The Secretariat paid special attention to an apparent split in the group's goals. That is, one principal reason for the IRDG's problems was mixing parliamentary activities with the group's role as a center of democratic political activity in Moscow. "This indisputably useful work led to the loss from the group of a significant contingent of deputies that consider legislative activity as their principal deputorial responsibility and not participation in the formation of new political organizations." To cure these problems, the Secretariat suggested that:

> operation of the IRDG as an [effective] parliamentary group [will require] an organizational division between the IRDG's two

main lines of activity: the IRDG as a parliamentary group and the IRDG as a democratic center demand different organizational structures and inner mechanisms... [Moroever], a requirement for the election of anyone into the working organs of the IRDG should be the intention of the candidate to consider this activity a [high] priority and give it a sufficient amount of strength and time.

In May 1990, the IRDG's General Assembly met to discuss its first year of work. The deputies and co-chairman Gavril Popov offered criticisms similar to those outlined above.[58] Popov, however, added one point: the IRDG's unifying cause, the elimination of the CPSU's constitutionally-mandated leading and guiding role, had been eliminated. Popov proposed a new goal, creating a framework for a genuine federation of free republics. "We must work out a new conception for a Union parliament. And this parliament should please the republics and the democratic movements and allow for the creation of a solid majority."[59]

In the fall of 1990, the IRDG apparently found the strength to revitalize its activities, if only on paper. Most noticeably, it started to issue group declarations at sessions of the Supreme Soviet calling for government action on various questions.[60]

Soiuz

The third session of the CPD took place in March 1990, before most republican legislatures had started to declare independence, so the appearance of a group called '*Soiuz*' (in Russian, Union, as in Soviet Union) at the fourth session, when the USSR was threatened with disintegration at the end of 1990, was not surprising. Some observers argue, in fact, that *Soiuz* was created by Lukianov, that he was its 'godfather,' and that he favored it in procedural matters. One Soviet commentator pointed out that some deputies had set their sights on the republican legislatures early on, but that for other, less-farsighted deputies "the train had left the station: all the spots in the republican legislatures were full." As a result, the stage was set for an alliance between these deputies and the federal leadership.[61]

In the fall and winter of 1990, *Soiuz* actively opposed Gorbachev's policy in the conflict in the Persian Gulf. When Eduard Shevarnadze resigned in December 1990, he pointed to members of *Soiuz* as part of the right wing backlash that threatened the country and forced him to resign in protest. In the spring of 1991, Soiuz became more active in the Supreme Soviet. The bloc obstructed ratification of treaties with Germany and the confirmation of Gorbachev's nominees to the Security Council and the Federation Council. Maxim Sokolov, a parliamentary correspondent for one Soviet independent newspaper claimed that:

> the strongest faction in the federal parliament is the Soiuz group of deputies; virtually every piece of legislation requires the assent of Soiuz and its sympathizers to pass successfully in the parliament. Since he had little in the way of a base of support, the Soviet president was forced to chart his "new course" with the help of the only strong right-wing faction, the Soiuz group, whose loyalty to Gorbachev was far from absolute at the beginning. Gorbachev's 'cordial agreement' was actually based on the credo of the German princes, which said: "The power of the king is absolute so long as he obeys our will."

In conclusion, Sokolov quoted Deputy Igor Griazin, who contended that "Gorbachev has created a Frankenstein, and he does not know how to control it."[62]

Power, Leadership, and the 'Center' vs. the Republics

The problem that Gorbachev faced as President in 1990–91 was that republican elites in both newly-elected Supreme Soviets and newly-threatened republican Communist Parties were increasingly unwilling to listen to advice or orders from Moscow. Moreover, he could not convince his own Council of Ministers of the urgent need for radical economic reform. Virtually all of the Supreme Soviets elected in the late winter and spring had declared sovereignty or independence of one type or another. Perhaps the best example of this so-called "paper war" was the self-evident necessity but frustrating difficulty of working out a common approach to economic reform if Russia was to remain part of the Union. On 10 September 1990, discussing the agenda for the USSR Supreme Soviet's fourth session, Deputy G.E. Burbulis, Yeltsin's campaign manager in the 1990 contest for the Russian Supreme Soviet and later a high official in the Russian government, pointed out that despite agreements between the President and the republics in July to work out a common approach to economic reform, the all-union government "boycotted the President's decision and practically took no part" in the work of a joint group. He urged the Supreme Soviet, to no great effect, to take action. The next day, Burbulis returned and declared that the Russian Supreme Soviet had ratified the radical '500 days' Shatalin–Yavlinskii plan.[63] From this point on, the economic contradictions between Russia and the Union would grow ever worse. Gorbachev initially supported the radical plan, but later backed away and proposed a national referendum on land ownership.

From mid-1991 until the coup, the twin themes of political power and republican sovereignty, a euphemism for republican demands to dictate the agenda in a renewed union, never left the center of political debate. The Supreme Soviet's fourth session witnessed growing deputorial frustration with the legislature's lack of power. Once again, the power of the purse was both a sore point for deputies and a good indication of the Supreme Soviet's secondary role. On 21 September 1990, Deputy K.D. Lubenchenko told his colleagues that "we in fact have no power... We did not control the government's expenditures or budget and do not use our powers for controlling the executive." Lubenchenko argued that introducing the presidency had "liquidated the division of powers and practically reduced the role of the Supreme Soviet to zero." Gorbachev, in his view, had become a defender of the Council of Ministers. Deputy E.A. Pamfilova, who took the floor immediately after Lubenchenko, pointed out that the legislature had failed to introduce a "control system for the financial activity of the highest organs of state power, including the apparats of the Council of Ministers and the Supreme Soviet."[64] On 17 November, Deputy Iu.A. Ryzhov stated the problem: "Today, we are not only in an economic crisis, but in the deepest constitutional and political crisis..." He proposed discussing, "the role, place and responsibility of the USSR Supreme Soviet," and suggested that if the legislature continued "along its sorry path to a decorative structure," it would soon have no reason to exist.[65]

The Supreme Soviet spent a good deal of time in the fall of 1990 and winter of 1991 debating republican sovereignty. This issue became a favorite reason for deputy groups to make bold declarations. For example, speaking for Soiuz, Deputy G.A. Komarov complained that "now all who wanted to have now declared full sovereignty, completely forgetting that there exists the sovereignty of the USSR backed up by the constitution." He asked why Gorbachev had not used his "enormous powers... to defend the sovereignty of the country?..." Soiuz proposed that Gorbachev "declare a moratorium on all [declarations of] sovereignty and, [where republics refuse], introduce direct presidential rule... Deputy V.Ia. Kariagin, following a similar line of reasoning concerning the question of power, asked: "Do you remember that while we were electing the president one main argument dominated: when we have a president we will have order? What did we get? There is a president but there is no order. We strengthened presidential power—but there is no power or order. The Supreme Soviet has become a decoration... Laws are not working..."[66]

Gorbachev himself was fascinated with the question of power: he seemed to think that it could be defined into existence. In September 1990, he asked the CPD and Supreme Soviet for and was granted additional presidential powers to deal with questions of economic reform, including the right to issue decrees on wages, prices, the budget, and law and order. His first decree permitted the Council of Ministers to keep economic plans intact for another 15 months. He ordered the republics to stop disrupting planned production and threatened tough action. Nonetheless, the republics continued on their determined ways to self-sufficient political and economic futures. They might be willing to enter a renewed union, but only as sovereign states.

In December 1990, at Gorbachev's request, the USSR CPD once again revised the government's structure. A vice-presidency, Security Council, and Cabinet of Ministers were created. A Council of the Federation, consisting of representatives from each of the republics, was formed to give subjects of the federation a clearer voice at the highest level.[67] In March 1991, Gorbachev issued a draft union treaty, but by April had yielded to republican demands for more power. Submitting to the obvious, Gorbachev was merely following events, hoping to maintain a viable political future. With more formal powers than any leader in Soviet history, as well as a repressive apparatus unmatched anywhere in the world, Gorbachev was forced to submit to the desires of republican political elites backed up by the institutional strength of independent Supreme Soviets.

Notes

1. "O treitei sessii Verkhovnogo Soveta SSSR," Moscow: Supreme Soviet, 1990. The Supreme Soviet's first year of work is discussed by T. Dudko, chairman of one of the legislature's committees, in "Predely polnomochii," *Narodnyi deputat*. No. 7, 1990, pp. 16–22.

2. "O treitei sessii..."

3. For a discussion of Lukianov's role in directing the work of the USSR Supreme Soviet see Iu. Bychkov, "Slishkom 'seryi kardinal dlia perestroiki," *Stolitsa*, No. 2, January 1991, pp. 9–12. Laptev's election elicited a good deal of conflict, much of it centered on an attempt by disgruntled deputies to elect an independent chairman who would push for real power for the chamber. See "Vydvizhenie i obsuzhdenie kandidatur na post Predsedatelia Soveta Soiuza," *Verkhovnyi Sovet SSSR, Tretia Sessiia, Biulleten No. 6 Zasedanie Soveta Soiuza*, 28 March 1990, esp. pp. 10–12.

4. This system did not, however, resolve the question of anonymity—individual voting records were not published. Moreover, in an interview in the summer of 1990, jurist M.A. Fedotov (who later argued Russia's case against the CPSU in the Russian Constitutional Court) argued that the new system created two additional problems. First, the voting buttons clicked when depressed, so hesitant deputies who did not want to be caught in the

minority (or think for themselves) could listen for a reassuring cascade of clicks as the chairman slowly recited the formula 'for,' 'against,' and 'abstain.' Second, deputies found ways around the electronic system to allow them to vote for absent colleagues. For confirmation by Deputy V.D. Iudin, see *Verkhovnyi Sovet SSSR, Tretia Sessiia, Biulleten No. 36 Sovmestnogo Zasedaniia Soveta Soiuza i Soveta Natsionalnostei*, 27 April 1990, pp. 6–7. Skimming the results of virtually all the recorded votes in the Supreme Soviet's published stenogram, it is remarkable how seldom the deputies seem to divide on questions of principle. Practically all the votes were nearly unanimous. Perhaps detailed roll-call analysis will identify ideological groups or other interesting patterns among blocs; however, if deputies were voting for more than one absent colleague without an explicit system of proxy ballots, any analysis of roll-calls faces severe data problems.

5. One day during the summer of 1990, I was in the Presidium's building in central Moscow and had the good fortune to find a deputy willing to help me approach the head of the Secretariat's financial administration, V.V. Kasatkin. We caught him by surprise in his enormous and luxurious (in comparison to the cubicles given to the deputies) office. Kasatkin invited us in, visibly suppressed an initial reaction somewhere between shock and panic, ordered his secretary to bring us tea and biscuits, spoke with us politely for ten minutes, and promised to help. He never answered subsequent calls and inquiries.

6. Interviews with Deputies Iu. Andreev and A. Murashev, summer 1990. For an overview of parliamentary budget practice in Europe see *Budgets of Parliaments*, National Parliaments, Series 2, 08–1988, European Parliament, Directorate General for Research in cooperation with the European Centre for Parliamentary Research and Documentation.

7. Lukianov appears to be underreporting expenses. A calculation based on reports that deputies receive a monthly salary of 500 rubles, 300 rubles per month for secretarial support, and 15 rubles for *per diem* expenses suggests that the true figure is closer to 2.7 million rubles. Unless absenteeism is even worse than reported, it is difficult to explain the missing 600,000 rubles. For confirmation of deputorial salaries see the Kasatkin interview cited above.

8. See "V 222 milliona rublei oboidëtsia nam v etom godu soiuznyi parlament," *Izvestiia*, 5 November 1991, p. 2. One deputy from the Committee on Defense and State Security reported in 1990 that the Supreme Soviet had an annual budget of 40 million rubles. This report also notes the Supreme Soviet's dependence on the executive for operating funds. See *The New Soviet Legislature: Committee on Defense and State Security*, Report of the Committee on Armed Services, House of Representatives, One Hundred First Congress, Second Session, 11 April 1990. Washington: U.S.

Government Printing Office, 1990, p. 8.

9. *House Appropriations Committee Report on Fiscal Year 1991 Legislative Branch Appropriations.*

10. During the third session, the Supreme Soviet's committees and commissions met more than 300 times, or an average of approximately 13 times each. A commission on deputorial ethics was formed along with three committees, one on law and order and crime, one for the affairs of veterans of the war in Afghanistan, and a third on education. The committee on questions of legislation, legality and law and order was renamed the committee on legislation. The Committee on questions of construction and architecture was renamed the Committee on questions of architecture and construction.

11. Interview with Deputy Iu.A. Ryzhov, summer 1990, Moscow.

12. "O tretei sessii...," p. 13. There is evidence that deputies knew little about the Secretariat's internal structure. See *Verkhovnyi Sovet SSSR, Tretia Sessiia, Biulleten No. 14 Sovmestnogo Zasedaniia Soveta Soiuza i Soveta Natsionalnostei,* 19 March 1990, p. 12.

13. One old-time staffer maintained that while the Secretariat's staff had grown in numbers and its wages had improved significantly since the demise of the old Supreme Soviet, it had become, on average, much less experienced. New staff members, like new deputies, learned only by trial and error.

14. Interviews with Deputies Iu.E. Andreev and Iu.A. Ryzhov, summer 1990, Moscow.

15. Lubenchenko's evaluation of the committees can be found in "Kak obnovliiat verkhovnyi sovet?," *Narodnyi deputat,* No. 15, 1990, pp. 28–33. For his remarks at the session see *Izvestiia,* 14 March 1990. Deputy complaints about scheduling and other problems can be found in *Verkhovnyi Sovet SSSR, Tretia Sessiia, Biulleten No. 14 Sovmestnogo Zasedaniia Soveta Soiuza i Soveta Natsionalnostei,* 19 March 1990, esp. pp. 10, 21, 35, and 43.

16. "O tretei sessii...," p. 24.

17. Interview with Deputy Iu.Iu. Boldyrev, summer 1990, Moscow.

18. Interviews with Deputies A.N. Murashev and S.B. Stankevich, summer 1990, Moscow.

19. Interviews with Deputies Iu.E. Andreev and A.N. Murashev, summer 1990, Moscow.

20. Interview with A. Makovsky, fall 1991, Durham. In the spring of 1990, Deputy Iu.Iu. Boldyrev exploded at the what he considered to be Lukianov's latest violation of voting procedure at a joint session of the Supreme Soviet. "Believe me," he insisted, "there cannot be legality in this [country] if legality is violated in parliament. There cannot be order in

[this] country if order is violated every day and every hour in parliament." See *Verkhovnyi Sovet SSSR, Tretia Sessiia, Biulleten No. 38 Sovmestnogo Zasedaniia Soveta Soiuza i Soveta Natsionalnostei*, 28 April 1990, p. 7.

21. The improvements pointed out by Lukianov included: the renovation of rooms and offices; installation of radios to listen to sessions in 19 meeting rooms, creation of a dictation center; installation of an inter-city (long distance) telephone system and additional telephones; opening an office for psychological counseling and medical care; the renovation of the cafeteria."O tretei sessii...," p. 40.

22. Interviews with Deputies Iu.E. Andreev and Iu.A. Ryzhov, summer 1990, Moscow. Remarks by Deputy N.V. Bosenko confirm this point. See *Verkhovnyi Sovet SSSR, Tretia Sessiia, Biulleten No. 14 Sovmestnogo Zasedaniia Soveta Soiuza i Soveta Natsionalnostei*, 19 March 1990, pp. 33-34.

23. Interview with Deputy Iu.Iu. Boldyrev, summer 1990, Moscow. Deputy A.A. Sobchak provided a clear summary of the inadequacy of the Secretariat's support. See *Verkhovnyi Sovet SSSR, Tretia Sessiia, Biulleten No. 36 Sovmestnogo Zasedaniia Soveta Soiuza i Soveta Natsionalnostei*, 27 April 1990, pp. 15-16.

24. This is confirmed both by the pamphlet "O tretei sessii..." and "Progulivaiut izbranniki naroda," *Argumenty i fakty*, No. 15, 1990, p. 2. Indeed, attendance had been a problem since the first session. See Deputy R.A. Medvedev's complaints in *Pervaia Sessiia Verkhovnogo Soveta SSSR: Stenograficheskii otchet*, Moscow: 1989, Vol. 2, p. 223. Remarks about the problem of attendance and voting at joint sessions can be found in *Verkhovnyi Sovet SSSR, Tretia Sessiia, Biulleten No. 19 Sovmestnogo Zasedaniia Soveta Soiuza i Soveta Natsionalnostei*, 28 March 1990, p. 49, and No. 36, 27 April 1990, pp. 6-7.

25. Lukianov was presiding over the session and offered a brief reply to Lopatin—Gorbachev, as President, had taken over all questions of military reform and state security. See *Verkhovnyi Sovet SSSR, Tretia sessiia, Biulleten No. 76, Sovmestnogo zasedaniia Soveta Soiuza i Soveta Natsionalnostei*, 14 June 1990, pp. 38-40. For more useful citations on the work of the defense committee see note 63 in Chapter 6.

26. For a discussion in the official press of work on this law see "Etot zakon rozhdalsia v sporakh," by A. Sebentsov, a deputy who particpated in the work of the committee, *Nedelia*, No. 24, 1990, p. 2. A marvelously detailed discussion of the law on the press, an essential contribution to our understanding of the legislative process in the Supreme Soviet, can be found in Thomas F. Remington's chapter in Robert T. Huber and Donald R. Kelley, eds., *Perestroika-Era Politics: The New Soviet Legislature and Gorbachev's Political Reforms*, New York: M.E. Sharpe, 1991.

27. *Pozitsiia*, No. 6, 1990.

28. Ibid.

29. Ibid.

30. Interview with Deputy Sebentsov, summer 1990, Moscow.

31. Significant articles on the presidency by Soviet scholars include B.M. Lazarev's "Prezident SSSR," *Sovetskoe gosudarstvo i pravo*, No. 7, 1990, and "Ob izmeneniiakh v pravovom statuse prezidenta SSSR," *Sovetskoe gosudarstvo i pravo*, No. 8, 1991. See also Iu. Skuratov and M. Shafir, "Prezidenstvo: genezis i perspektivy," *Narodnyi deputat*, No. 9, 1991, pp. 6-12. F.M. Burlatskii's observations can be found in English in *Journal of Soviet Nationalities* in a forthcoming article, "The Introduction of the Presidential System."

For an overview of the session and the creation of the presidency see David K. Shipler, "A Reporter at Large (Politics in the Soviet Union)," *The New Yorker*, 25 June 1990, pp. 42-57. See also, Dawn Mann, "Gorbachev Sworn in as President," *Radio Liberty Report on the USSR*, 23 March 1990.

32. *Vedomosti sezda narodnykh deputatov SSSR i Verkhovnogo Soveta SSSR*, No. 6, 1990, Art. 74. The revised agenda was published in a postanovlenie on 14 February, No. 8, Art. 95.

33. For a review of the IRDG's position at the second session of the CPD see *Golos izbiratelia, Informatsionnyi biulleten' Moskovskogo ob"edineniia izbiratelei, Ekspress-vypusk*, December 1989. For a discussion of Gorbachev's about face on this issue see S. Sulakshin, "Nuzhen li prezident?," *Doverie*, No. 5, May 1990, p. 2.

34. See *Izvestiia TsK KPSS*, No. 3, 1990, pp. 3-6.

35. *Pravda*, 6 February 1990.

36. *Vedomosti sezda narodnykh deputatov SSSR i verkhovnogo soveta SSSR*, 1990, No. 7, Art. 94. Deputies Gorbachev, Lukianov, Primakov, Nishanov, Aitmatov, Vorotnikov, Gorbunov, Dzasokhov, Kalmykov, Kudriavtsev, Pivovarov, Ryzhov, Tarazevich, and Shchevchenko were members.

37. *Pravda*, 13 February 1990.

38. *Vedomosti...*, 1990, No. 12. Art. 185.

39. *Izvestiia*, 13 March 1990.

40. Ibid., 14 May 1990.

41. *Izvestiia*, 17 March 1990.

42. "Prezident i pravitelstvo," *Pravitelstvennyi Vestnik*, No. 12, March 1990, p. 1. See also Elizabeth Teague, "The Powers of the Soviet President," *Radio Liberty Report on the USSR*, 23 March 1990, pp. 4-7.

43. For these remarks see debates on the agenda for the CPD's fourth session in *Verkhovnyi Sovet SSSR, Chetvertaia Sessiia, Biulleten No. 46 Sovmestnogo Zasedaniia Soveta Soiuza i Soveta Natsionalnostei*, 19 November 1990.

44. On 27 December 1990, the USSR CPD elected 193 new members to the Supreme Soviet. None of the radicals who stood won election while others never made it to the ballot. *Radio Liberty Daily Report*, No. 243, 2 January 1991. For a pointed discussion of rotation see remarks by Deputy K.D. Lubenchenko, "Kak obnovliat verkhovnyi sovet?," *Narodnyi deputat*, No. 15, 1990, pp. 28-33. For a third opinion see M. Deich, "Anatolii Ivanovioch beretsia za karandash," *Demokraticheskaia Rossiia, Ezhenedelnaia gazeta dvizheniia 'Demokraticheskaia Rossiia'*, 19 April 1991, pp. 1-2.

45. For a report on groups in the CPD see *Radio Free Europe/Radio Liberty: Daily Report*, No. 243, 2 January 1991. For the list of groups in the Supreme Soviet see "Verkhovnyi Sovet SSSR: poltora goda raboty v zerkale tsifr," *Narodnyi Deputat*, No. 1, 1991, p. 15. For an example of the political position of a workers' group see "Obrashchenie deputatskoi gruppy rabochikh Verkhovnogo Soveta SSSR k trudovym kollektivam, k trudiashchimsia strany," *Sovetskaia Rossiia*, 16 January 1991, p. 1. Deputy N.S. Sazonov presented the Social Democrats' proposals for the agenda of the Supreme Soviet's fourth session. See *Verkhovnyi Sovet SSSR, Chetvertaia sessiia, Biulleten No. 1, Sovmestnogo zasedaniia soveta soiuza i soveta natsionalnostei*, 10 September 1990, pp. 28-29. For a detailed summary of groups and members in mid-1991 see A. Kravtsov, "Gruppovye igri," *Ogonēk*, No. 25, 1991, p. 8.

46. "Mezhregionalnaia deputatskaia gruppa: vzgliad iznutri," *Vestnik Sekretariata mezhregionalnoi gruppy narodnykh deputatov SSSR*, March 1990. For a review of the IRDG's work up to and including the second session of the USSR CPD see "Vtoroi sezd: nadezhdy, itogi, uroki," *Pozitisiia*, No. 2, February 1990, p. 1. For one rank-and-file member's point of view see the almanac of the founding congress of the Association of Social Democrats, N. Tutov, "Vybor sdelan," *Otkrytaia zona*, No. 11, 1990, pp. 22-23.

47. See "Vitse-prezident SSSR Gennadii Yanaev," *Kommersant*, No. 58, 1990, p. 28, and L. Malash, "Sekretar TsK KPSS—Vitse-Prezident," *Kuranty*, 4 January 1991, p. 1.

48. The creation of the Russian Communist Party, the election of I.K. Polozkov as its leader, and the new organization's challenges to Gorbachev's reforms were clearly part of the transformation of the CPSU in the summer of 1990. Unfortunately time and space limitations make a sound analysis of this development impossible here.

49. For a description of the *OFT* and other organizations see "Za kem poidut massy?," *Narodnyi deputat*, No. 5, 1990, pp. 40-48. Ronald J. Hill describes the platforms in the CPSU in "The CPSU: From Monolith to Pluralist?," *Soviet Studies*, No. 2, 1991, pp. 217-237.

50. *Izvestiia*, 27 February 1990.

51. "Govoriat aktivisti 'Demplatformy' v KPSS," *Put*, 25 February 1990, p. 6. A short history of the Democratic Platform movement can be found in *Neformalnaia Rossiia: o neformalnykh politizirovannykh dvizheniiakh i gruppakh v RSFSR*, Moscow: Molodaia Gvardiia, 1990, pp. 302-306. See also "Chego khotiat predstaviteleti demplatformy?," *Izvestiia TSK KPSS*, October 1990, pp. 126-128 and "Dokumenty II vsesoiuznyi konferentsii demokraticheskoi platformy v KPSS" *Izvestiia TsK KPSS*, August 1990, pp. 129-132. For a discussion of the movement after a year of development see "The Democratic Opposition: An Insider's View," *Report on the USSR*, RFE/RL Research Institute, Vol. 3, No. 18, 1991, pp. 12-14.

52. *Neformalnaia Rossiia: o neformalnykh politizirovannykh dvizheniiakh i gruppakh v RSFSR*, Moscow: Molodaia Gvardiia, 1990, p. 305.

53. For an evaluation of the conference see "Politicheskaia karta KPSS: obnovlenie ile raskol?," *Vybory-90, Khronika Izbiratelnoi kampanii*, Vypusk No. 6, p. 6.

54. *Pravda*, 1 February 1990.

55. For a discussion of this see "Politicheskii dnevnik: Ianvar," *Pozitsiia*, No. 2, February 1990, p. 1. For a discussion of Democratic Platform's participation in the Central Committee's preparations see V. Lysenko, "Kak ia byl na plenume TsK KPSS," *Pozitsiia*, No. 5, 1990, p. 2.

56. V. Lysenko, "Kak ia byl na plenume...," p. 2.

57. "MDG segodnia i zavtra," and "Vystuplenie G. Popova na zasedanii Mezhregionalnoi deputatskoi gruppy 29 aprelia 1990," *Doverie*, No. 6, 1990, pp. 1-2. S.B. Stankevich clearly laid out the group's attitude toward the presidency. See *Verkhovnyi Sovet SSSR, Tretia sessiia, Biulleten No. 1, Sovmestnogo zasedaniia soveta soiuza i soveta natsionalnostei*, 14 February 1990, pp. 43-44.

58. Not surprisingly, Popov evaluated the IRDG's parliamentary work more positively in public than in the private report written for the group's Secretariat. Deputy V. Logunov, another member of the IRDG, offered an optimistic look at the group's work in "Mezhregionalnaia deputatskaia gruppa: god v oppozitsii," *Narodnyi deputat*, No. 12, 1990, pp. 19-27.

59. "Vystuplenie G. Popova na zasedanii Mezhregionalnoi deputatskoi gruppy 29 aprelia 1990," *Doverie*, No. 6, 1990, pp. 1-2.

60. See, for example, a statement for the IRDG by Deputy N.D. Tutov in *Verkhovnyi Sovet SSSR, Chetvertaia sessiia, Biulleten No. 51, Sovmestnogo zasedaniia soveta soiuza i soveta natsionalnostei*, 26 November 1990, pp. 31-32.

61. "IV Sezd narodnykh deputatov SSSR: Soiuz ostalsia nerushimym, i neplatezhesposobnym," *Kommersant*, No. 50, 1990, p. 3. See also "Soiuz group gaining prominence despite internal divisions," *FBIS Trends*, 3 January 1991, pp. 14-19. A debate about Soiuz can be found in an exhange of

letters to *Izvestiia* from A. Kivy, a doctor of jurisprudence and Deputy V. Alksnis, a leader of the group. See "Soiuz oderzhimykh," *Izvestiia*, 11 May 1990, p. 3 and "Za soiuz v otvete," *Izvestiia*, 14 May 1990, p. 2. A political statement by member deputies from soviets at all levels tells much about the group's values in "Zaiavlenie koordinatsionnogo soveta vsesoiuznogo ob"edineniia narodnykh deputatov vsekh urovnei soiuz po itogam IV sezda narodnykh deputatov SSSR," *Narodnyi Deputat*, No. 3, 1991. pp. 28–29. See also E. Teague, "The Soiuz Group," Report on the USSR, RFE/RL Research Institute, Vol. 3, No. 20, 17 May 1991, pp. 16–21. For an example of the groups's taste in parliamentary delarations, including an accusation of CIA plots invloving Ukrainian and Lithhuanian political groups, see a speech by Alksnis in *Verkhovnyi Sovet SSSR, Chetvertaia Sessiia, Biulleten No. 46 Sovmestnogo Zasedaniia Soveta Soiuza i Soveta Natsionalnostei*, 17 November 1990, pp. 5–7.

62. "A sleeping giant awakens," *Kommersant*, No. 10, 1990, p. 14.

63. See *Verkhovnyi Sovet SSSR, Chetvertaia Sessiia, Biulleten No. 2 Sovmestnogo Zasedaniia Soveta Soiuza i Soveta Natsionalnostei*, 10 September 1990, pp. 4–5, and *Verkhovnyi Sovet SSSR, Chetvertaia Sessiia, Biulleten No. 4 Sovmestnogo Zasedaniia Soveta Soiuza i Soveta Natsionalnostei*, 11 September 1990, pp. 8–9.

64. *Verkhovnyi Sovet SSSR, Chetvertaia Sessiia, Biulleten No. 10 Sovmestnogo Zasedaniia Soveta Soiuza i Soveta Natsionalnostei*, 21 September 1990, pp. 22–24.

65. *Verkhovnyi Sovet SSSR, Chetvertaia Sessiia, Biulleten No. 45 Sovmestnogo Zasedaniia Soveta Soiuza i Soveta Natsionalnostei*, 17 November 1990, pp. 10–12.

66. *Verkhovnyi Sovet SSSR, Chetvertaia Sessiia, Biulleten No. 51 Sovmestnogo Zasedaniia Soveta Soiuza i Soveta Natsionalnostei*, 26 November 1990, pp. 27–29.

67. "Further restructuring of the Soviet Political System," A. Rahr, *Report on the USSR*, RFE/RL Research Institute, Vol. 3, No. 14, 1991, pp. 1–4. Deputy A.M. Emelianov cynically summarized the proposed changes: further limits on the Supreme Soviet's powers. See *Verkhovnyi Sovet SSSR, Chetvertaia Sessiia, Biulleten No. 56 Sovmestnogo Zasedaniia Soveta Soiuza i Soveta Natsionalnostei*, 4 December 1990, pp. 16–17.

Chapter 9

The 1990 Elections

The 1990 elections were both a product of and a catalyst to the rebirth of politics in the USSR.[1] The analysis of the 1990 campaign presented in this chapter is based on two premises. First, many participants viewed the 1990 contest as a continuation of a struggle that started in 1989. Both individuals and campaign teams struggled to use their hard-won knowledge to win electoral contests. Second, any analysis of the elections must take into account the political structure that was being contested. Successful campaign teams took advantage of the fact that the RSFSR elections were held on three different levels on the same day: for regional soviets, city soviets, and the RSFSR Congress of People's Deputies. This schedule gave interested activists a chance to pool efforts in races at different levels. In short, this chapter suggests that both time-sequential and institutional aspects of the 1990 elections played key roles in the outcome.

The Electoral Law

Republican and local elections were originally scheduled in the Soviet Union for the fall of 1989. Local party bosses, after suffering a crushing defeat in 1989, demanded more time to prepare for the next round. At a Central Committee Plenum in April 1989, Gorbachev not only assented to a delayed schedule, but agreed to make the election of party first secretaries as chairmen of the corresponding soviet optional.[2]

In October 1989, the RSFSR Supreme Soviet published for public discussion drafts of a new law on elections and related constitutional amendments. Newspaper reports of the discussion and TASS summaries of meetings of the Presidium of the old RSFSR Supreme Soviet suggest that, in substance, little had changed from old-fashioned apparat-dominated politics. Nonetheless, complaints about shortcomings of the 1989 all-union law led to some significant differences in the two documents. To avoid a public battle, revisions were introduced in the original drafts. Perhaps the most important change was that election through social organizations—roundly despised as a method of protecting conservative CPSU interests—was dropped. The law also eliminated the registration meetings that were criticized in 1989 for being a tool used by the apparat to eliminate candidates it considered threatening. Public criticism was not, however, the final arbiter. For example, indirect elections to the Supreme Soviet, another aspect of all-union practice that was widely criticized, were maintained. In a structure analogous to the 'matryoshka' system of nested legislatures at the all-union level, the amendments provided for 1,068 deputies to be elected to a Congress of People's Deputies, which would then elect a bicameral Supreme Soviet with 126 deputies in each of two chambers, the Soviet of the Republic and the Soviet of Nationalities. The law on elections created 900 territorial and 168 new national-territorial districts. The national-territorial districts, along with the new bicameral Supreme Soviet, accounted for the multinational character of the Russian Federation.

The RSFSR Supreme Soviet (elected in 1985) ratified this legislation on 2 November 1989.[3] Preparations for the session were made according to the old style, in the Presidium of the RSFSR Supreme Soviet.[4] The session itself, however, was not without dramatic moments. Deputy D.A. Volkogonov, for example, complained to his colleagues in the RSFSR Supreme Soviet that "we ratified laws this way 10, 20, or 30 years ago. The essence of [our discussions] is being lost." He argued that many proposals made by the deputies had disappeared and some had been rejected as insignificant. "In practice, we are only voting on amendments to the amendments [and not on basic principles]...I think that this is undemocratic, that such an approach stinks of the past."[5]

Despite Volkogonov's criticism, the deputies continued the quick and quiet completion of their appointed task. Shortly after the end of the session, a schedule was published. Election day for soviets at all levels in the RSFSR would be 4 March 1990. The nomination period lasted from 4 December until 4 January, the registration of candidates from 4 January until 4 February, and the most active period of the elections, the campaign in the streets, took place between 5 February and election day.[6]

Links Between the 1989 and 1990 Campaigns

The 1990 electoral campaign actually started during the 1989 elections, which served as a five-month training program for political activists, providing a way for them to meet one another, organize, and start thinking about the future. In the spring of 1989, after the elections to the all-union CPD, some participants realized that without further efforts their struggle to elect progressive candidates would disappear, as they said, "into the sand." Eager to participate in elections for local and republican soviets, they decided to organize from the bottom up. The postponement of the elections by the April 1989 Central Committee Plenum gave independent activists a chance to form electoral blocs, organize individual campaigns, and, in general, prepare more thoroughly.

Perhaps the best example of the links between the 1989 and 1990 campaigns was at the USSR Academy of Sciences, where a decision was taken on 21 April 1989—the day that Andrei Sakharov was elected to the CPD— to form an electors' club. A working group was established to prepare the club's first meeting, a founding conference held in Moscow on 30 June 1989, a date chosen to maximize participation because it coincided with the formation of another organization of intellectuals devoted to democracy, the Union of Scientists. In all, 158 representatives of 58 academy institutes from Moscow, Leningrad, Novosibirsk, Irkutsk, Sverdlovsk and elsewhere, discussed the club's goals and structure. Instead of trying to agree on a platform, the delegates decided that the club, using a decentralized organizational structure, would promote democratization by spreading information and sharing experience. The club would also help democratic forces prepare for the 1990 republican and local elections by promoting the formation of local electors' clubs. A council and central working group were formed to coordinate the club's activities and a 24-member board of directors was elected, including Andrei Sakharov, Stanislav Shatalin and five other full and corresponding members of the Academy.[7]

Electors' clubs and political action groups took root at the local level across the USSR. Some groups grew out of the deputies' campaign teams in the 1989 elections. Many others popped up independently. By 11 January 1990, 76 electors' clubs were registered by the executive committees of Moscow's regional soviets.[8] In Moscow's Babushkinskii Region, for example, a club was formed by citizens who supported USSR People's Deputy Iurii Andreev during the 1989 electoral campaign. The club started meeting in the late spring and summer of 1989 with the explicit goal of preparing for the 1990 elections. In Yaroslavl, the Council of Electors, a group assisting USSR people's deputy V.S. Podziruk, the Yaroslavl People's Front, and a splinter group of the front, For Popular Sovereignty, joined forces in the summer of 1989. The first edition of the group's news bulletin declared:

> Uniting in a movement, we genuinely will be able to participate in the formation of the soviets of people's deputies. Today, there is no more important task than this. Only by achieving a transfer of power from the hands of the party-state apparat into the hands of popularly-elected representatives will we be able to move ahead...The elections [are] a question of life and death for the local elite. Therefore, the apparat will make all possible efforts to survive and preserve its right to command and decide everything...Will we succeed in breaking up [the party] mafia system...? The question today is clear. The answer depends on all of us.[9]

The party apparat tried half-heartedly but usually failed to stop the formation of independent clubs both by sponsoring organizations of their own and by refusing to register others as official organizations with the right to nominate candidates. In Kaluga, the CPSU *gorkom* created a voters' club to compete with seven others that had already been founded. The chairman of the Kaluga *gorkom*, V. Gorchakov, became one of three co-chairmen of the new voters' club.[10] An interview with one of the leaders of an electors' club in Pskov demonstrated the basic conflict between informal groups and the party: two groups were founded, the Union of Voters of Pskov (UVP) and the Electors' Club (EC). "The party leadership completely supports the EC—naturally, the club has a permanent [headquarters]...and materials about it are published in the press." The UVP, an opposition organization, received no help. "The local press is silent about us. And this is the best advertising."[11]

Conservative forces also learned lessons in 1989 and organized for the 1990 campaign. On 24 October 1989, at the editorial office of the newspaper *Sovetskaia Rossiia*, a meeting was held by USSR people's deputies, voters of Moscow, and representatives of social organizations to form a deputies' club, 'Rossiia.' The club was founded to unite voters and deputies interested in politicizing Russian nationalism. It planned to participate in the 1990 republican elections and assigned one of its members to work out a proposal for the electoral law. The club's co-chairmen included V.A. Iarin, a USSR Supreme Soviet deputy who later became a member of Gorbachev's presidential council, and D.A. Barabashov, an official from the apparat of the CPSU Central Committee.[12]

In addition to electors' clubs, other 'informal' political organizations, the so-called *neformalye*, played a role by sharing electoral experience. One example of this influence was a brochure on campaign strategy and tactics written by Sergei Stankevich, USSR people's deputy, and Mikhail Shneidr, his campaign manager in 1989. Both men were members of the coordinating council of the Moscow People's Front. They wanted to share the experience that they gained in the 1989 campaign because even "the [apparat is] using approaches and methods of organizing electoral campaigns that were tested and demonstrated by democratic forces in 1989." The 1990 campaign, they insisted, would demand "greater organization, much wider participation, and the application of untraditional, still-unpublicized methods of electoral agitation."[13] The brochure, originally distributed to approximately 1,000 participants, was written in a popular style and contained practical advice on how to organize and conduct a winning campaign, including principles for forming campaign teams, the qualities of winning candidates, the basics of political agitation, and how to compete with candidates from the apparat.[14]

Electoral umbrella organizations began to form out of the local clubs and *neformalye*. The Moscow Union of Voters (MUV), founded at a conference at Moscow State University in July 1989, initially united electors' clubs and other groups from 30 regions of the capital and 34 major factories.[15] Later, electors' clubs from more than 100 other institutions, including the USSR Academy of Sciences, entered the MUV.[16] A study of the capital's independent political organizations conducted for the CPSU *gorkom* argued that a "politicized independent movement" was actively involved "*in a real struggle for power.*"

> The principal and immediate goal [of this movement] is the [elections]. Active and persistent work is already being conducted in this direction. The first stage was preservation of the *aktiv* and organizations that formed in [1989] at the district level and the transformation of candidate's support groups into organs for helping... deputies maintain contact with voters. Further, on this basis, with the active participation of USSR People's Deputies, district electors' clubs and associations were formed that subsequently founded the Moscow Union of Voters... The creation and activity of MUV is an example of the consolidation of the most different independent, self-motivated, politicized associations and groups on an 'anti-apparat,' 'anti-official' position against all official candidates.[17]

The MUV's statute declared that its members were "united in the effort to promote the creation of a civil society and a system of genuine popular sovereignty through democratic elections ..."[18] The conferences of the MUV were useful in several ways. First, they helped to keep interest and awareness high in the most active sections of the populace. Second, they allowed participants in the 1989 elections from across the city to become acquainted and share experience to prepare for the 1990 elections. Third, the MUV created an institutional structure for interaction with the Moscow city government. One should note, however, that even the MUV was a relatively loose umbrella group. Local chapters were sometimes suspicious of its central leadership and often refused to listen to its suggestions.

Electoral Blocs

Electoral blocs were established in the RSFSR to endorse and work for candidates at all electoral levels. It is essential to stress, however, as participants often did, that these groups were, in fact, blocs rather than political parties. Like the CPSU itself, they united individuals with radically different political ideas—often Communists—into a loosely disciplined team. Remarks made by a representative of the 'New Wave' bloc in Novosibirsk suggested the character of these organizations. "Forming this block, we, Communists, non-party members, and representatives of various social movements... are united principally by a resolve to change the existing situation..." Two main blocs contested the elections in the RSFSR.

The Russian Patriotic Bloc

In December 1989, several Russian cultural and political groups, including the United Council of Russia, Edinstvo, Rossiia, the All-Russian Cultural Fund, the United Front of Russian Workers, the Social Committee to Save the Volga, and four others, formed the Russian Patriotic Bloc to promote 'conservative' positions such as environmental protection and greater control over Russian natural resources, protection of ethnic traditions for Russians and other "nationalities indigenous to Russian territory," and promotion of traditional Russian spiritual values. Timothy J. Colton neatly characterized this bloc when he noted that, "The primary chord was recoil against the kernel of the Westernizing reforms launched since 1985..."[19]

Declaring that "the Fatherland is in danger!," the patriotic bloc's platform criticized the CPSU, "the guarantor of political and social stability," for assuming a "defensive-capitulationist position." "The CPSU," it argued, "has not made sufficient efforts to consolidate society or its own ranks while step by step retreating before the the bloc of 'separatists' and left radicals that is prepared to dismantle the USSR and sell to western 'partners' our national riches." The program went on to ask, "Will Russia preserve its political and economic independence, its cultural integrity?— these are the things that every Russian must think about before voting in the elections on March 4th." Among the measures proposed in the platform were: (1) the creation of a Russian Communist Party, (2) sovereign control by Russia over its natural resources, (3) the elimination of alleged subsidies to other Soviet republics, (4) long-term leases of land to the peasantry, (5) protection against discrimination of Russians living in other republics, and (6) the revival of the Russian Orthodox Church and other religious organizations.[20]

Although the Russian Patriotic Bloc published a platform, other self-styled patriotic organizations that joined the bloc issued their own statements. V.N. Osipov, one of the leaders of the Russian Christian-Patriotic Union, ran as a candidate of the bloc in Moscow's Sevastopolskii RSFSR territorial district No. 47. In December 1989, the union published a call to vote for its candidates. This program suggests that the patriotic bloc, like the democrats, united forces with significant differences of opinion. Pointing out that "We profess neither capitalism nor socialism. We are for Russia," the program blamed Russia's problems on 'the virus of atheism.' The Christian-Patriotic Union argued that the way to save the country was through a renaissance of Russian Orthodoxy. The country should move from "a one-party dictatorship to a non-party system." "We can be saved only by a return to a religious understanding and acceptance of the world. Not ideology—faith, not politics—spirituality, not democracy—*sobornost*, not a union of republics—a Unified Great Power."[21]

On 4 February 1990, the Russian Patriotic Bloc published a list of candidates for *Mossovet* and the RSFSR CPD from Moscow.

Elections-90 and Democratic Russia

A group called Elections-90 was formed in October 1989 "to collect information about candidates for the RSFSR CPD and help them make contact with one another and with support groups, to encourage cooperation and mutual aid during the electoral campaign, to help coordinate nominations during repeat elections, and to help organize a conference to prepare strategy for the first session of the RSFSR CPD." Members of this coalition included representatives from the IRDG, the Electors' Club of the USSR Academy of Sciences, Memorial, Moscow Tribune, the Moscow People's Front, Aprel, the MUV, the Interregional Electors' Union, Shield, The RSFSR People's Front, the Interregional Association of Democratic Organizations, the Confederation of Anarcho-Syndicalists, the Moscow Buro of the Social-Democratic Association, and the social-democratic fraction of the Democratic Union. In a letter sent to organizations throughout the RSFSR, the group's headquarters asked for information about the elections and candidates as well as suggestions on future activities.[22]

On 20 November 1989, Elections-90 met in Moscow to discuss whom the group would support for election to the RSFSR CPD. Nearly 40 candidacies were identified, discussed, and agreed upon, including a wide range of representatives from the group's component organizations. Representatives of the Moscow Union of Voters, which did not enter the bloc, participated in the meeting, expressed its support and hopes for a positive relationship, and promised to report to district electors' clubs the list of candidates proposed by Elections-90.

Elections-90 developed contacts with Moscow voters' clubs and other relevant organizations. These links were both personal and organizational. Members of some of the component groups of Elections-90 were members of the coordinating council of MUV. On 23 November Elections-90 invited V.P. Mironov, the editor of *Khronika*, a popular *samizdat* newspaper that played a role in advertising democratic candidates in 1989, to speak. This meeting was arranged because *Khronika* was published by the All-Union Association of Electors, a group that had a semi-competitive relationship with MUV. The same day, representatives of Elections-90 also met with USSR People's Deputy Gavriil Popov in his capacity as co-chairman of the Interregional Deputies' Group.[23]

At the initiative of MUV and the Interregional Union of Voters, 116 candidates for RSFSR deputy along with more than 50 candidates for republican, city, and regional soviets from Moscow, Leningrad, 3 autonomous republics, 16 oblasts, and two *krai* gathered on 20–21 January 1990 in Moscow to form an electoral bloc. Representatives of the component groups of Elections-90 as well as USSR People's Deputies and members of the IRDG G. Popov, S.B. Stankevich, M. Bocharov, and A.N. Murashev also participated. The bloc, after some discussion, adopted the name Democratic Russia (henceforth, *Demrossiia*) and a common platform, a long list of proposed socio-economic and political reforms prefaced by the declaration that, "We have no greater task than to stop [our country] from sliding toward the abyss...Our future depends to a great degree on what kind of [Congress] we elect in Russia and what kind of local soviets."[24]

Among the 'political landmarks' included in the platform were: (1) guaranteeing the right of Russian citizens to participate in political parties, (2) rejection of the two-tier Congress-Supreme Soviet government structure, (3) true freedom of the press, (4) democratic control over the KGB and the Ministry of Internal Affairs, (5) a market economy with government intervention on a Western model, (6) "all forms of ownership," a euphemism for private ownership of means of production, (7) a price freeze on main food products and consumer goods until the market could guarantee an acceptable price level, (8) sovereignty of the Russian Federation, (9) a democratic resolution of national problems. Although some of the planks of *Demrossiia*'s platform appear to be mutually exclusive and others rather vague, the most interesting point to note is that *Demrossiia* did not start its existence with an emotional appeal to Russian sovereignty. The platform concluded with a short statement, "Our country confronts not only elections, which will decide a great deal, but faces a choice: Will we follow the majority of European countries along the difficult but peaceful and democratic parliamentary path of changes that in the end will give bread and freedom to all, or does bloody conflict await? A call to voters ratified at the conference ended with the following declaration: "We do not summon voters to vote for 'Soviets without Communists', we call them to vote for 'Soviets without the party nomenklatura.'"[25]

Demrossiia published a list of candidates for the CPD and *Mossovet* in late February in the newspaper *Pozitsiia*.[26]

The CPSU's Preparations

The CPSU, after the crushing defeat it suffered in 1989, prepared carefully for the 1990 elections. Party organizations attempted to analyze the disastrous experience of 1989 and apply it to the republican and local contests. Addressing the *aktiv* of the Leningrad party organization after arriving to force its first secretary into retirement because of a crushing electoral defeat in 1989, Gorbachev argued that the party faced "enormous work in preparing and conducting the elections for local soviets."

He argued that party members should reject the illusion that the CPSU's leading role and authority were guaranteed: "We all need to master the art of political struggle and political methods of working among the people." Gorbachev suggested that the reason for the defeat of many candidates was "the critical relationship of the workers to the activity of the party in a number of areas of perestroika" and that "the appearance of certain forces, consciously trying to discredit the party, its organs, and communists did not "always and everywhere[receive] counteraction from party committees, party organizations, society, and...the CPSU Central Committee."[27]

The Central Committee demonstrated its interest in the campaign at both the federal and republican levels. On 11 October 1989, the Central Committee's commissions on party cadres, legal policy, and ideology met under the leadership of Politburo members Medvedev and Razumovskii to discuss elections to the union republic and local soviets. Participants noted that "it is important that the necessary lessons were learned from the [1989] elections." Electoral guidelines were set out for party organizations. Their attention was directed first of all to decisions made on the national question by the Central Committee in September 1989. Organizational questions about the campaign were also discussed. Preparations, it was emphasized, should proceed openly and in consultation with workers and all forces in support of perestroika. The socialist idea should be defended. Only the resolution of pressing socioeconomic problems could guarantee success.[28] A second meeting was held in the Central Committee on 18 November 1989 to discuss the RSFSR elections. Gorbachev addressed an assembly of cadres from across the republic, where he led a discussion of the elections as a part of the reform program. The key role that primary party organizations would play in the elections was emphasized. Winners of the elections, it was stated, would be responsible for instituting the CPSU's economic program and converting the soviets into "real organs of popular power."[29]

The CPSU in Moscow

The Moscow party organization suffered a crushing defeat in 1989. One result was the promotion of second secretary Iurii Prokofev to the top position in the Moscow *gorkom*: former First Secretary and Politburo member Lev Zaikov had little hope of winning in a free election. Prokofev, at least, had a chance; moreover, he was expected to do a better job leading the capital's preparations for the elections.[30] Although he was promoted late, in November 1989, Prokofev undoubtedly had participated in the *gorkom*'s electoral work throughout the spring and summer.

By late May 1989, the *gorkom* already had drafted a detailed list of measures to be taken to prepare for the 1990 elections.[31] The list reflected the party leadership's desire both to study the needs and political inclinations of its citizens and to correct problems in the city's economic and social infrastructure. The *gorkom* planned to propagandize its own views through the mass media but also planned to work with existing informal political organizations while creating new voters' clubs. Among the 28 measures planned for completion by the end of 1989 were:

> 7. Work out a detailed plan for the electoral campaign. Create electoral headquarters in every region... Concentrate on the formation of electoral organs and initiative groups for the nomination and support of candidates and the identification of possible candidates while taking into account the opinion of workers' collectives and local organs of self-management...
> 13. Conduct a seminar for CPSU *raikom* secretaries and leaders of the executive committees of local soviets on the theme, "The work of party and soviet organs in the [1989] electoral campaign... and the problems of increasing the effectiveness [of this work] during the [1990] elections...
> 20. Create at the [*gorkom*] House of Political Education

and...regional party committees specialized groups of consultants for the timely analysis of the political situation...and for working out recommendations for party and soviet organs...

In addition to back-stage organizational preparations, the *gorkom* conducted several public demonstrations of electoral zeal, essentially political spectacles. Secretaries of the Moscow *gorkom* met with secretaries from the capital's primary party organizations on 24 November 1989 to discuss the party's platform. Prokofev led the meeting and made some unpublished closing remarks.[32] The Moscow *gorkom* met again on 20 December to ratify an electoral platform that advocated "the further deepening of perestroika and the realization of political and economic reform, democratization, and the widening of glasnost," and called for strengthening Moscow's rights as a city. In addition to an abundance of political boilerplate, the platform demonstrated the *gorkom*'s poor grasp of electoral strategy by calling for voting for the "bloc of Communist and non-Communist candidates." This slogan, popular when the party assumed that Soviet society was unified behind its leadership, was ludicrous in conditions where many candidates were actively campaigning against the CPSU.[33] (On 26 January 1990, the Russian Buro of the CPSU Central Committee joined with the Presidium of the RSFSR Supreme Soviet and the RSFSR Council of Ministers to issue a similarly-vague plea 'To the peoples of Soviet Russia.')[34]

Although the Moscow *gorkom* ignored tough political choices in its platform, it spared little effort in other areas. It enlisted the help of several CPSU institutions in the capital to provide support to selected candidates. Scholars at the Moscow Higher Party School created and conducted a series of role-playing electoral games that were intended to give participants: a deeper understanding of the electoral law; a command of basic skills; techniques, and technologies useful at various stages of the electoral campaign; and better interpersonal skills.[35] The *gorkom*'s House of Political Education provided consulting services both prior to and during the campaign. Candidates had the opportunity to attend seminars on writing campaign programs, giving campaign speeches, and answering questions from voters.[36] Materials distributed by the party contained suggestions on how to organize campaigns, including writing a strategic plan, choosing campaign tactics, choosing a district, forming a campaign team, writing a campaign program, studying public opinion, and conducting meetings with voters.[37]

The ideological department of the Moscow *gorkom* took a different approach to independent organizations in 1990 than in 1989. One study recommended that regional party committees develop "constructive and principled" relationships with the *neformalye*. The CPSU should "hasten the registration of independent formations" to avoid giving them non-registration as an "an excuse to use in the electoral campaign." While it would be possible "to support certain activists and leaders of the independent movement who are dedicated to the cause of socialist renewal," "even temporary agreements and blocs on the basis of joint platforms of party committees and informal groups" were considered undesirable. The report was particularly cautious concerning "adherents to traditional and national-patriotic views" who often "demonstrate their support of the CPSU." The report warned that "the conservative or at times frankly chauvinistic character of these programs" could discredit the CPSU "in the eyes of the working masses." Support could be given to "those who subsequently will conduct within social formations party policy," but "a principled party evaluation should be given to nationalist, conservative, and liberal views."[38]

Moscow's 33 regional party committees prepared carefully for the elections. Some party organizations, in Pervomaiskii Region for example, went so far as to publish their own programs for the elections.[39] In Dzerzhinskii Region, the party apparat prepared "Recommendations for restructuring the work of party organizations with the population for...elections to the local soviets of the RSFSR." Arguing that in 1989 the region's party *aktiv* had conducted itself according to old stereotypes instead of concentrating on "flexible political work asserting the CPSU platform and defending and advancing the party position," and complaining that political agitation had been undermined by demands for "organizational-technical help by the district electoral commission," the recommendations outlined a plan for improving the work of the regional party organization's political campaigners. Suggestions included: (1) reviewing the competence of the present staff of *agitatory*, (2) creating and working with electors' clubs, (3) studying public opinion in the regions through survey techniques, (4) contacting and working with initiative groups and independent organizations, (5) creating an electoral headquarters in the *raikom* to coordinate the campaign, and (6) changing the structure of the apparat to include a sector for working with local residents.[40]

One of the leading figures in the CPSU's Moscow campaign was A. Briachikhin, the first secretary of Sevastopolskii Region. Briachikhin, who lost in the 1989 elections to the CPD to liberal economist Oleg Bogomolov, drew what he claimed to be the necessary lessons. "Elections today are a political battle...If we want to confirm our authority and our position in society, simple participation in the battle is not enough—we must be able and willing to win." Briachikhin pointed out, perhaps unwittingly, the CPSU's chief weakness: "Without a clear program of concrete actions it makes no sense to appeal to the voters. All the more so because many of them are disenchanted by unfulfilled promises...There is a share of the population that can still be won over by beautiful phrases but their numbers are falling sharply." Briachikhin mentioned "removing ballast" and passive members from the CPSU, but was unwilling to discuss a political split in the party's ranks. He suggested that electing hardworking and 'worthy' candidates was the only way to solve the country's problems and that 'concrete' ideas were necessary. Both suggestions arise from the party's main failing in the campaign—concentrating on 'objective' organizational and socioeconomic questions and not conducting a clear-cut political battle.[41]

The Campaign

The 1990 electoral campaign grew directly out of the 1989 campaign. Thus, it is important to note that the vast majority of violations of the electoral law in 1989 went unpunished. If Gorbachev and the CPSU apparat were serious about enforcing the electoral law, one would have expected a well-publicized, all-union campaign to punish Communist violators of the 1989 law through party channels, followed by a corresponding series of civil criminal proceedings. Nothing of the kind took place. This was a signal that local authorities could act as they pleased.[42]

Electoral Commissions

The RSFSR Central Electoral Commission met for the first time on 10 November 1989. The commission's figurehead status was confirmed when, on the first day of its operation, it created and defined 1,068 electoral districts for the RSFSR CPD, set up a schedule for all elections in the RSFSR, and established the budgets for all other electoral commissions. The RSFSR party apparat undoubtedly used the CEC's staff, 67 specialist divided into 8 groups, to monitor and control the elections. One should also note that the RSFSR CEC faced in 1990 many of the same problems that the USSR CEC faced in 1989, including public unfamiliarity with a complex new law, thousands of requests for information, and insufficient resources to investigate accusations.[43]

Electoral commissions were formed to supervise the campaigns for soviets at all levels. In Moscow, there were separate electoral commissions for the elections to the Moscow City Soviet and each of the capital's 33 regional soviets. These commissions, just as in 1989, were a political tool of the local CPSU apparat. The central element of the apparat's power was that the commissions continued to be staffed by full-time employees of the executive committee of the corresponding soviet. The fact that the commissions were created on 11 November 1989 and started work on 12 November suggests, similar to the herculean agenda of the RSFSR CEC's first meeting, that their work was heavily influenced by full-time staff.

Although the membership of the election commissions continued to consist principally of political amateurs, some significant changes took place. Unlike 1989, independent activists and political blocs understood the importance of representation on the commissions. A report to the executive committee of *Mossovet* pointed out that

> in contrast to the past, in many districts a battle flared up at the stage of the formation of electoral commissions. If in the past we ourselves searched for [potential committee members] and organized the nomination, today many [nominations to the electoral commissions] came at the initiative of residents and workers' collectives. More than 50 nominations were made for 21 places in the city electoral commission. Although the law on elections allowed the formation of electoral commissions by the executive committees of soviets, we took a non-traditional course and decided the procedural question at a session of *Mossovet*. The [CPSU] party group and the chairmen of *Mossovet*'s standing commissions participated in preparing the session. Many local electoral commissions were formed in a similar way. In contrast to the [1989 elections], there are more representatives of voters [from local apartment complexes], local self-management committees, and electors' clubs.[44]

One example of changes in the CPSU's relationship to electoral organizations was that A. I. Muzykantskii, a member of Yeltsin's inner circle in the 1989 campaign and founder and member of the coordinating council of the Moscow Union of Voters became a member of the electoral commission for the Moscow City Soviet.

Despite the changes in the electoral commission at the city level, the protest resignation of 11 of 15 members of the electoral commission in Moscow's RSFSR territorial district No. 47 highlights the difficulties and inequalities that remained in the relationship between committee members and staff. The local CPSU *raikom* reportedly was unhappy about the nomination of P. M. Kudiukin, an active member of the Moscow chapter of Memorial who was supported by *Demrossiia*. The chairman of the executive committee of the local soviet, S. V. Zhavronkov, pressed the leadership of the Institute of Oceanology, the organization that nominated Kudiukin, to sign a document stating that the nomination was invalid for procedural reasons. When the institute's leadership succumbed to this pressure, 250 of its employees signed a protest addressed to the local electoral commission. When the commission decided in favor of Kudiukin, Zhavronkov appealed to the RSFSR CEC and, with the help of pressure 'from above,' succeeded in overturning the decision. Subsequently, the RSFSR CEC also overturned decisions in the district on the candidacies of Mikhail Maliutin, nominated by a new, independent trade union and Alexander Shaltaian, nominated by an independent Moldavian cultural society. In protest, 11 members of the local commission, including its chairman, resigned. Memorial's monthly bulletin, the source of this account, undoubtedly would have mentioned the resignations of any committee staff members in order to strengthen its case against the CEC and the local electoral commission. The absence of such a report suggests the loyalties of the staff—to the chairman of the soviet's executive committee and, ultimately, the corresponding party committee.[45]

Electoral commissions throughout the RSFSR were accused of violations of the electoral law; nonetheless, it would be unfair to argue that decisions made by local electoral commissions were always and everywhere politically motivated. Just as in 1989 at the federal level, the 1990 RSFSR law on elections was complex, vague, difficult to interpret, and therefore difficult to enforce.[46] Discussing whether problems in the interpretation of the electoral law were a result a lack of knowledge of the law or the quality of the legislation itself, of M.I. Kukushkin, a deputy chairman of the RSFSR CEC, argued that the commission had organized seminars to explain the law and that the CEC's instructions had been sent to the electoral commissions. "[One should] speak not as much about ignorance as about a fear to take responsibility for making decisions in each concrete case."[47] M. Sork, chairman of a local electoral commission in Moscow oblast sent a letter to *Izvestiia* that outlined some of the difficulties from the commissions'point of view.

> I am chairman of a city electoral commission for the seventh [time]... It would seem that I have some experience. But when the new RSFSR electoral laws were published we had to learn everything from scratch. Previously, electoral commissions did not register candidates, did not ratify the text of electoral bulletins, and did not decide many other questions that appear in the course of daily work. Today, all this has become part of our circle of responsibilities, but there are no instructions to be found in the law on elections. As early as November, I turned to the [RSFSR CEC] but... this organ only deals with the elections to the [RSFSR CPD]. It was then necessary to bother the organizational-instructional department of the Presidium of the RSFSR Supreme Soviet... [Their] answer came too late.[48]

Sork described problems that his commission faced in the interpretation of the law as well as financial difficulties that arose from budget constraints and unclear procedures. He concluded by despairing that the Presidium of the RSFSR Supreme Soviet would do anything to improve the situation.

The complexities of the electoral law make it difficult to decide where problems with interpretation end and politically-motivated abuse begins; nonetheless, it is clear that both existed. One good example of the ambiguous problems that arose out of the electoral law was a requirement that candidates compete on an equal basis. Although selective enforcement and creative interpretation of this article of the law allowed for political influence through the electoral commission, difficulties could also have been a result of inexperience. At times, electoral commissions would simply ignore the rule and allow candidates to use all resources that they could gather. This meant, of course, that heads of enterprises and other candidates well-endowed with resources could do a better job. Other electoral commissions took a different approach and attempted to control all aspects of the campaign. Politically motivated violations of the electoral law were much more common in this situation. Thus, candidates unacceptable to the local apparat could be eliminated from the race for petty violations.[49]

Electoral Districts

Electoral districts were formed in 1990 according to the same criteria that were used in 1989—primarily administrative convenience. If, in 1989, there was little direct evidence of gerrymandering outside the Baltic and little awareness of the potential problem, in 1990, people were at least conscious of the possibility for abuse. In the summer of 1989, the executive committee of the Moscow City Soviet commissioned a study of the capital's electoral districts by geographers from Moscow State University and the USSR Academy of Sciences. These scholars made a series of suggestions, noting, for example, that, although the districts answered the administrative needs of the city government, they could be improved upon to better represent the city's population.[50] For the RSFSR CPD, the result in Moscow, however, was that electoral districts were formed to coincide with the administrative subdivisions of the city. One group of scholars argued convincingly that Moscow was an example that "the preservation of the network of administrative bounds is an insurmountable barrier to the realization of the rule, one person—one vote." In addition to the mathematical facts, one should note that the old administrative system found it easier to control the electoral commissions through its existing network of soviets.[51]

Nomination and Registration

Nomination of candidates began on 4 December 1989 and ended formally on 3 January 1990. Nominations could be made in three ways. First, work collectives were able to nominate candidates for any district in the elections. A second nomination method was through "public organizations" that had to be registered as such *prior* to promulgation of the RSFSR election law. This element of the law gave the apparat a powerful tool to control nominations. Third, neighborhood caucuses of no less than 300 citizens in the district where the candidate resided had the right to make nominations to the RSFSR CPD and caucuses of 150 citizens could nominate candidates to the Moscow City Soviet.

Just as in 1989, the apparat had many tools at its disposal to disrupt nomination meetings. The requirement that a certain number of citizens be present throughout the caucus meant that opponents of a specific nomination could drag out or disrupt the meeting so that supporters would grow frustrated and leave. Moreover, one should not forget that almost all official business comes to a complete halt in the days just before and after New Year's Day. As Sergei Odarich, the coordinator of Rukh's electoral campaign in Ukraine pointed out, this time factor served the interests of the apparat, especially in nominations by local caucuses. "Nomination by law ended January 3rd but, in fact, in connection with the New Year holidays, [nominations] ended somewhere in the third week of December... They put us in a very complex situation."[52] Although the number of candidates nominated in neighborhood caucuses was comparatively low, in absolute numbers more than 500 such meetings were held in Moscow in 1990, a significant increase compared to the 22 held in 1989.[53]

There was a key strategic difference between neighborhood caucuses and nominations in the workplace. While liberal or reform-minded groups could be controlled at neighborhood caucuses controlled by the electoral commission, nominations in the workplace could be controlled by the workers themselves. Thus, liberal 'workers' at one institute of the USSR Academy of Sciences were able to nominate a large number of candidates for elections in districts all across Moscow. Although the Helsinki Report on the 1990 elections was generally correct when it argued that "reform and anti-apparatus candidates tended to be nominated by neighborhood caucuses or public organizations while party loyalists were put forth by labor collectives," these tactical exceptions should be noted.[54]

The politics of the nomination stage were more highly developed in 1990 than in 1989 because of the phenomenon of political endorsement by blocs. If, in 1989, well-known candidates like Yeltsin or Sakharov either tried not to get in each other's way or simply ignored one another's efforts, in

1990 democrats fought with one another over nomination. Indeed, there was some tension involved in putting together a list of unknown candidates that could satisfy both local electors' clubs and the leadership of *Demrossiia*. Inevitably, mistakes were made. For instance, one participant pointed out that "it is unknown how V. Burkov...wound up on *Demrossiia*'s list...Activists of the patriotic organization 'Otechestvo' campaigned for Burkov...and it became known that Burkov is a member of its coordinating council."[55] Several other incidents involving confused identities as well as conflicts between the central leadership and local clubs were reported in Moscow. Perhaps the most widely reported such conflict was the feud that economist Larisa Piasheva conducted with Ilia Zaslavskii and Gavriil Popov. Piasheva was excluded from the democratic bloc after she criticized in *Izvestiia* economic reform proposals made by Zaslavskii and Popov.[56]

Like Democratic Russia, the party apparat did not ignore tactical aspects of the nomination process. The two types of seats in the RSFSR CPD had different nomination requirements. While nominations for territorial districts demanded that the nominee live or work in the district, nominees to national-territorial districts were only required to prove residence in the RSFSR. This loophole gave apparatchiks the opportunity to run in relatively safe districts. Nearly 50 leading party figures were nominated in the autonomous areas of the Russian Republic. Control over the electoral process meant almost certain victory and, subsequently, when it came time to create the Supreme Soviet at the RSFSR CPD, these party leaders were included automatically.[57]

In all, 8,254 candidates were nominated for 1068 CPD seats in the Russian federation, or nearly 8 candidates per seat. Some districts had over twenty contenders while 26 others had only one candidate: 7% of the candidates were women, 8.5% workers, 3.2% collective farmers, and 1.5% Komsomol members. Only 3.2% of the candidates were nominated by neighborhood caucuses. Only 3.3% of the candidates had experience as deputies.[58]

Even after nomination, independent candidates could not feel safe. The Helsinki Commission reported that electoral commissions "heavily infiltrated by party officials attempted to disqualify reform candidates nominated by public organizations or neighborhood organizations on specious or trivial grounds." All things considered, however, the registration stage of the 1990 campaign proceeded in a much calmer atmosphere than in 1989, when bitter complaints surrounded the registration meetings that eliminated nominees from further contention in the election. In 1990, registration meetings were not held and electoral commissions registered virtually all nominees. As Colton argued, in Moscow, in comparison to 1989, "there was far less of an effort...to choke off entry of unorthodox candidates, probably because nomination chicanery the year before was widely seen to have aroused popular suspicions..."[59]

Campaigning for Office

How did candidates get their messages across to voters? The official meetings organized by electoral commissions did not play a great role. During January, electoral commissions in Moscow organized a mere 200 meetings with the participation of 1500 candidates for soviets at all levels.[60] Candidates took the campaign into their own hands. By law, they were allowed to nominate five campaign supporters to help them throughout the course of the elections. (In 1990, in Moscow alone, nearly 31,000 such supporters were officially registered.[61]) These campaign supporters, as well as electoral blocs, multiplied the resources available to candidates. Stankevich and Shneider pointed out in their campaign handbook that

> if, in the [1989] campaign, [campaign teams] were constructed on the basis of the [supporters] of ONE candidate, today, taking into account the necessity for simultaneous agitation for republican and local soviets, and also the presence in some districts of several progressive candidates competing for one [spot], it is more appropriate, apparently, to create teams united around a united democratic bloc of candidates for Soviets of three levels: region, city, and republic.

Colton pointed out that "Moscow *Demrossiia* had no stylized decision-making structure;" nonetheless, its local branches were well organized.[62] They campaigned according to a so-called 'vertical' principle of organization, which was well illustrated in remarks made by Vladimir Bokser, a leader of the MPF and MUV. He argued that "the voter should know...that it is appropriate and useful to vote not only for particular candidates for the regional soviet, *Mossovet* or the RSFSR CPD, not only for a good person, but for an entire 'team' since only the interaction [of these team members] will guarantee success."[63] In Timiriazevskii Region, for example, candidates for the *raion* soviet, the Moscow City Soviet, and the RSFSR Congress of People's Deputies worked together under the guidance of a general headquarters staffed by the local electors' club, *Pozitsiia*. Arkadii Murashev, the USSR people's deputy elected from Timiriazevskii Region in 1989, worked in concert with the local electors' club to help with the campaign.[64]

Political endorsements were widely used throughout the 1990 campaign. In Timiriazevskii Region, for instance, Murashev and other leaders of the IRDG issued posters with endorsements. Candidate for the RSFSR CPD

Sergei Krasavchenko convinced Boris Yeltsin and Gavriil Popov to pose with him for a photograph that became part of a campaign poster. The signatures of Yeltsin, Popov, and Iurii Afanasev, identified as co-chairmen of the IRDG, as well as five other USSR People's Deputies, including Iurii Chernichenko and Sergei Stankevich, followed a statement of support at the bottom. Deputies used organizational endorsements as well. Viktor Sheinis, a candidate for the RSFSR CPD in another district, published a campaign poster that, in addition to listing Galina Starovoitova (a well-known liberal USSR people's deputy) and *Demrossiia* as his supporters, also included the Electors' Club of the USSR Academy of Sciences, Memorial, Moscow Tribunal, and the local electors' club 'Golos' as supporters.

Party leaders naturally had trouble earning endorsements from leading democrats; nevertheless, they had many advantages, including, of course, the party apparat.[65] Local press, radio, and television played a significant role in the campaign. Although it would have been impossible to give information about all candidates in the press, the choices that were made about coverage were more often than not on the side of the *status quo*. One writer noted that "The local press supported some candidates quite actively... *For some reason or other*, 'official' candidates... enjoyed greater attention from local newspaper writers... radio programs, and on television ..." This type of influence often backfired. "Voters have already learned quite well how to identify candidates that the apparat [dislikes]... In the absence of other information such a 'recommendation' often turns out to be decisive."[66] That is, in a manner similar to the 'Yeltsin phenomenon' in 1989, voters suppported candidates that the apparat disliked.

The apparat found it easy to obstruct both mass rallies and meetings arranged by individual candidates. In Khabarovsk, for example, Iurii Strugov, a candidate for the RSFSR CPD, was denied access to the workers of a large factory in his district by the secretary of its *partkom*. The secretary explained that a meeting was already scheduled at the factory with Strugov's opponent, G. Goncharova, a secretary of the CPSU *kraikom*.[67] In Saratov, an independent group called the 'Club-Seminar for Candidates' decided to hold a meeting to protest that 45% of the districts in the city soviet and 58% in the oblast soviet had only one candidate. The local authorities took prompt action to preempt the event. Despite signatures from 77 candidates, a petition for official permission for the meeting was denied. Fences were erected around the central square where the organizers wanted to hold the meeting. Alternate meetings conducted by officials from the electoral commissions in each of the city's six regions were announced for the same date and time.[68]

Local party and industrial leaders had several other tools at their disposal, for example, the distribution of scarce goods to voters. A letter to

Izvestiia from Omsk noted that a large number of televisions had been delivered to one collective farm in January. "Why? Perhaps it is because an electoral meeting for the first secretary of the CPSU *raikom*, a candidate for the oblast soviet, and [a local trade official], a candidate for the RSFSR CPD, were scheduled there?"[69]

Although mass meetings and street picketing played a role in the 1990 campaign, better-organized campaign teams recognized that such meetings only reach a small section of the population.[70] Thus, citywide meetings focussed on national, republican, and local issues but could not help specific candidates a great deal. While meetings were typically attended by supporters, it was the broad masses of the undecided that had to be reached. The 'Patriotic Bloc,' for example, conducted a public meeting on 27 January under the slogan 'For the rebirth of Russia.' Approximately 1500 people heard speeches about difficulties in the economic, social, and political life of the country. Speakers called for the creation of a Russian Communist Party, a Russian academy of sciences, and a series of other Russian organizations. Press reports claimed that 'openly nationalistic' statements were made, including criticism of the central media for 'Russophobic' practices. The meeting also called for an end to the conflict between Armenia and Azerbaijan and collected funds to aid Russian refugees from the conflict.[71]

Election Day

If local authorities were unable to eliminate unwanted candidates earlier, it was possible, of course, to cheat on election day. One complaint sent to the RSFSR CEC outlined alleged cheating by a local party organization in Smolensk. Among the alleged violations, typical of other districts across the republic, were: (1) members of the electoral commission left polling stations to avoid receiving the credentials, and thereby facing the observation, of representatives of workers' collectives; (2) people voted without proper identification; (3) people voted for family members, (4) residents of a factory dormitory were forced to vote when it appeared that a 50% turnout was threatened in one district; (5) ballot boxes were carried to apartment blocks and passers-by were asked to vote; (6) vote totals were filled out in pencil; (7) voting protocols were sent from the polls to "some sort of regional electoral commission" located in the headquarters of the Smolensk *raikom* before going to the district electoral commission.[72]

Voters in Moscow faced a complex task. They voted for regional and city deputies as well as for candidates in territorial and national-territorial districts for the CPD. Each of these districts typically had several candidates (on average, 6 for *Mossovet* alone), each of which distributed campaign literature and held meetings.[73] Information problems were acute in many areas of the RSFSR, where newspapers limited themselves to reprinting the photos and brief campaign programs produced by the local electoral commissions.[74] Because of limited media access and legal restrictions on independent campaign financing, many voters were unfamiliar with their candidates and were forced to rely on cues from the brief descriptions of the candidates on the ballot.[75] In a letter to *Izvestiia*, one citizen pointed out that voters often knew nothing about the candidates. "A voter sits at home. He comes home from work tired and angry at office quarrels. He is apathetic. Why should he go off to a meeting with a bunch of unknown candidates?"[76]

An independent survey of Moscow's voters conducted the week before the election concluded that people did not know their candidates and had little idea whom they would vote for. Reporting the results, one article noted that people had expected "a repeat of the...flood of information, posters, and leaflets that occurred in [1989]." In reality only one in seven respondents said that they had seen such materials and only one in nine was able to name even one candidate.[77] Facing such conditions, the simplest solution to the problem of whom to vote for was provided by electoral blocs. *Demrossiia* posted a list of candidates that served as an important element of its success. One Soviet political commentator drew an analogy between *Demrossia*'s list and a popular method used by students to cheat on written exams.

> In the conditions in which democrats were placed before the elections the choice of a tactic other than [crib notes] was impossible. The CEC threatened to look upon any homemade leaflets...as material aid to candidates—therefore, to hope for success similar to 1989 in a leaflet war would have been short-sighted...To help voters decide 'who is who' only one method was possible: a list, or crib notes...Democratic Russia did just this in Moscow—and won the elections.[78]

A joint declaration of the leadership of the IRDG and the Moscow Union of Voters pointed out the difficulties voters faced and offered a solution.

> Dear friends! On the 4th of March you will vote for deputies in territorial and national-territorial districts to [the RSFSR CPD] and for the Moscow and regional soviets. The old apparat made great efforts to make this choice more difficult for you. Every democratic candidate faces a few obvious or masked [puppets] of the apparat. Moreover,...visual agitation was limited in this campaign. Everything, as if by chance, is being done to guarantee that you will vote according to the meager descriptions printed on the ballot.

But there is one clear mark by which you can identify candidates who stand for decisive democratic and socioeconomic change, membership in the bloc "Democratic Russia." A list of candidates of this bloc will be published in a few days... Only by electing candidates [supported by] "Democratic Russia" will you receive deputies in the Russian, Moscow, and regional soviets, our colleagues [who share our positions]... According to data not published in the official press, more than 75% of all Muscovites support the political position of the IRDG. Thus, can we really even consider handing victory in the elections to the apparat and right-wing conservative forces?

Results: Accountable Again

In Moscow, candidates from *Demrossiia* won 63 out of 65 seats for the RSFSR CPD. In Leningrad, "democrats" won 25 out of 34 spots. *Demrossiia*'s success in Russsia's largest cities was not mirrored in the rest of the RSFSR, where the bloc's candidates won approximately one-third of the mandates. The patriotic fronts fared poorly and lost virtually every campaign that they contested with *Demrossiia* and similar groups.[79] As a whole, the social composition of the RSFSR CPD was revitalized: only 60 'workers,' and 47 kolkhoz members were registered as elected deputies as of March 27. In short, the traditional Leninist principle of demographic representation no longer functioned.

In all, 86.3% of the newly-elected deputies in the RSFSR CPD were communists. More than 75% of the *obkom* first secretaries and chairmen of executive committees of oblast or *krai* soviets won their elections.[80] This is almost certainly due more to the control that they had over the campaign than to their popularity. One should not forget, moreover, that 25% of the *obkom* secretaries lost. Clearly, competitive elections, with consequences similar to 1989, were held in some districts.[81] The new bloc electoral politics were clearly demonstrated at the local level. Democratic Russia had a striking victory in the elections in Moscow. By the beginning of May, the bloc had won approximately 65% of the seats to the Moscow City Soviet. Although *Demrossiia* succeeded in Moscow, Andrei Berëzkin, a political geographer at Moscow State University, pointed out both its failures as well as the less-trumpeted successes of other contestants. His detailed political-geographic analysis shows that in various parts of Moscow the relationship of voters to *Demrossiia* was not identical. First, candidates did not run from the bloc in all districts. In the eastern part of the city, a quarter of the districts nominated no candidates from *Demrossiia* for elections to the Moscow City Soviet. In the southwestern and central areas, typically 100% of the districts had candidates from the bloc. However, the fact that a candidate belonged to a bloc, even if the voters were informed of this, did not guarantee victory. In Zheleznodorozhnii Region, where candidates from the bloc were nominated in all nine districts, they won only in two. Berëzkin shows that the Patriotic Bloc won little electoral support from Muscovites. Only two of its candidates were elected to [the RSFSR CPD] and only three made it into *Mossovet*. The CPSU's results in the capital were ambiguous. Although more than 58% of those elected belonged to the CPSU, more than half of the deputies from Democratic Russia were also party members. Two Moscow *gorkom* secretaries were elected to *Mossovet* as was the *gorkom*'s first secretary and seven *raikom* party secretaries.[82]

The 1990 elections to the RSFSR CPD revolutionized the membership composition of the USSR's largest republican legislature. Whether these revolutionary new members and their new-born political organizations could take further steps toward political power is another question, a question covered in the following chapter.

Notes

1. A detailed study of the 1990 elections in Moscow was published by Timothy J. Colton, "The Politics of Democratization: The Moscow Election of 1990," *Soviet Economy*, Vol. 6, No. 4, 1990, pp. 285–344. A comprehensive survey of the republican elections was published in *Elections in the Baltic States and Soviet Republics: A Compendium of Reports on Parliamentary Elections Held in 1990*, compiled by the Staff of the Commission on Security and Cooperation in Europe, Washington: U.S. Government Printing Office, 1990. The electoral campaign in one Russian district is covered in-depth in V. Shchepotkin, "Put k mandatu," *Izvestiia*, 3 April 1990. A. Nazimova and RSFSR people's deputy V. Sheinis published a detailed analysis of the new deputies in the RSFSR in "Deputatskii korpus: chto novogo?," *Argumenty i fakty*, No. 17, 1990, pp. 1–2. The most detailed analysis of the Russian deputorial corpus can be found in A. Sobianin and D. Iurev, *Sezd narodnykh deputatov RSFSR v zerkale poimennykh golosovanii*, Moscow: 1991.

2. See I. Kliamkin, "Logika vlasti i logika oppozitsii: Pochemu Gorbachev soglasilsia na prezidentskuiu sistemu?," *Cherez ternii*, Moscow: Progress, 1990, p. 708.

3. The second session of the CPD passed a number of constitutional amendments to remove contradictions between federal and republican

laws. For a discussion of the electoral laws in the republics see "Edinstvo i mnogoobrazie," *Narodnyi deputat*, No. 1, 1990, pp. 61–67.

4. See *Pravda*, 22 October 1989, for an announcement concerning the Presidium's meeting and discussion of the amendments and the law on elections.

5. *Izvestiia*, 28 October 1989, p. 4.

6. For an initial schedule of the elections nationwide see *Izvestiia*, 4 December 1989.

7. Despite this distinguished board, or maybe because of it, G. I. Marchuk, chairman of the Academy, refused to allow the new organization to be officially affiliated. *Protokol Uchreditelnoi Konferentsii Kluba Izbiratelei pri AN SSSR. Listok Kluba Izbiratelei pri AN SSSR*, 12 June 1989. *Predlozheniia po osnovnym napravleniiam raboty kluba izbiratelei AN SSSR.*

8. *O polnomochiiakh nekotorykh klubov i ob"edinenii izbiratelei, a takzhe dobrovolnykh obshchestv v voprosakh vydvizheniia kandidatov v narodnye deputaty. V Moskovskuiu gorodskiiu izbiratelnuiu komissiiu po vyboram narodnykh deputatov Moskovskogo gorodskogo Soveta narodnykh deputatov RSFSR.*

9. E. Kovalev, "Pobediat izbirateli ili pobediat izbiratelei?," *Za narodovlastie!*, No. 1, September 1989, pp. 2–3.

10. *Pravda*, 6 December 1989, p. 2. For an example in Saratov, see 'Sblizhaet doverie,' *Pravda*, 30 December 1989.

11. *Sluzhba ezhednevnykh novostei BIO. Vybory-90*. 14 December 1989. On this point see also "Udushiaiushchie obiatiia," *Za Narodovlastie*, Yaroslavl, No. 4, 1989.

12. "V dobryi put" and "Ustav kluba Rossiia," *Rossiia, Izdanie izbiratelei i narodnykh deputatov kluba Rossiia*, No. 1, November 1989, p. 1.

13. S. Stankevich and M. Shneider, *Rekomendatsii po taktike kandidatov demokraticheskogo bloka i ikh komand v izbiratelnoi kampanii 1989-90 g. g.*, Moscow: Informtsentr Moskovskogo Narodnogo Fronta.

14. Ibid. Interview with M. Shneidr, May 1990.

15. For a discussion of the birth of MUV see an interview with V. Bokser by A. Popov, "Stolitsa pered vyborom," *Moskovskii Komsomolets*, 27 January 1990.

16. V. Bokser, *Argumenty i fakty*, No. 50, December 1989.

17. *Informatsionno-analiticheskii material. O nekotorykh tendentsiiakh v samodeiatelnom obshchestvenno-politicheskom dvizhenii*, pp. 10–11, Moscow: Moscow City Soviet, 1990.

18. *Ustav Moskovskogo obedineniia izbiratelei.*

19. Colton, "The Politics of Democratization...," pp. 285–344.

20. *Rossiia. Izdanie izbiratelei i narodnykh deputatov SSSR kluba 'Rossia,'* No. 3, January 1990, p. 1. See also *Literaturnaia Rossiia*, 29

December 1989 and *Sovetskaia Rossiia*, 30 December 1989. "Za narodnoe soglasie i rossiiskoe vozrozhdenie. Predvybornaia programma Bloka obshchestvenno-politicheskikh dvizhenii Rossii," *Rossiia. Izdanie izbiratelei i narodnykh deputatov SSSR kluba 'Rossiia'*.

21. "Obrashchenie khristiansko-patrioticheskogo soiuza k izbirateliam" and "Predvybornye predlozheniia khrsitianskogo-patrioticheskogo soiuza," *Demokrat*, No. 12, 1989, pp. 16–19.

22. Form letter from A.A. Sobianin, "Po porucheniio shtaba Vybory-90," undated.

23. V. Pribylovskii, "Vybory-90," undated leaflet. 24. "Dos'e 'Vybory-90' Izbiratelnyi blok Demokraticheskaia Rossiia." *Vybory-90: Khronika izbiratelnoi kampanii*, Vypusk 6, pp. 4–5. *Sozdan blok demokraticheskikh kandidatov Rossii!* undated leaflet.

25. "Dos'e Vybory-90. Izbiratelnyi blok Demokraticheskaia Rossiia." *Vybory-90. Khronika Izbiratelnoi Kampanii*. Vypusk 6, p. 4. See also *Argumenty i fakty*, No. 8, 1990, p. 7 for an interview of Deputy N. Travkin concerning the birth of the bloc.

26. *Pozitsiia*, No. 3, February 1990, pp. 2–3.

27. "Vystuplenie M.S. Gorbachev pered uchastnikami plenuma Leningradskogo obkoma KPSS," *Ekonomicheskaia gazeta*, No. 29, 1989, pp. 1–2.

28. *Izvestiia*, 10 October 1989, p. 2.

29. *Pravda*, 19 November 1990, p. 1. Further advice was distributed to party committees and published later in "O khode izbiratelnoi kampanii v RSFSR po vyboram narodnykh deputatov v respublikanskie i mestnye sovety," *Izvestiia TsK KPSS*, February 1990, p. 20.

30. A. Danilov discusses Prokofev's career in, "Politicheskii portret v personalnom kabinete," *Pozitsiia*, No. 5, 1990, pp. 7–8. See also an interview with Prokofev, "Reforming the Party," *Moscow News*, No. 36, 1989, p. 5. Inside sources reported that Prokofev assigned a team of sociologists and political scientists to identify an electoral district where he stood a good chance of winning.

31. *Plan meropriiatii MGK KPSS po podgotovke k vyboram v mestnye Sovety narodnykh deputatov.*

32. *Moskovskaia pravda*, 25 November 1989, p. 1. Moscow, of course, was not alone in its preparations. In the city of Tiumen in early December, the CPSU *obkom* conducted a meeting of local party and soviet officials 'to work out united tactics.' *Izvestiia*, 3 December 1989, p. 3. For an interesting summary of the work of the Volgograd obkom during the elections see "Uchit'sia vzaimodeistviiu," *Izvestiia TsK KPSS*, No. 12, 1990, pp. 68–70.

33. See *Pravda*, 21 December 1989. Colton discusses the platform and its problems in "The Politics of Democratization..." The platforms of several party organizations were published in "Vybory v sovety: platformy

partiinykh komitetov," *Izvestiia TsK KPSS*, January 1990. pp. 75-87. For more platforms see also "Soviet local election platforms," *FBIS Trends*, 4 January 1990, pp. 7-16.

34. *Pravda*, 26 January 1990.

35. The course is described by N. Mikhaleva and L. Morozova in "Pobedil tot, kto luchshe gotovilsia," *Narodnyi Deputat*, No. 7, 1990, pp. 34-41. The handbook for the games, written by N.V. Borisova, V.I. Naumov, and Iu.V. Puzdrach, was *Izbiratelnaia Kampaniia: Vydvizhenie, Agitatsiia, Vybory (Delovye igry)*, Moscow: Moscow Higher Party School, 1990.

36. This program is mentioned in *Informatsiia o proshedshikh vstrechakh kandidatov v narodnye deputaty s izbirateliami g. Moskvy (po sostoianiiu na 7/02/90), No. 2, Otdel po rabote sovetov Mosgorispolkoma*, Moscow, 7 February 1990, p. 2.

37. *Metodicheskii material, Vozmozhnye deistviia kandidatov v narodnye deputaty po organizatsii i provedeniiu izbiratelnoi kampanii, MGK KPSS*.

38. *Informatsionno-analiticheskii material, O nekotorykh tendentsiiakh v samodeiatelnom obshchestvenno-politicheskom dvizhenii*, p. 13.

39. "Platforma Pervomaiskoi raionnoi organizatsii KPSS na vyborakh v Sovety narodnykh deputatov," *Izmailovskii Vestnik. Informatsionno reklamnoe izdanie Pervomaiskogo raikoma KPSS goroda Moskvy, raionnogo Soveta, Spetsialnyi vypusk*, 1990. This phenomenon demands closer attention in view of the abstract quality of the *gorkom*'s program. Perhaps the task of filling-out the skeletal program was left to local organizations?

40. *Dzerzhinskii RK KPSS: Rekomendatsii po perestroike raboty partiinykh organizatsii s naseleniem v period podgotovki k vyboram v mestnye Sovety narodnykh deputatov RSFSR*.

41. For an interview with Briachikhin see *Moskovskaia Pravda*, 2 December 1989, p. 2.

42. There is evidence from some districts that politically active citizens were hounded in the courts. See *Pravo golosa: Organ ob"edineniia izbiratelei proletarskogo raiona*, No. 6, February 1990, for a description of how electoral observers were charged, tried, and absolved in Moscow's Proletarskii Electoral District.

43. *Izvestiia*, 11 November 1989. For a review of the RSFSR CEC's dispute resolution process see "Chto takoe Tsentrizbirkom i ego konfliktnaia komissiia," *Vybory-90: Khronika izbiratelnoi kampanii, Vypusk 6*, p. 6. A. Ivanchenko, a consultant to the Presidium of the USSR Supreme Soviet offers some interesting thoughts on the commissions in "Izbiratelnaia kampaniia—Uroki na zavtra," *Kommunist*, No. 11, 1990, pp. 83-93.

44. *O podgotovke k vyboram 4 Marta 1990 goda*, undated memo.

45. "Bespretsedentnyi sluchai," *Put,* 25 February 1990, p. 6. *Sevastopolskie pretsedenty,* undated leaflet. For a description of pressure placed on one commission and its subsequent resignation in Ukraine see "Izbiratelnaia komissiia podaet v otstavku," *Izvestiia,* 7 April 1990.

46. The Central Electoral Commission decided to send instructions to the local commissions on how to interpret the law in a way that would emphasize "the observation of democratic norms and principles, openness, and glasnost." *Izvestiia,* 25 November 1989.

47. "Moskva: Za nedeliu do vyborov," *Vybory-90: Khronika izbiratelnoi kampanii, Vypusk 9,* p. 6.

48. *Izvestiia,* 18 January 1990. For the views of another chairman see a letter in *Ivzestiia,* 17 January 1990.

49. See, for example, "V ravnykh li usloviakh?," *Izvestiia,* 2 January 1990.

50. See *Predlozheniia po narezke izbiratelnykh okrugov v Moskve. Geograficheskii fakultet MGU. Institut Geografii AN SSSR.*

51. *Otchet po nauchno-issledovatelskoi teme: "Izuchenie territorialnykh faktorov organizatsii i provedenie vyborov narodnykh deputatov po g. Moskve, Moskovskii gosudarstvennyi universitet, Geograficheskii fakultet,* pp. 26–27.

52. *Sluzhba ezhenedelnykh novostei BIO, Vybory-90,* 14 December 1989.

53. *Izvestiia,* 14 January 1990. For an account of difficulties in neighborhood caucuses see *Pravda,* 11 January 1990.

54. *Elections in the Baltic States and Soviet Republics...*

55. V. Pribylovskii, *Golosovanie po shpargalke,* undated leaflet.

56. Ibid.

57. On this point see S. Shakrai "A delo u nas odno: Rossiia," *Izvestiia,* 13 May 1990. That the average number of candidates in autonomous regions was much lower than elsewhere see "O khode izbiratelnoi kampanii v RSFSR po vyboram narodnykh deputatov v respublikanskie i mestnye sovety," *Izvestiia TsK KPSS,* February 1990, p. 20. For a statistical analysis of this question see V. Vorontsov, "Kto i ch'i interesy budet predstavliat v palate natsionalnostei Rossii," *Argumenty i fakty,* No. 21, 1990, p. 4.

58. *Pravda,* 13 January 1990.

59. Colton, "The Politics of Democratization...," p. 294.

60. *Informatsiia o proshedshikh vstrechakh kandidatov v narodnye deputaty s izbirateliami g. Moskvy (po sostoianiiu na 2/02/90), Otdel po rabote sovetov Mosgorispolkoma,* Moscow, 2 February 1990, p. 1.

61. *Informatsiia o proshedshikh vstrechakh kandidatov v narodnye deputaty s izbirateliami g. Moskvy (po sostoianiiu na 12/02/90), No. 3, Otdel po rabote sovetov Mosgorispolkoma,* Moscow, 13 February 1990, p. 1.

62. Colton, "The Politics of Democratization..."

63. V. Bokser, "Stolitsa pered vyborom," *Moskovskii Komsomelets*, 27 January 1990, See also A. Ivanchenko, "Izbiratelnaia kampaniia—Uroki na zavtra." *Kommunist*, No. 11, 1990, p. 91. *Klub izbiratelei Timiriazevskogo raiona, Pamiatka dlia raboty na stadii vydvizheniia kandidatov v deputaty mestnykh sovetov*, leaflet, 1990.

64. Interview of Valerii Kaganov, team leader for A. Tarasov, July 1990, Moscow.

65. For an overview of the resources that were at the disposal of the apparat in Iaroslavl see "Put k mandatu,' *Izvestiia*, 3 April 1990.

66. *Izvestiia*, 6 April 1990.

67. Ibid., 1 February 1990.

68. Ibid., 10 February 1990.

69. Ibid., 7 February 1990. See also *Izvestiia*, 23 January 1990.

70. Interview with Valerii Kaganov.

71. *Vybory-90: Khronika izbiratelnoi kampanii, Vypusk 9*, p. 1.

72. *Zaiavlenie v Tsentralnuiu izbiratelnuiu kommissiiu po vyboram narodnykh deputatov RSFSR, Doverennye litsa kandidata v narodnye deputaty Borokhova, Ermolaev, Kosenkov, Manoim*.

73. After casting his ballot on March 5th, Gorbachev spoke with the press. Through an endorsement of the politically protean concept of perestroika, he highlighted the problem behind the 1990 election: it was often impossible to tell what the candidates stood for. See *Pravda*, 5 March 1990, p. 1.

74. *Elections in the Baltic States and Soviet Republics...*, p. 2.

75. Ibid.

76. *Izvestiia*, 12 February 1990.

77. "Moskva: Za nedeliu do vyborov," *Vybory-90: Khronika izbiratelnoi kampanii, Vypusk 9*, p. 2.

78. V. Pribylovskii, *Golosovanie po shpargalke*, undated leaflet.

79. For the views of one leading member of the bloc on the reasons for the loss see "Chem nedovelen V. Skripko?," *Narodnyi Deputat*, No. 7, 1990, pp. 54–56.

80. *Sovetskaia Rossiia*, 17 May 1990.

81. *Elections in the Baltic States and Soviet Republics...*, p. 2.

82. A. Berëzkin, "Moskovskie vybory glazami geografa," *Moskovskii Universitet*, 4 May 1990, p. 14. For an interview with a *raikom* first secretary who lost see L. Staroselskii, "Otkazatsia ot dogm i stereotipov," *Izmailovskii Vestnik*, No. 5, 1990, p. 3.

Chapter 10

Politics in the RSFSR CPD

After the first sessions of the new USSR Supreme Soviet and CPD and the 1990 elections, the political spotlight turned to the first sessions of new republican legislatures. Disenchanted with federal institutions, many politicians decided to try and make a difference at the republican level. The new republican Supreme Soviets started a process that became known as 'the war of the parliaments.' By declaring sovereignty and refusing to enforce federal law, the republics challenged Moscow's rights to dictate policy. As early as March 1990, the Lithuanian parliament voted 124–0 to restore independent statehood. In June, the Moldovan parliament approved a declaration of republican sovereignty and asserted that its decisions superceded federal law. This process led eventually to the disintegration of the Soviet Union and the birth of the Commonwealth of Independent States.

This chapter examines the birth of politics in the RSFSR Congress of People's Deputies. Although attention is primarily given to the appearance and influence of deputorial blocs, a summary of activity in the CPD and Supreme Soviet covers the development of Russian politics up until the August 1991 coup.[1]

Preparing the Congress

Preparations for the first session of the RSFSR CPD were controlled by the apparat of the Presidium of the RSFSR Supreme Soviet and ultimately, of course, by the CPSU's Politburo.[2] In a manner similar to the procedures used for the first session of the USSR CPD, apparatchiki orchestrated the preparations while attempting to give the appearance of deputorial participation. A new twist on this theme was the creation by the apparat of a 93-member deputorial preparatory commission.

Shortly before the session opened in May 1990, RSFSR Deputy Sergei Shakrai, a member of the preparatory commission, argued that it was still unclear whether the CPD would become a tool of the apparat or a working institution. "[We] received a vivid lesson about 'who is who' during the work of the preparatory commission...The apparat used a strict system of filters. Documents prepared by the deputies were filtered and the deputies themselves were filtered."[3] Shakrai maintained that the apparat used this system to eliminate a proposal to gather all the deputies before the start of the session to elect a legitimate deputorial organizational committee. The apparat also defeated a proposal to expand the membership of the original preparatory commission. Moreover, in order to head off any attempt by the deputies to organize independently, the apparat, despite "repeated requests and then demands," refused to hand over a list of the newly-elected deputies with their telephone numbers. "[They decided that] until the final stage the deputies should know nothing." Shakrai argued that the reason for these backstage manipulations was clear. "In all these variants the filtering and directing role of the apparat would have been set aside."[4]

Blocs

Democratic Russia. On 31 March 1990 in Moscow, RSFSR deputies who shared the Democratic Russia platform in the 1990 elections assembled for the first time in an effort to overcome the apparat's interference and to prepare for the congressional session.[5] More than 200 deputies representing 40 oblasts, 9 autonomous republics, and 6 other territorial subdivisions of the Russian Federation participated. A survey of participants suggested that no less than 350 RSFSR people's deputies (out of the 1,008 registered at the time) supported the Democratic Russia movement. Participants in the March Democratic Russia conference announced the formation of a parliamentary bloc and agreed that the platform published in *Ogonēk* for *Demrossiia*'s electoral campaign would serve as the basis for its program.[6] Seven working groups were created to prepare materials for the session, and a temporary group was formed to manage the bloc's organizational affairs. At a press conference, a spokesman stressed that the bloc would have an open-door policy: "Democratic Russia is not a party, it is an association of RSFSR people's deputies [created for] joint work in parliament."[7] Despite general agreement over the need for unity, the bloc was by no means a political monolith: Nikolai Travkin found only 63 colleagues to sign his somewhat provocative draft of a call to voters to rally around the bloc.[8]

On 14 April 1990, *Demrossiia* held a second preparatory meeting. More than 200 deputies from across the Federation discussed the bloc's candidate for Chairman of the RSFSR Supreme Soviet. No one was surprised when that nominee turned out to be Boris Yeltsin, the most popular politician by far in all of Russia becuase of his opposition to the party apparat. Nikolai Travkin, Mikhail Bocharov, and Nikolai Vorontsov declined nomination, but Travkin and Vorontsov reserved the right to compete with Yeltsin if direct presidential elections eventually were held. Other questions discussed at the conference included the agenda for the CPD, a decree on power, and the persecution faced by some Communist members of the bloc from local party organizations.[9]

Communists of Russia. The bloc 'Communists of Russia,' at first composed primarily of conservative members of the party apparat, was a second group that participated in the work of the first session of the RSFSR CPD. A group of 61 Communist deputies—opponents of the bloc—prepared an announcement that pointed out its connections to the CPSU Central Committee.

> During the course of the first session... the CPSU Central Committee apparat conducted regular meetings with Communist People's Deputies of the RSFSR, to which they invited only Communists from the group 'Communists of Russia.' As we know, a minority of the Communists participating in the session, 216 out of 917, [belong to] this group. We, Communist People's Deputies, protest against such a selective principle... We demand an end to this depraved practice, which violates the rights of the main mass of Communist deputies... We call for publication in the party press of the content of [these] meetings.[10]

Although it is unclear exactly when the bloc was formed, it is unlikely that it took part in the preparations for the CPD. The Communists of Russia bloc, as a creature of the apparat, was almost certainly obliged to pursue the goals defined by the party elite. Deputy G.S. Bondarev, a representative of a rival bloc of Communist deputies, the Democratic Platform in the CPSU, declared his group's objections to the behavior of the Communists of Russia. "They are behaving destructively... We think that comrades from the apparat of the Central Committee who conducted separate meetings with deputies from this group played a role [in encouraging such activity.]"[11]

The First Session of the RSFSR CPD

The RSFSR Congress of People's Deputies convened for the first time on 16 May 1990. The chairman of the RSFSR's Central Electoral Commission, V.I. Kazakov, conducted the meeting until the election of the chairman of the Supreme Soviet.[12] *Izvestiia* noted that Kazakov "seized power and...tried to move the CPD in a [conservative direction]." Suggesting that Kazakov was working for the party apparat, one correspondent listed several problems with his conduct: ignoring proposals from the floor; unjustified attempts to speed the discussion; reading telegrams on his own initiative from anonymous 'workers' collectives' to the CPD with angry denunciations of 'demagogues' (i.e. *Demrossiia*); and, cutting short discussion that was necessary to resolve basic principles but that was unprofitable for the apparat. Kazakov's behavior, the correspondent argued, hastened the political maturation of deputies: "Hundreds of people who did not know one another coalesced and decided that questions of principle would be decided by their own will."[13]

The first confrontation between Democratic Russia and the apparat, a debate on the agenda, took up the entire first day of the session. According to the agenda proposed by the Presidium and the Assembly of Representatives (another filter), the third point (after the report of the mandate commission and ratification of temporary standing rules) was election of the chairman of the RSFSR Supreme Soviet. That is, the apparat wanted to elect the chairman first, without any potentially controversial preliminary discussion that might hurt the chances of their candidate. Democratic Russia wanted to hear from the RSFSR Council of Ministers *before* the vote in order to help convince fence-sitters of the need for change by voting for Yeltsin.[14] Despite Kazakov's efforts to prevent a vote on this question, *Demrossiia* convinced enough deputies to earn a majority. *Demrossiia* also advocated including the sovereignty of Russia as the fourth point on the agenda instead of saving it for the end of the session. Voting on this question produced a record consensus: 1,004 deputies voted for the proposal, one against, and four abstained.

Victory in the agenda debate was the first triumph for *Demrossiia*, a triumph that was noted by the apparat, which opened the session's second day with an attempt to discredit the bloc. Deputy V.I. Berestovoi, the second secretary of the Belgorod oblast party committee, took the floor and argued that the first day of the session showed that 80–90% of the speakers had been from *Demrossiia*. "We," he declared, "are talking about an attempt by *Demrossiia* to seize power."

Electing the Chairman of the Supreme Soviet. On 25 May the RSFSR CPD turned to nominations for the chairman of its Supreme Soviet. Thirteen candidates were nominated, including I.K. Polozkov, at that time first secretary of the Krasnodar *obkom* and later first secretary of the Russian Communist Party, and V.I. Morokin, a professor at an aviation institute in Kazan. The first person nominated was Boris Yeltsin.

Three candidates were placed on the first ballot, Yeltsin, Polozkov, and Morokin. Each outlined his program to the deputies. Yeltsin's speech should be viewed as the continuation of remarks he made about Russian sovereignty when he first addressed the Congress on 22 May. This address, in essence, contained an alternative program to that which was presented to the CPD on 21 May by Politburo member Vorotnikov, for whom Russian sovereignty meant little more than a widening of existing republican rights, not qualitative change in the relations between the RSFSR and the USSR. Yeltsin argued that the sovereignty of the RSFSR demanded qualitative changes in its constitution and its relationship with the USSR. His vision of a Russian Republic consisted of a sovereign, democratic, law-based state voluntarily uniting national groups with equal rights. All political power in the RSFSR would belong to the people, who would exercise it through the soviets. Relations with other republics and the USSR would be regulated by separate treaties. Yeltsin emphasized that Russia should think about what functions to give 'the center' and which to reserve to itself. Within the RSFSR, relations between subjects of the federation would be regulated by a treaty guaranteeing sovereignty, economic independence, autonomy, cultural and national integrity, and just and equal representation in all federal institutions. The constitution of the Republic should guarantee political pluralism, a multi-party, democratic system with strict divisions between executive, legislative, and judicial powers. The Republic's economic rights, he claimed, could only be guaranteed by creating republican property and implementing an independent foreign trade and currency program. A republican bank with the right to print money should be separate from the all-union bank and subordinate to the Russian parliament. The RSFSR constitution should protect all forms of property.[15]

In his nomination speech, Yeltsin spoke briefly and sharply. He argued that Russia needed bold and forward-looking policy, and proposed a metaphor: he did not want to break the old system down but planned to construct next to it a new building. He rejected the CPSU's monopoly on power and proposed empowering the people through genuinely revitalized soviets. A market system, he argued, would make the command economy obsolete. He claimed that a series of laws should be passed immediately: a new constitution, a law on the sovereignty of Russia, a law on the sovereignty of the autonomous republics, a law on the economic independence of oblasts, and a law on the judicial system. He proposed direct elections of an RSFSR president no later than May 1991. Next, Yeltsin dealt with his own complex personality and attempted to convince deputies that he would be able to compromise, to listen to various points of view. He assured his colleagues that he would work in a businesslike manner with Gorbachev and the federal government—but without hurting Russia's interests.[16]

Polozkov's nomination speech supported the *status quo*. He argued that the government had everything it needed to take control of the situation, stabilize the economy, improve the political and spiritual atmosphere in 'our Russian home' and move ahead along a socialist path, which he suggested was the 'historic ideal of the Russian people.' He argued that there should be no divisions between the Union and the RSFSR, which would lead to a geopolitical catastrophe.

The nomination speeches were only one element of a complex political game. Gorbachev's political and personal rivalry with Yeltsin intensified during the session. In fact, Gorbachev's inability to desist from attacking may have been one reason why Yeltsin was elected chairman of the RSFSR Supreme Soviet. The morning after Yeltsin spoke on Russian sovereignty, Gorbachev found an excuse to address the CPD, claiming that he had arrived "at the request of deputies." He called for the Congress to think carefully before accepting the arguments of 'certain forces,' i.e. *Demrossiia* and Yeltsin, who, he alleged, claimed to be able to solve all problems quickly. Gorbachev called for the deputies to be faithful to perestroika, to "the choice made in 1917," and to democratic socialism. After these general remarks, he asked the deputies if they wanted to hear his opinion on Yeltsin's speech. Without waiting for a clear answer, he forged on. First, he suggested that Yeltsin was over-ambitious and power hungry. Next, he accused him of attempting to separate Russia and socialism and reproached him for not mentioning socialism even once during his speech. Yeltsin's remarks, he claimed, were a rejection of socialism and "soviet power." He accused Yeltsin of a confrontational approach to the question of sovereignty. Yeltsin and *Demrossiia*, he argued, were calling the people to unite under the banner of a sovereign Russia, and this would lead to the destruction of the Union.[17]

Gorbachev's address elicited a flood of reactions, both positive and negative. Deputy N.V. Bogaenko, a worker from Novosibirsk, rose to defend Yeltsin. He noted sarcastically that "Gorbachev, again 'by invitation',...gave an emotional 45-minute speech, and I think that he significantly influenced the opinion of the deputies." The moderator, a creature of the apparat, interrupted Bogaenko three times and finally asked him to return to his seat. Shouts from Gorbachev's supporters included, "Outrageous! Slandering the president!!"[18] In a pointed reply to Gorbachev, Deputy G.V. Starovoitova defended Yeltsin's rejection of socialism. She noted that deciding Russia's fate demanded principled discussion and asked, "Are we prepared to continue the prolonged experiment on ourselves, our children and millions of our fellow citizens?"[19] "Today, the center of political life of the country is actually moving...out of the Supreme Soviet and away from the [CPD] to the republican parliaments." She pointed out that, for the first time, 'Russia' and 'the center' could not be considered as one. The federal Supreme Soviet and CPD, she argued, were no longer capable of leading the country, and new elections should be held to close the gap between the people and their representative institutions.[20] Deputy F.G. Gosporian reminded the deputies of Gorbachev's contention that "certain forces" were trying to seize power. "The thought is correct, but let us look whether the accents here are placed correctly. Power today is given to us, people's deputies. The forces that want to seize power from us [are in] the anonymous administrative-command system which is approaching the end of its life stubbornly, but holding on to its power and privileges."[21] Deputy S.A. Kovalev took Gorbachev to task by suggesting that he had spent too much time listening to the advice of analysts from the KGB.[22] Deputy O.M. Poptsov argued that it had become stylish to talk about "certain forces struggling for power" and that "images of these people with teeth bared seeking power are unattractive" but that it was just as unattractive to see "people who had already sunk their teeth into power and were unwilling to give it up."[23]

Arguments against Yeltsin followed two lines, 'Yeltsin as destroyer of the union' and 'Yeltsin as dictator.' Deputy I.S. Savchenko contended that the election of the chairman of the RSFSR Supreme Soviet would determine Russia's path, either into the union or out, and that Yeltsin stood for disintegration of the USSR. Deputy Iu.K. Karanets pointed out that if one sat and read the telegrams that had been sent to the congress it was clear that some people wanted a boss, a prophet, or a messiah and saw Yeltsin in this role. Karanets said that he feared such people and argued that Russia needed a calm leader who would not tell people how to live but would give them freedom to create.[24]

The first round of elections ended without a winner: 1,034 deputies voted; Yeltsin received 497 votes for, 535 against; Polozkov 473 for and 559 against; Morokin 32 for and 1,000 against. The results were announced at the morning session on 26 May. A second round was held between Yeltsin and Polozkov, but neither earned enough votes to be elected: Yeltsin, 503 for, 529 against, Polozkov 458 for, against 574.

Immediately after the results of the first round were clear, representatives of the apparat proposed that Yeltsin and Polozkov should decline second nominations. Deputy A.A. Chernyshev, second secretary of the Orenburg obkom, reminded Yeltsin that he had spoken about consolidation and that "now is the moment to show the sincerity of your statement" by rejecting a second nomination.²⁵ The apparat also tried to change the standing rules in order to eliminate Yeltsin's chances. Yeltsin argued that the CPD should continue according to its old rules and declared that if he was nominated again he would attempt to form a coalition with representatives of all the principal groups of deputies.

Repeat nominations included Yeltsin, Vlasov, Polozkov, and seven others, including a self-nomination by S.S. Peruanskii, who later played a key tactical role: he renounced his candidacy at the last minute in favor of Yeltsin. The bloc conflict sharpened during this second round of elections. Deputy M.G. Arutiunov pointed out some of the consequences.

> One bloc wants Yeltsin and is supported by the majority of the population. The second bloc could be called the party bureaucratic apparat. They do not have a clear leader. They propose many different candidates. This shows that they are prepared to accept anyone just to block Yeltsin. The proposal that the candidates should decline nominations was another attempt to block Yeltsin. What will we get from a representative of the second bloc? Violation of the laws similar to their attempts to change the standing rules to block Yeltsin. The apparat considers us a herd of cattle that can be led where it wants.²⁶

The ballot for this round on 29 May included Yeltsin, Vlasov, and Tsoi. 1038 ballots were cast. Yeltsin received 535 votes for, 502 against; Vlasov, 467 for, 570 against; Tsoi, 11 for, 1026 against.²⁷ In all, Yeltsin was elected by a margin of 4 votes.

After the results were announced, Yeltsin addressed the deputies. He confirmed that "for the sake of the future unity of the Supreme Soviet, national harmony of RSFSR deputies and the whole CPD," the formation of the Supreme Soviet and the government would be "conducted only on the basis of consultation with registered deputy groups after consulting and accounting for their proposals."²⁸ Yeltsin's first act as chairman was to create a compromise committee consisting of five deputies from each of the 27 registered groups plus one representative from each of the autonomous republics, oblasts, and okrugs. To end discussion of the possibility that he would favor *Demrossiia*, Yeltsin declared that he had suspended his membership in the bloc and would defend "the interests not of separate groups or parties or organizations but the interests of the peoples of the Russian Federation." "This means," he emphasized, "that I no longer am a member of *Demrossiia* and therefore am not its prisoner."²⁹

Electing Yeltsins's Deputies and the Supreme Soviet. The battle between *Demrossiia* and the Communists of Russia next raged over the election of vice-chairmen of the RSFSR Supreme Soviet. As Yeltsin promised, he gave up his prerogative as Chairman of the Supreme Soviet and allowed the compromise committee to select candidates. Nominees for vice-chairmen were presented to the CPD for discussion on May 30. Four candidates were proposed for first deputy chairman and for the three second deputy chairmen, three candidates each. All four candidates for first deputy were representatives of the Communists of Russia. Three women, representatives of *Demrossiia*, were nominated for one of the second secretary spots. The other two posts received a mixture of nominees, apparently reflecting a decision to compete. Deputy Sergei Shakrai, for example, was nominated by *Demrossiia* for one post and B.M. Isaev, chairman of the Cheliabinsk oblast soviet, almost certainly a candidate from the Communists of Russia, was nominated for the other post.[30]

The first round of voting elected one of the three second deputies, Isaev, but failed to fill the other positions. *Demrossiia* argued that the Communists of Russia, despite the existence of the compromise committee, was acting to block the elections. A second tour of voting produced one more winner, a woman, S.P. Goriacheva. She claimed to belong to no bloc and was included on the ballot only after one candidate dropped out of the race.[31] Attempting to resolve the impasse, Yeltsin nominated one candidate for each of the two remaining posts. For first deputy chairman, he nominated R.I. Khasbulatov, and for the remaining second deputy position he nominated, once again, Sergei Shakrai. Neither candidate was able to get the required number of votes. Yeltsin proposed appointing them as temporary deputies and returning to the question at the end of the session. After a great deal of discussion, Yeltsin nominated Khasbulatov again and postponed the question of Shakrai's candidacy until the end of the session. Khasbulatov was elected.[32] Shakrai was not elected even at the end of the session. The post remained empty.

A debate over the procedure for forming the Supreme Soviet also was fought along bloc lies. *Demrossiia* proposed rejecting the constitutional equality of the Supreme Soviet's two chambers. Deputy V.L. Sheinis outlined *Demrossiia*'s position on 5 June. The Supreme Soviet, he argued, should reflect the political composition of the CPD. While allowing for regional representation, he claimed, it would be possible to defend the interests of deputorial blocs by increasing the number of deputies in the Supreme Soviet. Such an approach would guarantee the right of minorities in regional groups. Sheinis was thinking, of course, of representatives of *Demrossiia* elected in the depths of Russia. He proposed that instead of two equal chambers of 126 deputies, the Soviet of Nationalities should remain at 126 while the Soviet of the Republic was increased to 450. Arguing that the apparat wanted to portray the proposed changes as a conflict between *Dem-*

rossiia and the autonomous regions, Sheinis declared that "the CPD must make a responsible and difficult choice. Either it will subordinate itself to the scenario that was written for it... or it will demonstrate its own political will and create a Supreme Soviet capable of becoming a real parliament."[33] After further discussion, the constitutional variant of the formation of the Supreme Soviet was retained.

The inter-bloc struggle continued during the election of the Supreme Soviet. Just before the first ballot, Deputy V. P. Rasskazov reported that the Communists of Russia had, "in one night, analyzed the list of deputies included on the ballot and created special separate lists for both chambers to identify deputies that should be voted for and deputies that should be voted against." Rasskazov pointed out that this was especially crucial for the Moscow and Leningrad delegations, which had many candidates on the ballot. He demanded that the lists be published.[34]

The results of the first round of elections to the Supreme Soviet suggested that the lists circulated by the Communists of Russia had an effect. In elections to the Soviet of the Republic, out of 25 candidates from Moscow and 14 from Leningrad, none got the required number of votes. Among these 39 candidates were some of the most well-known representatives of *Demrossiia*, including V.F. Komchatov, N.I. Travkin, and V.L. Sheinis. Not one of the eight representatives of Kemerovo oblast, located in the strike-torn region of the Kuzbass, and therefore seen as strong supporters of Yeltsin and *Demrossiia*, was elected. In the Soviet of the Republic as a whole, out of 126 places only 81 deputies were elected. Representatives of *Demrossiia* had better luck, however, in the Soviet of Nationalities, where 121 deputies were elected in the first round. Both Father Gleb Iakunin and L.A. Ponomarev, well-known members of the bloc, received seats.[35]

Democratic Russia reacted promptly to its troubles in the first round of elections to the Supreme Soviet: it requested a one hour recess for consultation. When the Congress refused this request, the bloc asked for a break until the next day, which also was voted down. The bloc's third proposal was sharp and clear: it announced that it would not participate in a ballot to ratify the voting protocols for the Soviet of the Republic if it was not given the opportunity to meet. An extended debate raged over this question. Deputy N.I. Travkin, a representative of *Demrossiia*, made a proposal that, apparently, broke the tension.

> Normal democracy in a normal parliament [functions] when the amount of ambition is equal to the number of mandates. We have a situation where the democrats have a great deal of ambition but few mandates. I understand that it is unpleasant that we lost. It might have been better if we had [voted against] all

representatives of the Communists of Russia and then we would have been the only ones left. This did not happen... Moreover, if we crossed out names from the bloc Communists of Russia by one hand then, at the same time we, democrats, with the other hand crossed out one another... I am convinced that it is necessary to move forward... A normal battle of factions is taking place in parliament... We, *Demrossiia*, were unable to organize, we are amorphous and therefore cannot stand up to [a smaller group]. If we think that we should conduct a parliamentary battle in the future, then it is necessary to introduce party fractions. I myself will found a fraction during the break.[36]

After this discussion, nominations were reopened. To avoid obstruction by the Communists of Russia, the Moscow delegation nominated eight candidates for eight places, all representatives of *Demrossiia*. Six of the candidates had been nominated in the first round and two new names were added. Out of the eight, however, only three were elected, the two new nominees and one of the old. The minority of the Moscow delegation, i.e. representatives of the Communists of Russia, presented their own five nominees. Three of these candidates were elected.

The difficulties that the CPD faced electing the Supreme Soviet eventually led to a joint agreement between the factions. Deputy G.V. Saenko, second secretary of the Kursk CPSU obkom and a representative of the Communists of Russia, read to the Congress the text of a joint statement by the coordinating councils of his bloc and *Demrossiia*:

> We affirm a preliminary agreement concerning the joint support of all candidacies nominated to the Supreme Soviet by deputy groups on a non-alternative basis in correspondence to the quotas established for given territories. We ask the CPD to support the candidacies from Moscow, Leningrad, Murmansk, Rostov and Kemerovo oblasts nominated by the overwhelming majority of the deputy groups of the corresponding territories. In cases where the deputy groups... nominated alternative candidacies, we rely on the will of the Congress.[37]

Even given this understanding, after the next round vacancies remained, which clearly displeased *Demrossiia*. Deputy S.A. Filatov made an announcement in the name of the CPD's coordinating council.

> After the first round of voting for the RSFSR Supreme Soviet, the Congress expressed a desire to support in the second round deputies nominated on a non-alternative basis by deputy

territorial groups. Understanding the complexity of the situation, the coordinating councils of *Demrossiia* and the Communists of Russia, in a joint announcement, summoned the members of their groups and all people's deputies to support this proposal. The results of the second round showed, however, that the agreement was not kept. This eliminated the possibility of necessary consolidation... Deputies... who made the biggest contribution to the preparation of documents defining the effectiveness of the first stage of the Congress and who are prepared to work professionally in the Supreme Soviet were not elected. ... The bloc *Demrossiia* summons people's deputies of the RSFSR to keep the agreement reached earlier and, for the sake of consolidation, to support the deputies nominated by territorial deputies' groups.

Filatov then nominated Rumiantsev and Medvedev for the third time.[38] Deputies from Communists of Russia ignored this call to consolidation and nominated five additional candidates, none of which were elected. Only in the fourth round, when *Demrossiia* nominated two relatively independent 'centralists' who were acceptable to the Communists of Russia, were the elections completed.[39]

Bloc Politics and Political Outcomes at the First Session

After creating the Supreme Soviet, the RSFSR CPD turned to a number of policy questions. On 22 Juene, the last day of the session, Deputy A.N. Manokhin read a declaration from *Demrossiia* to voters, deputies of all levels, and social and political organizations. This declaration took credit for a series of policy decisions taken at the Congress, including, for example, the declaration of RSFSR sovereignty, the introduction of the practice of an annual report from the Russian government to the Congress, the election of Yeltsin as chairman of the Supreme Soviet, and a series of other constitutional amendments. He contended, however, that "the results of the Congress could have been more significant if not for the obstruction of a group organized by the party apparat, the Communists of Russia." Arguing that this group "does not reflect the opinions of the majority of Communist deputies," he called upon deputies and voters alike "to unite in a mass socio-political movement, Democratic Russia."[40] Addressing the closing session of the Congress, Yeltsin concluded that its deputies were making their first steps toward becoming "genuine civilized politicians" and summoned them to raise their qualifications by studying the experience of European parliamentarians. "It was especially important [to see that] our deputies have the potential to rise above group, bloc, and party interests and, in the most decisive moments, rise to a level of historic responsibility."[41]

Yeltsin's declaration about rising above bloc interests was more wishful thinking than political reality. A deep split between Democratic Russia and the Communists of Russia at the first session was demonstrated in a rollcall analysis of ten key votes on questions of principle by three members of the electors' club of the USSR Academy of Sciences. They argued that the evidence "clearly shows where the principal line of political demarcation lies." "On one side of the barricades," Democratic Russia's side, were workers and the intelligentsia, farm workers and junior army officers, lower-level police and former dissidents, party secretaries from small and mid-sized enterprises and non-party representatives of informal political groups. On the other side of the barricade stand "faithful fighters for the cause of the nomenklatura," the Communists of Russia.[42]

Development of Russian Legislative Politics

The All-Union Context

Gorbachev's ability to manage the political agenda was weakened considerably in 1990 when the union republics elected their own Supreme Soviets. Republican Supreme Soviets opposed his presidential decrees and refused to enforce them.[43] A struggle for republican sovereignty and the renewal of the Union on revised terms was played out between the summer of 1990 and the summer of 1991. Addressing the second session of the all-union Congress of People's Deputies in the fall of 1990, Yeltsin argued that, "processes of renewal, blocked [at the federal level], have moved to the republics." Republican Supreme Soviets had, "seriously weakened the totalitarian system's control over them," and "real opportunities to begin radical transformations," had appeared. "As Chairman of the Supreme Soviet of the Russian Federation," he declared, "Russia will not agree to the revival of the Kremlin's *diktat*..."[44] Yeltsin went on to argue that the union could only be reborn if conditions could be created for the flourishing of the republics. Decisions should be made on splitting both powers and property. The center should reject interference in republican affairs. The August 1991 coup came the day before a new union treaty was to have been signed that would have stripped the center of much of its power and given it to the republics.

Subsequent Sessions of the Russian CPD

While it is beyond the bounds of this study to analyze completely the evolution of Russian legislative politics, this chapter attempts to make two points. First, the political legitimacy of a new republican legislative institution, combined with the attempt of a new political elite to defend its gains from the elections, made leadership by 'the center' untenable. Second, politics in the RSFSR CPD typically revolved around the attempts of the two principal deputorial blocs, Communists of Russia and Democratic Russia, to rally a majority around any given point. Clearly, as Smyth pointed out, the radicals did not control the Russian parliament.[45] In fact, it would be wrong to say that *anyone* controlled it, except, perhaps on occasion, Boris Yeltsin, who was able to manipulate deputorial ire against 'the center' to his own advantage. Bloc politics in their peculiar 'soviet' form, weakened the legislature's ability to work effectively. There was little or no discipline inside groups and blocs. The electoral calendar—guaranteed places until new elections in an uncertain constitutional context—did little to encourage responsible behavior by deputies.

The CPD's second session (27 November to 15 December 1990) for the first time recognized, in principle, private ownership of land and ratified an agricultural program for the rebirth of the Russian village. The decision taken in the RSFSR contrasted quite markedly with indecision at the all-union level. Communists of Russia, however, weakened the property bill considerably and were able to engineer a number of other successes, including rejection of Yeltsin's first attempt to pass constitutional amendments creating a presidency, blocking Yeltsin's candidate for vice-chairman of the Supreme Soviet, and passing a resolution on the war in the Persian Gulf. Indeed, at the second session, Communists of Russia held the upper hand. If, at the first session, Democratic Russia could count on the enthusiasm for change of newly-elected deputies, especially when general declarations of popular democratic slogans were on the table, the second session's focus on economic bills weakened their ability to control the center.

The CPD's third session (28 March to 5 April 1991) came on the heels of a referendum held in March 1991 on the further existence of the USSR. In Russia, Yeltsin succeeded in attaching a second question to the referendum, a proposal to introduce a Russian presidency. More importantly, he successfully delayed the opening of the session until after the vote, which passed with a constitutional majority: more than half of all *registered* voters supported the change. The congressional session itself, summoned by a petition at the intiative of Communists of Russia, can be viewed as a premeditated attempt to remove Yeltsin before he could engineer constitutional amendments to create a presidency and summon elections that he was almost certain to win. The CPD did not approve Communists of Russia's gambit: on the contrary, riding the tide of popular support offered by the referendum, and helped by street demonstrations in Moscow in support of democracy, Yeltsin used the occasion to convince the CPD to give him additional powers to deal with economic reform: in essence, he could conduct economic reform by decree. By threatening to resign, Yeltsin cleverly convinced the Congress to set a date for presidential elections *before* constitutional amendments had been passed to create the office.

Yeltsin built on his successes at the third session in a series of subsequent, complex parliamentary moves in the Supreme Soviet, which drafted and ratified concrete proposals for the presidency. The fourth session of the CPD (21–25 May 1991), ratified the principle of a division of powers and called for creating executive and judicial branches of government. The new president, elected for no more than two consecutive 5-year terms, would be the highest official in the RSFSR and the head of its executive institutions, but was obligated to report to the CPD no less than once per year. The president was given the right to issue decrees that were obligatory across the RSFSR and was given the right to suspend decisions of executive organs if they contradicted the constitution or laws of the RSFSR. Both the Supreme Soviet and the CPD were given the power to revoke presidential decrees, but voting procedures were not specified. The CPD received the right to remove the president from office by a two-thirds vote on a report by the Constitutional Court issued at the initiative of the CPD itself, the Supreme Soviet, or one of its chambers.[46]

In June 1991, after a blitz two-week campaign against six opponents, Yeltsin was elected Russia's first president.[47] Shortly after his inauguration on 10 July, in a series of presidential decrees, Yeltsin reappointed Ivan Silaev head of the Russian Government, created a presidential administration, appointed a number of ministers, and, in a new round of his battle against the CPSU, banned the political activities of parties, including, of course, Communist Party cells, in all executive organs.[48]

The August 1991 coup led the RSFSR Supreme Soviet, hastily summoned back from summer vacation, to grant Yeltsin extraordinary powers to deal with an extraordinary situation.[49] In the fall, deputies granted Yeltsin still more powers, including the right, denied in June, to independently reorganize government structures, legal aspects of the relationship between the President and the Supreme Soviet were defined explicitly to prevent presidential power from turning into a dictatorship.[50]

Yeltsin presented a plan for radical economic reform to the Congress's fifth session (10–17 July, 28 October to 2 November 1991), which granted him still more formal powers. On 6 November he signed a decree appointing himself Russia's new prime minister and formally declared the RSFSR

Council of Ministers the Russian Government. Thus, he eliminated the possibility that the Council of Ministers could fall into the hands of a political opponent. On 11 November, he divided Russia's 24 ministries into four blocs, himself assuming control of defense and internal affairs. Russia took control of the property of all USSR ministries and enterprises on its territory. Subsequently, much of Russia's radical reform program, including the freeing of prices and the privatization program, was introduced by presidential decree.

The coup seemed to offer deputies an unprecedented chance to unite with the President to introduce wide-ranging change; nonetheless, it appears that executive-legislative conflict weakened any such feelings. The fifth session of the CPD elected both a constitutional court and a new chairman of the Supreme Soviet, Ruslan Khasbulatov. Both Khasbulatov, through his influence over the Supreme Soviet, and the new constitutional court, in a number of early decisions, played roles in opposing presidential power. That is, the long-sought system of division of powers started to play a real role in Russian politics. Moreover, deputies in the CPD started to see a common interest in opposing executive power. In fact, Deputy Sergei Baburin, a leader of the conservative Russian nationalist wing of the parliament, complained that Communists of Russia and Democratic Russia had *joined together* in an alliance of the old and new apparat. Although, like much of Baburin's inflammatory rhetoric, this statement was untrue, it did reflect a general trend: deputies wanted the legislature to play a real role. The principal difference, however, was that while some deputies wanted a working system of checks and balances, others wanted to restore parliamentary supremacy and make Yeltsin subordinate to legislative power.[51]

Although the Congress ratified Yeltsin's actions and endowed him with strong formal powers to rule by decree, Khasbulatov warned the new government to acquaint itself with laws passed by the deputies. Thus, the stage was set for a new round of conflict, this time between the president and the legislature.[52]

Notes

1. Regina A. Smyth, in "Ideological vs. Regional Cleavages: Do the Radicals Control the RSFSR Parliament?," *Journal of Soviet Nationalities*, fall 1990, pp. 112–158, demonstrated that regional, demographic, and other factors played an important role in cleavages at the first session. On this point see also Gregory J. Embree, "RSFSR Election Results and Roll Call Votes," *Soviet Studies*, Vol. 43, No. 6, 1991, pp. 1065–1084.

2. Deputy V.A. Rebrikov, for example, declared that, "We all know that during preparatory discussion in the Politburo over the proposed candidates for the chairmanship of the RSFSR Supreme Soviet a decision was taken to nominate three candidates: Iu.A. Manaenkov, A.V. Vlasov, and I.K. Polozkov. See *Sovetskaia Rossiia*, 27 May 1990.

3. S. Shakrai, "Delo u nas odno—Rossiia," *Izvestiia*, 13 May 1990. The proposal declared that "the existing practice of the preparation of the Congress...has demonstrated its ineffectiveness. The election by democratic means of an organization committee ... would significantly raise the authority of the Congress." *Obrashchenie deputatov bloka "Demokraticheskaia Rossiia" k Prezidiumu Verkhovnogo Soveta RSFSR*. See also the almanac of the founding congress of the Social Democratic Association, P. Kudiukin, "V parlamente i za ego stenami: opyt prognoza," *Otkrytaia zona*, No. 11, 1990.

4. S. Shakrai, "Delo u nas odno—Rossiia...," Deputy O.G. Rumiantsev contended that the agenda did not reflect the wishes of deputies because there was neither a unified point of view at the Assembly of Representatives nor discussion.

5. For information on the blocs registered at the first session of the RSFSR CPD see *Sovetskaia Rossiia*, 29 May 1990, 31 May 1990, 8 June 1990, and 20 June 1990. An analysis of the social composition of the two blocs was published by L. Efimova, A. Sobianin and D. Iurev, "Narod i nomenklatura ediny?," *Argumenty i fakty*, No. 29, 1990, p. 2.

6. *Ogonëk*, No. 6, 1990.

7. Iurii Bogomolov "Parlamentskii blok 'Demokraticheskaia Rossiia' sozdan," *Pozitsiia*, No. 5, 1990, p. 2. Informatsionnye soobshchenie o vstreche narodnykh deputatov RSFSR storonnikov platformy "Demokraticheskaia Rossiia. "Konferentsiia bloka Demokraticheskaia Rossiia," *Argumenty i fakty*, No. 14, 1990, p. 4.

8. *Obrashchenie k izbirateliam, deputatam vsekh urovnei RSFSR ot gruppy deputatov bloka "Demokraticheskaia Rossiia," Proekt Rezoliutsii, Blok "Demokraticheskaia Rossiia."*

9. "Demokraticheskaia Rossiia vydvigaet Borisa Yeltsina," *Doverie*, No. 5, May 1990, p. 1.

10. *Sovetskaia Rossiia*, 8 June 1990. For an account of the birth of the bloc and a description of its activities from a conservative point of view see "My za konstruktivnuiu rabotu v sovetakh," *Izvestiia TsK KPSS*, No. 2, 1991, pp. 32–34.

11. *Sovetskaia Rossiia*, 8 June 1990.

12. In 1,068 electoral districts there were 6,705 candidates. In 33 districts there was only one candidate. In 24 districts there were 20 candidates.

13. Deputies expressed this will for the first time when they refused to

agree with a proposal to include in an editorial commission V. Chikin, the editor of *Sovetskaia Rossiia*, the newspaper that first published the famous 'Nina Andreeva' letter. See *Izvestiia*, 17 May 1990.

14. RSFSR Deputy Anatolii Shabad suggested that a second tactical element played a role. Gorbachev was scheduled to leave the country. *Demrossiia* wanted to delay the elections until he was gone. Lecture, Jackson School of International Studies. University of Washington, November 1990.

15. *Sovetskaia Rossiia*, 25 May 1990.

16. Ibid., 27 May 1990.

17. Not all deputies accepted Gorbachev's attack peacefully. See, for example, the presentation by N.V. Bogaenko in *Sovetskaia Rossiia*, 26 May 1990.

18. *Sovetskaia Rossiia*, 26 May 1990.

19. Ibid.

20. Ibid.

21. Ibid., 29 May 1990.

22. Ibid.

23. Ibid.

24. Ibid.

25. Ibid.

26. Ibid., 30 May 1990.

27. Ibid., 31 May 1990.

28. Ibid., 30 May 1990.

29. Ibid., 31 May 1990. Yeltsin cited similar reasons when he resigned from the CPSU on the final day of its 28th Congress in the summer of 1990.

30. Ibid., 2 June 1990.

31. Ibid., 3 June 1990.

32. Ibid., 7 June 1990.

33. Ibid., 6 June 1990.

34. In reply, Yeltsin, who only rarely commented on remarks during debate, proposed that the Secretariat and the voting commission look into the question after the vote. *Izvestiia*, 12 June 1990.

35. Ibid.

36. Ibid., 13 June 1990.

37. Ibid.

38. Ibid., 19 June 1990.

39. In discussion before the final round, Deputy S.M. Akhmetkhanov summarized the situation by noting that the deputies had ended up in a dead end by turning the CPD into "a congress of political parties." *Izvestiia*, 21 June 1990.

40. Ibid., 23 June 1990.

41. Ibid.

42. L. Efimova, A. Sobianin, D. Iurev, *K voprosu ob antagonizme (po rezultatam analiza poimennykh golosovanii uchastnikov sezda narodnykh deputatov RSFSR)*.

43. For a discussion of this phenomenon see Dawn Mann, "Nongovernment by Decree," *Radio Liberty Report on the USSR*, 31 August 1990, pp. 1–4.

44. B.N. Yeltsin, "Vystuplenie na IV Sezd narodnykh deputatov SSSR."

45. This was one of the principal conclusions of the analysis of dozens of roll-call votes over the course of the first five sessions of the RSFSR CPD. See A. Sobianin and D. Iurev, *Sezd narodnykh deputtatov RSFSR v zerkale poimennykh golosovanii*, Moscow: 1991.

46. The president would have the power to initiate legislation, veto Supreme Soviet decisions (subject to an override), lead the activities of the Council of Ministers and with the Supreme Soviet's consent accept the resignation of the government, choose a Chairman of the Council of Ministers (with the Supreme Soviet's consent), appoint and remove ministers (according to proposals by the Chairman of the Council of Ministers), was the head of the RSFSR Security Council, conduct negotiations with other nations and sign treaties ratified by the Supreme Soviet, take measures to insure state security, and declare states of emergency. The president would not be allowed to dissolve the Supreme Soviet or alter the government's structure. The president was not allowed to be a people's deputy and, during his tenure, must suspend his membership in all political parties and social organizations and was prohibited from occupying any other post in state institutions or social organizations. See *FBIS Trends* 10 April 1991, 15 May 1991, 30 May 1991; *Vedomosti RSFSR*, No. 17, Art. 512, pp. 463–466; "Zakon Rossiiskoi Sovetskoi Federativnoi Sotsialisticheskoi Respubliki," "O Prezidente RSFSR, Vedomosti RSFSR," No. 17, 1991, Art. 512.

47. An excellent review of the results of the campaign across the RSFSR, including extensive statistical analysis of voting by region, can be found in D. Iurev, *Prezidentskie vybory*, Moscow: 1991.

48. For the structure of the presidential administration see S. Parkhomenko, "My–struktura chisto apparatnaia," *Nezavisimaia gazeta*, 26 June 1991, p. 2. For an outsider's view of the GPU see an interview with the minister of justice by N. Zhelnorovoi, "Est veshchi povazhnee politiki," *Argumenty i fakty*, No. 21, 1992, p. 2. For speculation on splits in Yeltsin's team see G. Shipitko, "Organizovannyi oppozitsii v apparate Yeltsina net," *Izvestiia*, 9 October 1991, p. 2.

49. RSFSR Supreme Soviet Decree, "O dopolnitelnykh polnomochiiakh Prezidenta RSFSR po obespecheniiu zakonnosti deiatelnosti Sovetov narodnykh deputatov v usloviiakh likvidatsii posledstvii popytki gosudarstvennogo perevorota v SSSR, 21 August 1991." For an inside discussion of the

new organs and a review of their performance see "Thirty Days After the Putsch," *Moscow News*, No. 39, 1991, pp. 8-9.

50. The Supreme Soviet and President were given the right to suspend union and republican acts blocking reform. Local executives were subordinated even more tightly to central institutions. "Prezidentu Rossii dan zelenyi svet na provedenie radikalnykh reform," *Izvestiia*, 2 November, 1991.; "Chtoby provodit reformy, prezidentu nuzhna vlast'," *Rossiiskaia Gazeta*, 31 October 1991, p. 1.; "Chtoby provodit reformy, prezidentu nuzhna vlast'," *Rossiiskaia gazeta*, 1 November 1991, p. 1.; I. Elistratov, "Khasbulatov nazval sezd istoricheskim ne zria," *Izvestiia*, 4 November 1991, p. 1.

51. See "Sezd: nadezhdy, realnost, prognozy," *Rossiiskaia gazeta*, 6 November 1991, p. 1.

52. For a description of the duties of the president's representatives, see "Glaza i ushi prezidenta," 30 January 1992, *Trud*, p. 3. For a list of Yeltsin's representatives see "Rossiia: institut doverennykh lits prezidenta protiv paralicha vlasti i upravleniia," *Izvestiia*, 11 January 1992, p. 2. For objections to this system by Yeltsin's supporters in Democratic Russia see, "My podderzhivaem Eltsyna uslovno," *Izvestiia*, 7 October 1991, p. 2.

Chapter 11

'Soviet Politics' and the End of the Soviet Era

The failure of the August 1991 coup led swiftly to a series of revolutionary changes across the USSR. The activities of the Communist Party were suspended or banned in a number of republics, several of which declared independence.[1] In October, the USSR Supreme Soviet rejected the oft-praised advantages of 'soviet-style government' and officially ended the country's failed political experiment.[2] On 7 November 1991, President Yeltsin signed a death warrant for the Communist Party of the Soviet Union, a decree outlawing its activities on the soil of the Russian Republic. On 8 December 1991, the presidents of Belarus, Russia, and Ukraine formed a Commonwealth of Independent States and declared the USSR defunct. By mid-December, eight other former Soviet republics had joined. Before the new year, Mikhail Gorbachev resigned the presidency, and the Soviet Union ceased to exist.

Despite the catalytic jolt of the coup, causes for the changes in Soviet politics clearly go deeper than the tanks that rumbled through Moscow or even what some have called Yeltsin's counter-coup. How can one explain the multi-year political hemorrhage that destroyed the USSR, soviet-style politics, and the CPSU? Why did *demokratizatsiia*, Gorbachev's attempt to create a truly *Soviet* Union lead to the collapse of the system? Can this collapse promote democratic transformations in the former republics of the USSR? This final chapter addresses these questions by using the theoretical frameworks outlined in Chapter 2 to explore the relationships between *demokratizatsiia* and democratization.

Demokratizatsiia and Democratization

By the early 1980s, the USSR's political elite understood that Brezhnev's 'developed socialism' was not working. Economic growth had dropped while a series of chronic socioeconomic and political problems appeared to be getting worse. Decisions shaped by the Politburo and Secretariat and ratified by the Central Committee on industrial, agricultural, social, and other issues often went unfulfilled. Worse, the USSR's economic infrastructure faced permanent backwardness in an international division of labor dominated by technologies and human resources that the Soviet system seemed incapable of producing. Later dubbed the 'period of stagnation,' the latter years of the Brezhnev era left the USSR—and therefore its political elite—in a critical situation.

The problem was easy to identify yet frighteningly complex: the political and economic levers wielded by the party's General Secretary, Politburo, and Secretariat no longer worked. Despite its constitutional 'leading role' and a firm practical grip on all nodes of the USSR's political and economic systems, the CPSU, as a party, had little fungible power.[3] The CPSU was unable to control in an effective manner the Council of Ministers.[4] 'Party leadership' meant little when Central Committee decisions were not fulfilled. Economic centralization and Brezhnev's policy of 'stability of cadres' encouraged a type of politics where personal and bureaucratic interests predominated at the expense of the long-range interests of the party.[5]

The failure of reforms attempted prior to the January 1987 Central Committee Plenum, acceleration or *uskorenie*, convinced the party leadership that economic change must be accompanied by explicit political change. Subsequent reforms, whether 'planned' or 'improvised,' can be viewed as Gorbachev's attempt to reempower the CPSU as a political organization, and himself first of all as its General Secretary, by creating new institutional mechanisms for political leadership and accountability. Internal party reforms alone, however, were politically unfeasible. Gorbachev was too familiar with Khrushchev's downfall to risk a similar fate. The soviets were an open avenue. At the 19th Party Conference, Gorbachev argued that revitalizing the soviets was part of the "logic of the development of socialism" and announced a program that included changes in the party, the soviets, and the executive apparatus. Popularly-elected, revitalized soviets could encourage party leaders to develop the art of political leadership; moreover, they had the added advantage, at least in theory, of helping legitimize a painful series of economic reforms while providing Gorbachev with an institutional shield from the wrath of his comrades in the Central Committee.

Gorbachev could not seriously propose a return to the soviet-style government of Leninist reality, a period when the soviets never developed the democratic potential they may have had before the party started down the road to what later became known as Stalinism. Instead, tapping into the post-Stalin consensus about expanding the role of the soviets, Gorbachev proposed a move toward the ideal proclaimed advantages of a 'soviet socialist democracy' that never existed.

The program and statute approved at the 27th Party Congress and many of Gorbachev's subsequent statements, including pronouncements at the 19th Party Conference, argued that party members should provide political leadership and withdraw from day-to-day economic decisionmaking.[6] Echoing Krushchev, he maintained that the CPSU could still be the avantgarde of Soviet society while party leaders and members spent more time leading through party groups in the soviets and less time ruling by fiat. The CPSU's apparat would no longer undermine the soviets; instead, acting *through* the soviets, party members could produce decisions that enjoyed, at least in theory, some measure of popular support. Echoing Brezhnev, he suggested that the soviets could help eliminate 'arbitrariness' and would help the party keep the executive under control. In hindsight, it is clear that Gorbachev wanted real change. But did *demokratizatsiia* equal democratization?

Democratic transformations in post-totalitarian systems, according to Di Palma's model of democratic crafting, begin when the party elite decides that there is 'no way out' of the problems that it faces other than assenting to the political contingency inherent in democracy. Social, economic, and political problems facing the country appear unsolvable and, if the party wants any claim to power or leadership, it must act in its own self-interest to expand the bounds of legitimate political participation. Gorbachev declared that *demokratizatsiia* was part of the 'logic of the development of socialism,' and repeatedly asserted that there was no alternative. But did these changes indicate that he was prepared to start a process of 'political crafting' leading to democracy, did he see no way out of 'the period of stagnation' other than a system based on procedural political contingency? Did he find the competitive aspect of democracy appealing, convenient, or compelling?

The first stages of perestroika and *demokratizatsiia* conformed in some ways to Di Palma's model. One might (and many did) see in Mikhail Gorbachev the personification of a democratic craftsman: a political figure capable of convening the chief institutional interests of an authoritarian state and demonstrating in an open-ended series of negotiations and political maneuvers that market democracy offers advantages to all participants. Activating the soviets was one way to start the process while keeping everyone in the game. He tapped into both the soothing political familiarity of the long-term formal activization process and the *soviet* roots of the revolution to create a reform program that rallied a wide spectrum of supporters. The revival of the Supreme Soviet and the system of republican and local soviets, was a brilliant political gambit, a compromise that promised to revitalize the system. The CPSU contained a number of ideological trends and the program seemed to offer some benefit to each of them. Conservatives could welcome a return to traditional soviet values while counting on the continued 'leading role' of the party. The apparat needed reassurance that it could remain in control: no better comfort could be given than accustomed rhetoric from the Khrushchev and Brezhnev years about strengthening the soviets. Liberals, without stretching their imaginations too far, could see the changes as the first step toward democracy.

At least two other aspects of democratic crafting might appear to fit into the first stages of the reform program. First, through glasnost and the elections, Gorbachev appealed to civil society as a tactical weapon against the entrenched apparat.[7] Second, Di Palma argues that agreements reached during the crafting process should at times be 'fuzzy,' i.e. contain ambiguities that allow players to remain in the game. That was certainly the case here. A massive number of unresolved questions remained after the end of the 1988 party conference and even after the reform amendments had been ratified by the Supreme Soviet. Perhaps the most significant element of uncertainty used by Gorbachev was the concept of socialism itself, an empty box that had been filled, refilled, and could be filled again to suit the needs of a developing political situation.

Demokratizatsiia is subject to mutually exclusive interpretations: 'Gorbachev the revitalizer' and 'Gorbachev the democratizer.' Both, of course, imply radical change, but in different directions. If Gorbachev felt that the CPSU was threatened with extinction and that the only way to retain power was to move toward democracy, if one is prepared to see Gorbachev as a political tactician and view many aspects of the reform program as strategic concessions to ensure that the party apparat would not boycott the democratization process, one might be tempted to consider the 19th Party Conference proposals an attempt to 'get the game started' and label Gorbachev a sly democratic craftsman. One must not exclude the possibility, however, that Gorbachev was never interested in democracy. Western analysts have not paid sufficient attention to the unique elements of 'soviet-style' government that allowed Gorbachev to rationalize his decision not to turn to tried and true democratic institutional models. In this view, Gorbachev wanted to revive the socialist project, to create a system where actually existing socialism could reach the potential that he believed it had. The revitalization of the soviets, inner-party liberalization, and the taming of the executive apparat would produce a system more in tune with the needs of the people and, more importantly for Gorbachev, a system capable of being led. One way to resolve the paradox inherent in these interpretations is to analyze the implementation of the post-1987 reform program using both 'Leninist' and democratic crafting criteria.

Electoral Politics

A Leninist Benchmark

Leadership and Accountability. For seventy years, Soviet voters selected representatives in noncompetitive elections for rubber-stamp soviets. In 1989, changes in the electoral law created a new political environment for the party's ruling elite by eliminating the Leninist split between leadership and accountability and moving toward a new type of contingent political relationship. As one Soviet political analyst noted, "earlier, a deputy depended not on [his electorate] but on the party organs... He did not have to look back at his voters, to take their position into account. Now the situation is completely different."[8] A revolutionary breed of independent candidate challenged the status quo and destroyed the already-tattered myth of party leadership. Although rank-and-file Communists won more than 80% of the seats in the CPD, party leaders were defeated in contests across the country: often, even massive cheating could not prevent embarrassing losses. A type of 'us vs. them' politics—the people vs. the party—was common during the campaign. 'Democratic' or 'progressive' candidates, for the most part, tried to stay out of each other's way and concentrated their fire on the party. This type of politics found its high mark in the 'Yeltsin affair,' when seemingly all of Moscow rose up to defend the maverick candidate against the party apparat.

After 70 years of a political monopoly, the CPSU apparat received a cold slap in the face. Lessons derived from electoral defeat, if taken to heart, could have served the party well.[9] First secretary of the Leningrad *gorkom* A. Gerasimov noted that "when more than 31 obkom first secretaries fail to receive the support of the people, then even if they objectively 'earned' this result, it is all the same reason for serious thought for any Communist."[10] Despite Gerasimov's comments, and the fact that Gorbachev took the unusual step of personally attending a plenum of the Leningrad party committee that removed him from office, few party leaders took the stunning electoral defeat as a signal that the CPSU needed fundamental reform. Instead, repeating tirelessly the phrase that "the party started perestroika and will finish it," CPSU leaders seemed intent on keeping their lock on power and the ability to define the bounds of political discourse.

The staggering blow to the CPSU's prestige in many high-profile areas could have been worse: local party officials and the central party apparat were often able to control outcomes. This should not be viewed as a centralized plan to produce the aggressively obedient majority in the Congress of People's Deputies that Afanasev complained about: it was in large part a natural result of the desire of local party officials to control an unfamiliar process that had enormous consequences for their political futures. Three points need to be emphasized here. First, multi-candidate elections are not necessarily more democratic than single-candidate contests. Without the labels, discipline, and incentive structures provided by political parties it is difficult or impossible for voters to determine whom they are voting for. Second, party officials *did not* control the elections in the Baltic and elsewhere. This aspect of the 1989 contest helped define the political character of the Congress of People's Deputies and Supreme Soviet. Elections supply the players and create an incentive system that structures the rules of the game in any representative institution.[11] A potentially unmanageable CPD and Supreme Soviet were direct results of this process. Third, the elections were held for offices with a five-year term. Thus, electoral incentives were weak for deputies, especially considering the uncertain institutional environment and the fact that many owed their posts to local party organizations and not the voters.

The decline of the CPSU and party leadership was so great in 1989 that one could argue that the campaign was conducted on a non-party basis. The CPSU did not compete as a national party; the elections were conducted in a different manner depending on the republic and region; the CPSU did not hold its members to its platform; the party did not insist on one Communist candidate per district. Many Communist candidates conducted their own campaigns with no support from the party while others ran *against* the local party apparat. In short, even if the CPSU could be considered an electoral bloc, it fell flat as a unified, leading party. An offical CPSU *gorkom* analysis of the electoral battle in Moscow pointed out that

> party organizations and especially their apparats were not prepared for such a previously unknown political battle. The old, now irrelevant mechanism of complete organization and a formal approach to the electoral process went into action. Many party organs and their workers chose not to open a dialogue with society... Their unpreparedness for discussion and arguments, ... the absence of a deep analysis of [public opinion] and the effect on it of informal political organizations also played a role.[12]

Finally, as Anatolii Sobchak and others have pointed out, the campaign further accelerated the growth of ideological, national, and organizational splits inside the CPSU. Instead of pulling the party together, the 1989 elections helped pull it apart.[13]

In 1990, thanks to Gorbachev's electoral reunification of the Leninist split between leadership and accountability, the CPSU, as in 1989, was called to account for its past. In the RSFSR, Democratic Russia, an electoral bloc with goals contrary to those of the Communist Party, won a resounding victory in Moscow and approximately one third of the seats in the new RSFSR Congress of People's Deputies. Nationalist blocs and parties took control of legislatures in six republics, casting aside Communist arguments about leadership and punishing party leaders for decades of mismanagement.

The CPSU failed to apply effectively the experience of 1989 to 1990. While Gorbachev declared that the party needed to conduct a political battle, he repeatedly denied the CPSU should become a parliamentary party. Not surprisingly, local party organizations failed to rise to the occasion. Reviewing the 1990 campaign, Timothy J. Colton described a problem that had also hindered the party in 1989: "there was now a slew of Communist candidates...[that] brought to mind more a herd of elbow-swinging marathon athletes, their CPSU sponsorship stenciled to their jerseys in barely legible letters, than a team swaying to a common rythm. It was predictable under the circumstances that Party propaganda would be wooly."[14] The party platform, an empty document, provided no political leadership and was, essentially, an attempt to avoid responsibility. None of the tough choices that needed to be made *inside* the party to produce an organization and program capable of leading the country into a new era were made.

Representation. Principles of representation underwent a fundamental change in 1989 from Leninist-symbolic to functional, from fictitious to real. As a Communist, Gorbachev could not reject outright a demographic, 'reflective,' principle of representation; nonetheless, he made it clear that "politically active, intelligent people" should become deputies and play a genuine role in working legislatures. For the first time, the public demanded competent representation, calling for lawyers and other educated professionals instead of tractor drivers, milkmaids, and party bureaucrats. Moreover, by legitimizing differences of opinion and calling for representation of a 'socialist pluralism of opinions,' Gorbachev suggested that a broader section of the population had legitimate interests that should be taken into account. In short, the 1989 elections were not a symbolic celebration of the unity of party and people, but, at least in some constituencies, a broad discussion of values and goals.[15]

There is little to say about a Leninist principle of representation in the

1990 campaign other than that it was buried for good. Electoral politics became bloc politics. This new system of representation was not, however, without its problems. First, the blocs were *not* organized parties, so many candidates who joined were poorly screened and turned out to be inadequate for their new tasks.[16] The new bloc politics were, moreover, a product of 'us vs. them' politics, i.e. the people vs. the party apparat or a minority nationality vs. the center. Although this type of politics may produce crushing victories under certain circumstances, it does not necessarily result in the triumph of a group with a viable program.

The CPSU's weak performance in the 1989 and 1990 elections demands explanation. Colton argued that the CPSU failed to act "like a normal political party" and claimed that it was "caught napping."[17] I suggest a different answer: the CPSU was *incapable* of acting like a political party because its internal incentive structures and the incentive structures that it perceived in its political environment had nothing to do with electoral politics. The CPSU was not "caught napping," it was *politically and organizationally incapable* of performing "like a normal political party." The vision of political leadership entertained by party cadres was fundamentally non-democratic. Thus, by substituting organizational busywork, a focus on technocratic solutions to socioeconomic problems, and the exaltation of personal characteristics for political vision and the creation of a competitive and clear political identity, most CPSU organizations failed to prepare *politically* for the elections.

Soviet Electoral Politics and Democratic Crafting

Did Gorbachev use elections as a tool for democratic crafting? If, as Di Palma points out, democratization in communist states can only begin when the core of the party elite recognizes that there is no other way, there are at least two possible answers. First, Gorbachev may have wanted the elections to demonstrate that the party had no choice but to move toward democracy. If this was the case, he sent a strong message. The CPSU was unprepared for political battle and suffered big losses in areas where a real choice was allowed. Circumstantial evidence that Gorbachev in fact used electoral failures to discipline recalcitrant party comrades was provided by the April 1989 Central Committee Plenum, where he forced a significant minority of the Central Committee to hand in their resignations. These 'dead souls' (older members or members who had lost their other positions in the party or the government) made up a conservative threat to further reform.

Di Palma suggests that the rebirth of civil society can serve as a signaling tool of democratic crafting. In the Soviet case, the 1989 and 1990 elections led to a process that got out of control. Soviet society participated in the 1989 elections in several ways: street demonstrations in Moscow in support of Boris Yeltsin were just one example of a new type of mass politics. The effect of the elections was summarized by the Moscow City Soviet's department for work with soviets in an internal memorandum that observed that "one of the principal results of the election was sharply increased political activity of Muscovites."

> Many layers of society were set into motion in the city. New, informal, independent organizations and initiative groups were formed. Most often, their members were united by ecological, social, national, and political problems. For the first time in the course of the elections the voters themselves became the initiators and participants of meetings and marches. Thousands of participants, [with] nontraditional slogans, posters, and leaflets appeared. The electoral campaign, [even] with all the ambiguity and contradiction of its content, became a mighty impulse for the mobilization of social and popular forces.[18]

The 1989 elections politicized a narrow layer of Soviet society by encouraging groups of politically active citizens to meet one another and organize. Directly or indirectly, in 1989 tens of thousands of Soviet citizens graduated from an electoral 'school of democracy.' Despite seven decades of electoral torpor, candidates quickly grasped the basics of campaign strategy and tactics. They built campaign teams and learned to direct them.

In 1990, 'graduates' of this 'school' used the skills learned in 1989 to form electoral blocs and compete.[19] In Moscow and Leningrad, *Demrossiia* and other areas liberal blocs arose out of the organizations created in the 1989 campaign. Although local CPSU organizations continued to enjoy the same advantages that control over the electoral process gave them in 1989, *Demrossiia* was able to win enough seats, to elect Boris Yeltsin Chairman of the CPD. Yeltsin's narrow margin of victory, literally a handful of votes, could easily have gone the other way if *Demrossiia* had not been so well organized and won an overwhelming majority in Moscow.[20]

A second, more likely interpretation of Gorbachev's attitude toward the elections is that he failed to accept the discipline of political contingency, the possibility that the CPSU might share the government or be voted out of office altogether. The elections were merely one step to stronger soviets. While it would be unreasonable to expect the leader of any party to call for its removal from office, Gorbachev did not appear to even entertain the possibility of an institutionalized opposition. In fact, he did what he could to help the party avoid this danger: republican and local elections originally planned for the fall of 1989 were postponed until the beginning of

1990. Gorbachev argued that the party needed to relearn political methods of leadership and that a series of economic problems that led to a loss of contact with the working class could and should be overcome. This attitude toward the non-replaceability of the CPSU was well expressed by A. Briachikhin, a regional party secretary in Moscow, when discussing the possibility of CPSU losses in 1990. He declared that there was "no other force [in society] except the CPSU that can lead to progress... After all, if the wrong people are elected, we will still be the ones who are guilty. The voters will end up telling us: you didn't warn us and things have now gotten even worse."[21]

In the Russian Federation, the 1990 elections were conducted, in many regions, in the old style.[22] That is, the party elite still did not want to admit that there was 'no way out' and that it would have to agree to procedural political contingency. Gorbachev did not trade constitutional articles mandating the leading role of the CPSU until it was too late to form or include alternative parties in the republican elections. No pacts or informal agreements were negotiated by the regime, which in December 1989 rammed an electoral law through the Russian Supreme Soviet in old-fashioned rubber-stamp style. Without an even playing field, victories in Moscow, Leningrad and elsewhere by Democratic Russia, were not matched across the Federation. In the provinces, the CPSU apparat still had a strong hand on the ballot box. The elections themselves, including the victory of *Demrossiia* in many areas, may have helped convince the apparat that changes were due, but, even if it still believed in its future as a ruling force, nationalist and democratic blocs were clearly the wave of the future. Just as clearly, thanks to the sequence of electoral reform, they would take control at the *republican* level.

Legislative Politics

The USSR Congress of People's Deputies

The first session of the USSR CPD was a watershed in Soviet political history. The nation sat virtually hypnotized in front of its televisions as an unprecedented political spectacle was played out daily. The tide of change that had seemed to exist throughout the electoral campaign could no longer be ignored. A quick review of the results of the first session alone is enough to demonstrate the fundamental nature of the changes.

Leadership. The question of political leadership was tied directly to the work of the CPD, an institution whose constitutional role was to define the principal directions of Soviet domestic and foreign policy. At the practical level, however, party leadership, understood as reviving the work of communist deputies in the legislature, was not effective. Gorbachev used a series of control mechanisms prior to the opening of the first session of the CPD to guarantee its outcomes. He was able to define the agenda as well as a series of cadres questions using old-fashioned methods. The locus of party power and influence, therefore, was still *outside* an elected institution. The old-style rules of Kremlin power politics continued behind a facade of representative government. There was no 'political leadership,' understood as a contingent relationship between party leaders and party-deputies interacting within an incentive structure defined by legislative and electoral politics.

Boris Yeltsin's address to the IRDG in September 1989 highlighted both the problems of party leadership at the Congress and some popular misconceptions. Noting that preparations for the session took place "under the *diktat* of the central Committee and the General Secretary," Yeltsin argued that the "archaic" division of the CPD by republican and oblast delegations guaranteed that the Central Committee apparat was able to manage the Congress.[23] He failed to note, however, one essential point—a qualitative change had been made in the relationship between the center and the republics. Republican delegations now contained deputies not dependent on the party apparat for their mandates. The Lithuanian deputy group, which, at one point, marched out of the Congress in protest, was the best example of this new phenomenon.

Accountability. The first session of the Congress demonstrated both a new type of political accountability and a strong element of political inertia. Perhaps the best example of this phenomenon was provided by Deputy Iu.P. Vlasov, a writer and former weight-lifting champion from Moscow, who attacked the CPSU, Gorbachev, and the KGB in a speech that was discussed on the street for days afterward. He argued that the tragedy in Tbilisi and the procedural maneuvering by Gorbachev at the Congress were evidence of a lack of political accountability. He called for a constitutional amendment to create an impeachment clause. Moving to an even more striking topic, Vlasov declared that the KGB was an 'underground empire' that conducted a policy to defend the party no matter the cost. Changes should be made, he argued, to bring the KGB under control, including the symbolic act of evicting it from its headquarters in the center of Moscow.[24] One must be careful, however, to separate rhetoric and reality. The difference between the two was perhaps best expressed by Deputy Chernichenko, who, discussing agricultural problems, sarcastically declared that nothing was said at the Congress about "the complete dictatorship of the party apparat. Not one hair falls off the head of a steer without the permission of the Central Committee's agricultural sector."[25]

Deputies expressed a new sense of accountability to their constituents in a number of ways, perhaps because live television coverage of the session told constituents more about deputorial conduct than they had read in 70 years of 'soviet power.'[26] Deputy A.G. Zhuravlev's comments on his relationship to his electorate echoed concerns mentioned frequently by his colleagues. Discussing his frustration with the slow tempo of debate, he argued that, "I had to ask for the floor because of a flood of telegrams and calls that, I suppose, are coming in from home to all of us. Let's try, after all, to hear the voice of our voters."[27] Deputy Iudin agreed, arguing that recorded votes raise "the responsibility of deputies to their electorate."[28] Deputy A.P. Ianenko argued that any draft legislation under consideration by the Congress should include the names of its author or authors. He maintained that many of his colleagues "propose one or another solution knowing that even if it ends up in colossal losses, they will not have to answer for it.[29] Finally, several deputies noted that accountability is weakened when voters do not have access to appropriate information about their representatives.[30]

Representation. Leninist standards of representation crumbled at the first session of the CPD. Several new types of representation joined the traditional "reflection" principle: (1) social organizations, (2) electoral district interests, (3) political factions, and (4) nationalities. Social organizations for the first time had their own representatives.[31] Deputy S.F. Kalashnikov, elected by the Komsomol, presented his organization's opinion on the election of Lukianov as vice-chairman of the Supreme Soviet.[32] He argued that before the Komsomol deputies could vote for the nominee, they needed to hear his opinion on problems confronting youth.[33] Other deputies expressed the purely local interests of their constituents. Deputy A. Trudoliubov asked for 500 million rubles for the social development of rural towns in near Smolensk.[34] Deputy Z.N. Tkacheva spoke for a group of deputies from regions affected by the Chernobyl disaster. Discussing the problems of radiation poisoning, she demanded compensation for its victims."[35] Representation by nationality and ethnic groups was expressed in many ways. Deputy N.S. Sazonov protested when only 4 out of twenty of the USSR's autonomous republics had been given the chance to address the Congress.[36] Deputy Oleinik took it upon himself to speak for Russia when he complained that, unlike other republics, the RSFSR had been deprived, "by not having its own Communist Party or its own Academy of Sciences. Moreover, Russia, having endured along with Belorussia and Ukraine the brunt of [WWII] is not even represented in the United Nations." Oleinik went on to complain about language, ecological, agricultural, and other problems in the Russian Federation.[37]

Executive-Legislative Relations. The relationship of the CPD to the executive organs of the Council of Ministers presented the fourth element of 'Leninist' change. The CPD, in theory, set the principal directions of foreign and domestic policy. As a working body, however, it was too large to work effectively in the day-to-day control of public policy; therefore, the Supreme Soviet was created. Deputy G.M. Khodyrev, the first secretary of the Gorky *gorkom*, claimed that "the deputies of Gorky oblast, 18 people, sent [an official] inquiry to the Council of Ministers concerning the fate of a [nuclear-powered] heating plant under construction five kilometers from Gorky," and that the relevant offical had answered "as if Chernobyl never happened." Khodyrev complained that "leaders of ministries should treat deputorial inquiries with a greater sense of responsibility." Unfortunately, the size of the Congress, the limited time and resources at its disposal, and the constitutional responsibilities given to the Supreme Soviet worked against deputies' attempts to play a role in controlling the executive.

The USSR Supreme Soviet

The new USSR Supreme Soviet was constitutionally required to implement the strategic course set by the CPD. Consequently, as a standing legislature in a system based on a 'socialist system of checks and balances,' the Supreme Soviet was responsible for controlling the Council of Ministers. With these requirements in mind, analysis of the new Supreme Soviet using a Leninist framework best explores the relationship between political leadership and executive-legislative relations.

Leadership and Executive-Legislative Relations. By rejecting the formalism of the old Supreme Soviet, by arguing that political leadership should be realized by Communist deputies in the legislature, by creating a separation of powers, by preventing ministers and executive officials from becoming deputies, by suggesting that the Supreme Soviet should play a role in all major decisions, Gorbachev was creating a specific type of legislative structure, a structure much more similar to the United States Congress or the German Bundestag, transformative legislatures, than the arena-type institution best symbolized by Great Britain's Parliament.[38] In short, by creating a 'socialist division of powers,' Gorbachev rejected one of the principal tenets of 'Leninist' soviet-style government.

Legislatures capable of playing an independent role in controlling the executive typically have well-developed, substantive committees. One respected survey of the comparative legislatures literature observed that "the stronger and more specialized the committees in a legislature, the more influence that each of them naturally has on policy making in its area of jurisdiction... The weaker and more general the committees in a legislature, the less chance it has to exercise any significant influence on policy."[39] In the new Supreme Soviet, Gorbachev, through the Presidium and the Secretariat, weakened the committees. This attempt to artificially split political decisionmaking and policy formulation between the party and the Supreme Soviet's committee system was based on an unworkable concept of political leadership. In this model, the party made strategic choices that were drafted into public policy by the Supreme Soviet's objective/specialist committees.[40]

Control over the committees was necessary because the attempt to divide political leadership and policy formulation by creating 'specialist' committees was unworkable. Political factors that the CPSU could not control strongly affected both the committees' legislative and monitoring functions. For example, the battle fought by Baltic deputies to gain representation on the defense committee demonstrated that nationalism played a role in politics inside the Supreme Soviet, and, therefore, that the defense committee could not be merely the group of objective specialists. That is, the party could not separate political decisionmaking and policy formulation to preserve for itself the special role of 'political leadership.' Political demands, both implicit and explicit, played a role in all aspects of the committees' work.[41]

In June 1989, Gorbachev gave an example of what he considered political leadership in the formulation of public policy. Addressing the CPSU Central Committee, he argued that the party's role in relation to the economy "is to give society a scientifically based, socially oriented economic program... [Therefore] we need to identify the meaning of this principled position as it applies to the concrete activity of different branches of the party."[42] Although Gorbachev's argument may at first seem workable, one should note that Soviet political leaders made similar statements concerning the relationships between political leadership, 'concrete' decisions, and the division of functions for nearly 70 years. In the daily grind of political practice it always was impossible to separate 'concrete' decisions from questions of 'political leadership' and strategy. Political reality at both the national and local levels, constantly pulled the party down from the lofty heights of 'strategy' into the so-called 'concrete' details of policy implementation. One Soviet political analyst summarized the problem that was at the heart of the division of functions among the CPSU, the Supreme Soviet, and the Council of Ministers in the following way:

> The 'division of functions' is unrealizable. In our country the party's power is hierarchical and total... therefore [the party] cannot help but be not only the only political power, but also [every other type] of power... A law-based state cannot be created if, as before, party leadership is understood as [a force]

that works out 'policy' that is later merely formulated and concretized through the 'power' of state institutions...[43]

In short, a workable division of functions was impossible to establish under conditions of a one-party monopoly in a centralized polity and economy.

In fulfilling their responsibilities to their constituents, Communist deputies in the Supreme Soviet faced a special problem related to party leadership. Discussing this issue at a Central Committee Plenum, Gorbachev himself pointed out the phenomenon of dual subordination, i.e. deputies are accountable to both the party and their constituents.

> We...cannot consider deputies free from party discipline, the fulfillment of party decisions. But to reduce deputorial activity to the formulation of party directives would be wrong. I think that it is the responsibility of Communist deputies to start from united positions on important questions, [positions] that follow from the party's political strategy on questions of principle...in all the rest, complete freedom of judgement, voting, and initiative.[44]

Gorbachev was unable to find an adequate way to define the differences between "questions of principle" and "all the rest," which probably was why he elected to control the committees and their members. Although reports of the discussions held in the party group seemed to confirm that the CPSU was moving toward the goal outlined at the 19th Party Conference to create "an atmosphere of principledness, openness, discussion, criticism and self-criticism," the split between "questions of principle" and "all the rest" was ultimately undefinable and therefore artificial.[45]

The phenomenon of ministerial programs, packages of ideas presented by nominees to the committees during confirmation hearings, demonstrated another weakness of CPSU leadership. Instead of a comprehensive party policy coordinated across the government, individual ministers campaigned for confirmation both in committee hearings and in joint sessions. In the confirmation battles fought both in the committee system and in joint sessions of the Supreme Soviet, it was not clear whether individual ministerial campaigning was based on 'strategic political decisions' and an overall plan approved by the CPSU Central Committee or its Politburo, or was merely improvised by individual nominees to serve the needs of the moment. The conflicts set up between ministerial nominees and deputies may have been good political theater but they were of doubtful practical utility. Responsible parties with legislative majorities pick their ministers and get down to the business of government.

Without the power of the purse or, in fact, much power at all, the committee system was not capable of helping the Supreme Soviet hold the

Council of Ministers accountable. The revitalization of the Supreme Soviet and the redistribution of functions at the highest level of the political system failed to meet the goals set at the 19th Party Conference. Indeed, the evidence presented here suggests that Gorbachev never intended to turn the Supreme Soviet into a genuine working institution. Despite an overwhelming majority of Communist members in the Supreme Soviet, Gorbachev never tried to lead a concerted effort to use it to control the executive. Gorbachev's failure to do so was a result of the half-measures taken in intra-party reform. As Hough pointed out, the possibility that Gorbachev would ever truly democratize the party was "little more than the dreams of radical Soviet intellectuals."[46] His inability, indeed his refusal, to turn the CPSU into a parliamentary party sealed the fate of the two legislatures. The spectrum of opinions among party members in the Supreme Soviet was too broad and Gorbachev's conception of political leadership too narrow to encourage parliamentary politics.

The New Russian CPD

Gorbachev's attempt to create a new *soviet* politics, based on rejoining political leadership and political accountability, served a limited purpose in a limited fashion through both the 1989 and 1990 elections. After the 1990 elections, politics were genuinely reborn beyond Gorbachev's control in revitalized soviets that, at the union republic level, enjoyed popular mandates. Deputies in the new soviets explicitly rejected Leninist forms. For example, the deputorial corpus in the RSFSR CPD contained two polarized blocs: Communists of Russia and Democratic Russia. *Demrossiia* and the wide range of deputies it attracted to its cause were able to elect Boris Yeltsin chairman of the RSFSR Supreme Soviet and implement a series of radical decisions because of the sense of responsibility that deputies felt towards their constituents and, conversely, not to the party apparatus represented by the Communists of Russia. Because of the general problems of bloc politics, however, the typical incentive system built into an electoral-legislative-party system was absent and neither bloc was able to meet its goals.

Soviet Legislative Politics and Democratic Crafting

Crafting at the Federal Level? Can the first session of the new Soviet legislatures help us distinguish between visions of 'Gorbachev the democratizer' and 'Gorbachev the revitalizer'? The institutional structure of the USSR CPD precluded any sort of productive work while the Congress was in session; clearly, it was created to serve as a political forum—but not the type of forum that could craft a democratic compromise. Although the dialogue that took place both at the first session and prior to it suggested that intra-party discussion would be encouraged, the CPSU was so enormous that a separate set of institutions *within the party group* would have been needed to create a democratic dialogue. Gorbachev's use of both the apparat and non-party mechanisms to control the preparations for the Congress, as well as the approach taken by many oblast and republican delegations, suggests that intra-party democracy was not developed. The party's rank-and-file may have influenced some decisions through the work of the party group or at the session itself; nevertheless, the agenda was decided ahead of time.

Gorbachev's call for consolidation around a "socialist pluralism of opinions," an attempt to define certain outcomes as out of bounds, gave reason to doubt his acceptance of contingency. Deputy Stankevich, discussing the role of the IRDG, pointed out the problems inherent in Gorbachev's advocacy of political harmony.

> The presence of parliamentary groups—is not a deception, not a pretense, not a conspiracy of a narrow circle of radicals struggling for power. It is the only possible way for a working parliament to exist... Some parliaments have existed for hundred of years and have seen much, but the one thing that they have not seen is any kind of unity. Where unity begins, a working parliament ends...
> Before consolidating, which they constantly are calling us to do, it is necessary to intelligently separate. We must clarify the platforms on which we stand, what views we are defending, what we understand by the universal term 'perestroika'... On this basis we can both consolidate and separate. And if [in this process] there appears among us various platforms and various views, there is nothing frightening in this. This is a normal spectrum of opinions appearing in society. We need to create a situation in which... these conflicts are decided... in parliament and not in the streets.[47]

By setting bounds to legitimate debate within the CPSU and denying the possibility of a multi-party system, Gorbachev rejected the idea of contingency essential to the democratic transformation of society. In Di Palma's model of democratic crafting, however, this attitude could be considered a tactical retreat to keep the apparat in the game. "Living with an imperfect agreement," he argues, "may not yet constitute a consensus on fundamentals, but, because it makes room for political actors with contrasting expectations, it is a useful approximation of it."[48] Would Gorbachev make way for actors "with contrasting expectations"? The Supreme Soviet provides further evidence.

The operation of the Supreme Soviet's committee system demonstrated that Gorbachev was not interested in procedural political contingency. The artificial split between policy and politics demonstrated his unwillingness to create any genuine sort of political competition in the Supreme Soviet, even through the controlled arena of the committee system. The apparat would not be a participant on an equal basis—it was the controller of the game. Deprived of traditional party discipline, Gorbachev turned to a management style based on what some deputies called *apparatnye igry*, two colorful words that roughly translated mean 'games played by the central party and state apparats,' but express a new twist on a familiar theme: old-style politics dominated by officials from the Communist Party's central apparat. This type of politics was most clearly visible in the Secretariat's manipulation of the Supreme Soviet's committee system. One major problem with *apparatnye igry* is that political tradeoffs and value judgements that should have been made more expeditiously to start moving the USSR away from the brink of the abyss were delayed. Decisions and tradeoffs in the apparat were made in the old-fashioned way, closed to the public. The Supreme Soviet was held at arm's length until a decision was made and then used, if possible, to legitimate it.

The Soviet case calls into doubt a key assumption of Di Palma's model of democratization in post-communist systems: that democratization guided by the party elite can work in a federal system. If democratization is a process of 'crafting' aimed at convincing participants of the merits of political contingency, neither Gorbachev nor the party apparat ultimately believed in a rule that one might call the 'or else' clause. Gorbachev could not tell his parliamentary party, "Follow my lead or we will go down to electoral defeat." The institutional structure of 'soviet power' and electoral schedule left them safe for five years without the discipline of the ballot. Moreover, the apparat believed too firmly in its own role and enjoyed its privileges too much for this argument to work. The party, even when the right wing tried before the coup, could not say to Gorbachev, "Stick with us or we will replace you." Gorbachev always had the option of moving to the left and conducting a popular fight against the apparat.[49] Because of these insititutional and electoral dynamics, perestroika never received any substance and difficult choices were not made. Initiative flowed to the republican level. This process condemned the USSR Supreme Soviet to second-class status.[50]

Gorbachev's 'power to the soviets' campaign, a brilliant political program in 1988, had failed by early 1990. The control system constructed to manipulate the Supreme Soviet's committee system, the birth of parliamentary blocs, and Gorbachev's treatment of the Democratic Platform movement during preparations for the 28th Party Congress all suggest that he needed a presidency because of a problem that has been clear since the first sessions of the CPD and the Supreme Soviet: he could not control the CPSU as a legislative party, and he was losing his control over it as a national political party. The Communist Party was an enormous umbrella organization, not a political party in any western sense and certainly not a parliamentary party. Without a genuine party system, even a one-party system, legislatures cannot produce politically workable solutions to complex questions. The creation of the presidency was a result of the failure of Soviet legislative politics in the curious hybrid form devised by Gorbachev and, specifically, the failure of the CPSU to function effectively.[51]

Like much of *demokratizatsiia*, the birth of the presidency and the constitutional changes concerning the party's role are liable to several interpretations. Perhaps Gorbachev merely wanted increased powers to safeguard the democratic game. More convincingly, one could argue that his assumption to the presidency at an engineered session of a weak legislature suggested that democracy was not the only game in town: it was not convenient, compelling, or appealing in the sense outlined by Di Palma. Gorbachev, either for private glory or driven by an urge to save the Union, wanted personal power. Kliamkin and others argue that the creation of the presidency and the revisions to Articles 6 and 7 of the Soviet Constitution were connected. Gorbachev needed the presidency to save himself and the party. The 1990 republican elections threatened not only to eliminate the leading role of the party *de facto* through a new deputorial corpus, but de jure through new constitutions. If the party elite wanted to keep a say in national affairs, a presidency was one way to guarantee it. F.M. Burlatskii offers a related interpretation: Gorbachev's move was a preemptive strike launched when he foresaw Yeltsin's election to the Chairmanship of the Russian Supreme Soviet.[52]

Crafting in Russia? Di Palma's model of democratic crafting can be applied separately to two stages of the political transformation in Russia. The first stage consisted of the elections and the preparations for the opening of the session, a process controlled by the apparat through the system of filters pointed out by Sergei Shakrai. Although preparations for the first session of the RSFSR CPD started around the same time that the Communist Party gave up its claims to a leading and guiding role in the USSR's political system, this did not mean that the party apparat was willing to negotiate to create a modern political democracy. The *de jure* multiparty system was a *de facto* one-party monopoly. The apparat was unwilling to share power. Indeed, the testimony of several witnesses who took the stand in the Russian Constitutional Court's review of the legality of Yeltsin's decision to ban the Communist Party suggests that the central party elite acted as if the party's 'leading and guiding role' had never been removed from the constitution.

Yeltsin and *Demrossiia* were interested, one might argue, in a process resembling Di Palma's democratic crafting. The RSFSR CPD provided an institutional structure within which to conduct the 'game.' After *Demrossiia* succeeded in electing Yeltsin chairman of the RSFSR Supreme Soviet, the game moved into a new stage: Yeltsin in 1990, unlike Gorbachev in 1989, appeared intent on negotiating with all principal institutional and organized interests to produce a compromise solution leading to genuine democracy. In addition to a willingness to create a negotiated settlement, both sides, represented by Democratic Russia and the Communists of Russia, were trapped by the structure: exit games became more unlikely from either side. This 'mode of decisionmaking' encouraged both sides to fight to convince deputies from the broad middle ground. Yeltsin's creation of a compromise committee to resolve cadres questions and other disputed issues, a second 'mode of decisionmaking,' encouraged negotiated outcomes. By the end of the first session of the RSFSR CPD, decisionmaking was closely monitored, if not managed, by the coordinating councils of *Demrossiia* and the Communists of Russia.

The End of the Soviet Era

Demokratizatsiia was neither a 'Leninist' solution to the problems of the 'period of stagnation' nor a conscious process of democratic crafting. Neither Gorbachev's incantations about 'democracy' nor Western eagerness to see democratic solutions should obscure this point. He advocated a third path, a political program that strategically accounted for the interests of the party apparat and the frustrated desires of Soviet citizens for economic security and political liberalization. *Demokratizatsiia* was not about sharing or devolving power, it was about *creating* power, first politically and later economically, to pull the USSR out of 'stagnation.'

Gorbachev's rejection of 'Leninist' views of leadership, accountability, representation, and executive-legislative relations, the basic elements of his attempt to reempower both the CPSU and himself as its leader, were *not* matched by a concerted effort to democratize the party or, in Di Palma's language, to demonstrate to the party that there was no alternative to democracy, that democratic competition was appealing, convenient, or compelling.

Although Gorbachev failed to revive 'Soviet socialist democracy', we should note its success, an unintended side effect: a massive authoritarian empire was dismantled with much less bloodshed then might have been expected thanks to discussion and debate in semi-democratic political institutions. The birth of the new politics in the former republics of the USSR—or the death of *soviet* politics—can be divided into three stages. If perestroika was an attempt to recreate power and leadership within a 'soviet' 'socialist' political system, and immediate post-perestroika politics the attempt to use soviet institutions left standing in the ashes of *demokratizatsiia*'s failure, post-coup politics will move into a new realm and create new political and economic institutions.

The first stage of the reforms, up to and including the 1989 elections, consisted in many areas of 'us vs. them' politics. That is, 'the people' rejected 'party leadership'. Society, however, was atomized and efforts, with some exceptions, tended to be individualistic or in small groups. Gorbachev called for consolidation and said the party should play the role of a harmonizer. *Demokratizatsiia*, however, set into motion forces that careened out of control. Gorbachev recreated a type of public power by rejoining political leadership and electoral accountability, yet did not provide tools for wielding that power—the institutional structures that could have produced real political leadership. He destroyed traditional communist solutions to the problems of power and leadership but did not provide workable institutional replacements.

The second stage of the transformation, started by the 1990 elections, was also characterized by 'us vs. them' politics, but organized in a new way. No longer were 'the people' atomized: Soviet citizens had not been politically neutered by decades of authoritarian rule. Coalitions fought against the party apparatus. More importantly, republican nationalists fought in the new republican Supreme Soviets first for sovereignty and later for independence. Legislative politics in 1990 started to move away from zero-sum 'us vs. them' model to a more sophisticated bloc system. In a corresponding shift, politics and power moved to the republican and local levels. Republican legislatures refused to implement federal law. The creation of republican presidencies, most notably the election of Boris Yeltsin to the presidency of the RSFSR in the spring of 1991, added a direct link between the people and their governments. This link, while far from the only reason for the failure of the coup in the RSFSR, was surely an important factor.

The challenge of post-coup politics is the same challenge that Gorbachev faced in 1985: economic and political reform to create institutions that will reempower the government and the people. The changes that took place over the past three years moved the citizens of the Soviet Union to the brink of an historic choice: whether to continue a 73-year experiment with a form of government whose alleged advantages never materialized, or to look elsewhere. The August 1991 coup pushed most doubters over the edge.

While some republics turned to principles and institutions tried and tested for centuries in the West, others faced a more difficult choice.[53] The nations of Central Europe westernized their political systems in the upheavals of 1989–90 with little hesitation—but many of them were separated from parliamentary government by a mere 45 years. The former republics of the Soviet Union, conditioned by the long absence or total lack of parliamentary traditions, the difficulties of economic reform, the centrifugal forces generated by multinational multi-ethnic populations, and ruling elites that may refuse to give up their newly-won positions in the Soviets without a battle, face a difficult future.[54] Even if they succeed, as Larry Diamond has pointed out, the "global zeitgeist for democracy," does not mean that popular government is indestructable. Between 1973 and 1989, 15 countries became democratic while 12 moved in the opposite direction.[55]

Several factors, each of which can be traced to the institutional legacy of 'soviet' power, may block democratization in Russia.[56] First, of course, soviet power impoverished the USSR, producing a curious type of economic backwardness. 'Soviet-style' reforms led to the disintegration of the Union while encouraging Gorbachev to delay making fundamental decisions on economic reform. The problem for the near future is that there may be no way to escape from the economic, social, cultural and other prerequisites for democracy discussed so widely in the literature and so obviously and sadly lacking all across Russia.[57]

Soviet-style government, with its electoral and legislative consequences, handicapped the development of parliamentary parties and will continue to do so until Russia ratifies a new constitution, dissolves its CPD and Supreme Soviet, and holds a genuine multiparty election.[58] Unfortunately, the electoral and legislative incentives that would drive the creation of modern parliamentary parties probably will not be put in place in the near future. Moreover, time, the passage of electoral and political cycles, is necessary for the institutionalization of any political incentive structure. If leadership can be viewed as the identification, discussion, and implementation, of alternate futures through a process driven by the 'carrot' of political perquisites and the 'stick' of the ballot box, the political incentives in the new system seem weak.

The future of 'soviet' politics, de-sovietization in the literal sense, was clear long before the USSR Supreme Soviet formally rejected soviet-style government in the fall of 1991 as one of its final acts.[59] After nearly a year as chairman of the Moscow City Soviet and more than two years as a USSR people's deputy and member of the coordinating council of the IRDG, Gavriil Popov argued that newcomers who had wielded power in the soviets at all levels were united by one thought, "the soviet political mechanism demonstrated during the course of perestroika that it is just as ineffective as the economic system of socialism."[60] Pointing to the peculiarities of bloc politics, Popov argued that the soviets were weakened by their composition. Deputies, especially the democrats, were elected not as representatives of a party but as personalities. The new soviets, he contended, act decisively in only two situations: "when it was necessary to break down the old [system] or when it is necessary to define in the most general terms policy for the future." When it is time to decide something concrete, he insisted, "endless debates began that were completely incapable of culminating in any kind of constructive decision." Ilia Zaslavskii, a leading member of *Demrossiia* who was elected chairman of the Oktiabrskii regional soviet in Moscow, maintained that the structure of 'soviet power' was inappropriate from the first day. He drew some broad conclusions:

> Almost all soviets at all levels are demonstrating their powerlessness and uselessness. The entire structure of Soviet power does not work as it should. The meetings and congresses [of this system] have turned into senseless debates far from real life...I must warn you that the slogan 'All power to the soviets!' is deceptive! It does not lead to democracy. It is a direct route to dictatorship.[61]

The RSFSR CPD could not escape the effects of 'soviet-style' organization. Claiming that the situation in the RSFSR CPD was so obviously bad that it "is boring to even talk about this," RSFSR Deputy Viktor Sheinis pointed out that, "in Russia a torturous process of the creation of parliamentarism," was taking place. "It would be nice to have different deputies... But we have a congress and parliament that reflect the situation in our society. Society looks in this mirror and is shocked."[62]

In addition to the problems that deputies had organizing soviets, they also faced opposition from the party apparat at all levels. This presented an interesting paradox. The Free Democratic Party of Russia claimed, for example, that "in both the local soviets and the [RSFSR] CPD the conservative wing of the administrative-party apparat, despondently clinging to power, and obstructing normal parliamentary activity, is leading the country to a social and economic catastrophe."[63] While the coup and subsequent developments solved the problem of the CPSU apparat at the federal level, it did not help resolve the long-range problem of eliminating entrenched mafias at the local level.

The Russian republic's presidential system was one product of republican battles with 'the center' and the inadequacies of 'soviet power.' Indeed, Yeltsin's constant requests for more and more formal power, first as Chairman of the Supreme Soviet and later as president, were reminiscent of Gorbachev's ill-fated attempt to rule by decree. As Juan Linz has pointed out, however, presidential government can threaten democracitic development. "The vast majority of stable democracies in the world today are parliamentary regimes," he argues, "where executive power is generated by legislative majorities and depends on such majorities for survival."[64] Linz argues that the winner-take-all element of presidential elections, the danger of staking more on a 'national mandate' than is warranted, rigid fixed terms of office, and the perils of possible standoffs between the president and the legislature make presidential systems a dangerous gamble. In conditions where economic reforms highly polarize the electorate the risks, it would seem, are even higher.

Paradoxically, 'soviet politics' led to the end of the Soviet era. Both the sequence of elections and the institutional forms selected for the process strongly influenced outcomes. Gorbachev's experiment with soviet government awakened civil society while giving republican political elites a legitimate institutional forum to press for sovereignty.[65] Moreover, in a system where electoral and legislative competition started to define political incentive structures, the CPSU was unable to function effectively. The final edition of *Izvestiia TsK KPSS*, the Central Committee journal that Gorbachev rescued from the party's dustbin to serve as a herald of perestroika, contained a Politburo decree lamenting the poor work of CPSU fractions in soviets at all levels.[66] The fragile net of interwoven political incentive structures, the nexus of elections, legislatures, parties, and executives that forms the institutional infrastructure of modern democracies, is only just appearing. Whether new political institutions and political actors will be able to create their own public power and lead the peoples of the former USSR to a peaceful and prosperous future is an open question. Power and leadership can be reconstituted in various ways. Anything less than market democracy may be a step backward, but a step that politicians frequently are willing to take.[67]

Notes

1. On 6 November 1991, Yeltsin signed a decree banning the activities of the CPSU and Russian Communist Parties. For the text of this decree see *Rossiiskaia Gazeta*, 9 November 1991, p. 2.

2. The USSR Supreme attempted to reorganize and restructure itself in the wake of the coup, but failed. See, "Sessiiu nesformirovannogo Verkovnogo Soveta SSSR ne smozhet otkryt dazhe gospod bog," *Izvestiia*, 10 October 1991, p. 1.

3. See M.S. Gorbachev, *Perestroika*, p. 17, and note 1, Chapter 1.

4. Gorbachev discussed this in *Perestroika* and in his speech at the 19th Party Conference. Yeltsin offers an interesting opinion on this question. See *Pervaia Sessiia Verkhovnogo Soveta SSSR: Stenograficheskii Otchet*, Moscow: 1989, Vol. VIII, p. 105.

5. This question is discussed by Elizabeth Teague in "Perestroika and the Party," in *Gorbachev and Perestroika*, Martin McCauley, ed. New York: St. Martin's, 1990, pp. 13–15. For an earlier view on the dispersal of power in Soviet society see William E. Odom, "A Dissenting View on the Group Approach to Soviet Politics," *World Politics*, No. 28, 1976, p. 565. In the terms used by Ken Jowitt, the CPSU was "unable to transform its elite members into deployable combat 'agents' to prevent the routinization of a party based on charismatic impersonal discipline into a neotraditional status organization of cadres primarily oriented to personal, familial, and material concerns." Ken Jowitt, "Soviet Neotraditionalism: The Political Corruption of a Leninist Regime," *Soviet Studies*, No. 3, 1983, pp. 275–297.

6. As Elizabeth Teague has pointed out, "Gorbachev resorted to drastic methods to separate the functions of the Party from those of the state." Teague, "Perestroika and the Party," p. 22.

7. Kliamkin, p. 707.

8. M. Piskotin, "Trudnyi put demokratizatsii," *Narodnyi deputat*, No. 2, 1990, p. 5.

9. An article published in *Pravda* shortly after the campaign took the Leningrad party organization to task for its failure to compete effectively. See "Vyvody bez deistviia," *Pravda*, 30 April 1989, p. 2.

10. "Poniat chto proizoshlo," *Izvestiia*, 23 April 1989. p. 2.

11. For initial Soviet reviews of the lessons of the elections see: "Vybory: Pervye Uroki," *Literaturnaia gazeta*, 5 April 1989, p. 10; "Zatianuvshaiasia pauza: Razmyshleniia o nekotorykh urokakh vyborov v Leningrade," *Pravda*, 20 April 1989, p. 2; "Voskhozhdenie k demokratii," *Pravda*, 4 April 1989, p. 3; "Etapy reformy," *Pravda*, 7 May 1989, p. 3.

12. *Moskvichi vybiraiut narodnykh deputatov SSSR. O nekotorykh itogakh vyborov narodnykh deputatov SSSR v g. Moskve v Marte-Mae 1989 g. Ispolnitelnyi komitet Moskovskogo Gorodskogo Soveta Narodnykh Deputatov. Otdel po rabote sovetov*, Moscow: 1989, p. 18.

13. For a discussion of this point see A.S. Sobchak, "Ot sezda k sezdu: stanovlenie novoi politicheskoi sistemy," *Cherez ternii*, Moscow: Progress, 1990.

14. Timothy J. Colton, "The Politics of Democratization: The Moscow Election of 1990," *Soviet Economy*, Vol. 6, No. 4, 1990, p. 304.

15. On this point and for a more general discussion see A. Ivanchenko, "Izbiratelnaia kampaniia—Uroki na zavtra," *Kommunist*, No. 11, 1990, p. 87. Ottorino Cappelli discusses changes in representation in "The Soviet

Representative System at the Crossroads: Towards Political Representation?," *The Journal of Communist Studies*, Vol. 7, No. 2, pp. 170-201. For an excellent discussion of the electoral law and its effects see S.A. Avakian, "Izbiratelnyi zakon v deistvii," *Vestnik Moskovskogo Universiteta, Pravo*, No. 6, 1989, pp. 9-19.

16. Interviews with M. Shneidr, V. Kaganov, and V. Kuznetsov, summer 1990, Moscow.

17. Timothy J. Colton, "The Politics of Democratization: The Moscow Election of 1990," *Soviet Economy*, Vol. 6, No. 4, 1990, p. 304.

18. *Moskvichi vybiraiut narodnykh deputatov SSSR*, pp. 1-2.

19. One good example of this process were the elections conducted by the Academy of Sciences (as a social organization), which helped politicize the intelligentsia, both in Moscow and in Academy institutes across the country. An 'Electors' Club' founded in 1989 by Moscow members of Academy institutes played a key role in both the 1989 and the 1990 elections. Another good example is that the campaign helped give the Moscow People's Front an identity and organization. On 20 May 1989, representatives of 46 socio-political clubs and regional groups of Moscow and Moscow oblast gathered at a founding conference and declared that the Moscow People's Front was "a movement for the revolutionary renewal of society. For the views of the head of the CEC on the Academy of Sciences see "Demokratiia nabiraet silu," *Sovetskaia Rossiia*, 14 March 1989, p. 1. For information on the birth of the Moscow People's Front see *50 otvetov na 50 voprosov 'Gaid-Parkov' Moskvy o Moskovskom Narodnom Fronte*, Moscow: August 1989.

20. The formation of new political identities received a strong stimulus from the 1990 elections. See "Anatomiia neformalnogo dvizhenie," *Izvestiia TsK KPSS*, April 1990, pp. 150-156 for an overview of informal political organizations that were formed in this period.

21. *Moskovskaia Pravda*, 2 December 1989, p. 2.

22. Di Palma's model of democratic crafting more closely fits several of the other 1990 republican elections. These are reviewed in *Elections in the Baltic States and Soviet Republics: A Compendium of Reports on Parliamentary Elections Held in 1990*, Compiled by the Staff of the Commission on Security and Cooperation in Europe, Washington: U.S. Government Printing Office, 1990.

23. *Informatsionnyi biulleten, Izdanie Mezhregionalnoi gruppy narodnykh deputatov SSSR*, 15 September 1989, p. 4.

24. *Izvestiia*, 31 May 1989, p. 3.

25. Chernichenko moved on to attack Egor Ligachev, head of the Central Committee's agricultural section. "Why is a politically vital industry that will define...the future of perestroika headed by a man who understands

nothing and was [even] a failure when [he headed the Central Committee's ideology section]?" *Izvestiia*, 30 May 1989, p. 1.

26. Ibid., p. 4. Deputy R.Kh. Solntsev, a writer from Krasnoiarsk, complained that the time difference between Siberia and Moscow meant that a flood of calls came in late at night, making it difficult to sleep.

27. Ibid., 30 May 1989, p. 2.

28. *Izvestiia*, 31 May 1989, p. 6.

29. Ibid., 1 June 1989, p. 4.

30. Deputy Zaslavskii, for example, argued that, "our bulletin is distributed only among the deputies, but voters have the right to know their deputy's point of view and what he advocates here." See *Izvestiia*, 31 May 1989, p. 5. Deputies Kiselev and Obolenskii pointed out that the session's stenogram published in *Izvestiia* contained inaccuracies, and urged deputies to take a closer look at it. For Kiselev, see *Izvestiia*, 31 May 1989, p. 5. *Izvestiia* excused inaccuracies by publishing a disclaimer that it merely made its pages available for text prepared elsewhere.

31. Despite new standards, one debate that took place throughout the session was the representation of the working class. Deputy A. Korshunov, a worker from a Tashkent factory, argued that he was not part of a "gray mass" of workers. "I have something to say, I have something to contribute to the agenda of the Congress and Supreme Soviet, and I have something to advocate there. Other workers and peasants here, I think, could do the very same thing."

Izvestiia, 28 May 1989, p. 2, and 3 June 1989, p. 3.

32. Ibid., 30 May 1989, p. 4.

33. Ibid., 9 June 1989, p. 3. The difficulty of balancing geographic representation and representation through social organizations was demonstrated several times. Addressing the CPD on May 29, Deputy Kiriak, elected by the Women's Councils, asked for more time to discuss women's problems, but did so in the name of the Moldavian deputies. Deputy Gorbunov, the head of the CPD's Secretariat, faced criticism from representatives of social organizations who complained that they were not allowed to speak. See *Izvestiia*, 31 May 1989, p. 4.

34. Ibid., 4 June 1989, p. 3.

35. Ibid.

36. Ibid., 4 June 1989, p. 7.

37. Ibid., 2 June 1989, p. 2.

38. For a review of Soviet thought on this question see, B. Lazarev, "Razdelenie vlastei i opyt sovetskogo gosudarstva," *Kommunist*, No. 16, 1988, pp. 42–51.

39. G. Loewenberg and S. Patterson, *Comparing Legislatures*, Boston: Little Brown, 1979, pp. 209–210.

40. Discussing the principles behind this legislative process, Deputy Alekseev, respected jurist and (at the time) chairman of the Supreme Soviet's legislation committee, emphasized the committees' specialist role. Committees "should conduct their own scientifically verified line and step by step pull social opinion up to a higher level of understanding of problems that face our society." See *Komsomolskaia Pravda*, 11 July 1989, p. 2.

41. Gorbachev recognized the problems that plagued the relationship between the soviets and the party. See, for example, *Pravda*, 19 July 1989, p. 2.

42. *Pravda*, 19 July 1989, p. 2.

43. L. Baktin, "Ostanetsia li vlast u partii?," *Vecherniaia Moskva*, 1 September 1989, p. 2.

44. *Pravda*, 19 July 1989, p. 2.

45. *Materialy XXVII sezda KPSS*, Moscow: Politizdat, 1986, p. 49.

46. Jerry F. Hough, "The Politics of Successful Economic Reform," *Soviet Economy*, Vol. 5, No. 1, 1989, pp. 3–46.

47. *Informatsionnyi biulleten, Izdanie Mezhregionalnoi gruppy narodnykh deputatov SSSR*, 15 September 1989, p. 4.

48. Di Palma, p133.

49. Gorbachev the party apparatchik was unpopular, but if he had 'unmasked' himself to crusade for democracy he could have shifted the polls in his favor.

50. Yeltsin made this argument, and contended that Gorbachev agreed, in an interview, "Kazhdyi den' neustupchivosti pravitelstva Ryzhkova otnimaet den' vlasti u Gorbacheva," *Demokraticheskaia Rossiia*, No. 3, September 1990, p. 6.

51. For a discussion of the party's failures see B.P. Kurashvili, *Strana na rasnpute*, Moscow: Iuridicheskaia literatura, 1990. Jerry F. Hough, "The Politics of Successful Economic Reform," *Soviet Economy*, Vol. 5, No. 1, 1989, pp. 3–46. See the exchange of articles on Gorbachev's leadership published in *Soviet Economy* in 1989, No. 4, 1990, No. 2, and 1991, No. 2. Contributors to the series include George Breslauer, Peter Reddaway, Archie Brown, Andranik Migranyan, and Jerry F. Hough.

52. Kliamkin, p. 713.

53. See B.P. Kurashvili, *Strana na raspute*, p. 27.

54. In November 1990, Gorbachev proposed renaming the Union of Soviet Socialist Republics a union of sovereign soviet republics. Apparently prepared to drop the pretense of socialism, he was reluctant to surrender the unique soviet cachet. The CPD rejected Gorbachev's proposal and retained the old name.

55. Larry Diamond, "Beyond Authoritarianism and Totalitarianism: Strategies for Democratization," *The Washington Quarterly*, Winter 1989,

pp. 141-142. See also Samuel Huntington, *The Third Wave: Democratization in the Late Twentieth Century*, Norman: University of Oklahoma Press, 1991, esp. pp. 290-316.

56. F.M. Burlatskii complained about the decision to install 'soviet-style' government in "Alternativa drobleniiu levykh sil—dvizhenie k sotsialnoi demokratii," *Literaturnaia gazeta*, 1 January 1991, p. 5. Charles H. Fairbanks, Jr. discussed some of the obstacles facing democratization in the RSFSR in "After the Moscow Coup," *Journal of Democracy*, fall 1991, pp. 3-11.

57. On this point see Bova, "Political Dynamics of the Post-Communist Transition," pp. 133-136. The transitional costs of reform may lead, as Przeworski (p. 189) pointed out, to a situation where authoritarian temptations are inevitable.

58. One can only hope that this process, which has already started, will not demand energies that could be better spent elsewhere. For a negative view of Democratic Russia see "Kuda idët Demokraticheskaia Rossiia?," *Izvestiia TsK KPSS*, No. 12, 1990, pp. 104-106.

59. "O rabote kommunistov v sovetakh narodnykh deputatov," *Izvestiia TsK KPSS*, No. 8, 1991, pp. 15-17.

60. On this point see Gavriil Popov, *Chto delat'? O strategii i taktike demokraticheskikh sil na sovremennom etape*, E. Savost'ianov and B. Pasternak eds., Moscow: *Moskovskaia Pravda*, 1990, pp. 12-15. The principal issues in the debate between executive and representative power at the local level can be found in a round table discussion, "Razdelenie vlastei: teoriia i praktika," *Narodnyi deputat*, No. 15, 1990, pp. 7-27, esp. pp. 22-27. See also A. Migranyan, "Dolgii put k evropeiskomu domu," *Novyi Mir*, No. 7, 1989, pp. 166-184.

61. I. Zaslavskii, "V strane nenuzhnykh sovetov," *Stolitsa*, No. 4, January 1991, pp. 3-4. Martin Malia noted that "seventy years on the road to nowhere," a slogan referring to the experiment in 'soviet power' was one of the most popular slogans in the USSR at the end of 1991. See "The Hunt for the True October," *Commentary*, Vol. 92, No. 4, October 1991, p. 27. For a discussion of Zaslavskii's district see Timothy Frye, "Oktyabrsky Raion: The Problems of Creating Democracy in One District," *Report on the USSR*, RFE/RL Research Institute, Vol. 3, No. 33, pp. 26-29.

62. Iu. Aidinov, "Portret v krovom zerkale," *Vecherniaia Moskva*, 1992.

63. *Svobodnyi Demokrat, Informatsionnyi listok orgkomiteta Svobodnoi demokraticheskoi partii Rossiia*.

64. See J. Linz, "The Perils of Presidentialism," *Journal of Democracy*, Vol. 1, No. 1, p. 72-84. Donald L. Horowitz and Seymour Martin Lipset respond to this article and Linz gives a rebuttal in Vol. 1, No. 4 of the journal. Linz's argument is applied in several different national contexts

in U. Liebert and M. Cotta, *Parliament and Democratic Consolidation in Southern Europe: Greece, Italy, Portugal, Spain, and Turkey*, New York: Pinter, 1990.

65. Juan Linz and Alfred Stepan make a similar assertion in "Political Identities and Electoral Sequences: Spain, the Soviet Union, and Yugoslavia," *Daedelus*, Spring 1992, pp. 123- 140.

66. This, of course, does not rule out the possibility that Communist parties will learn from their mistakes and make an electoral comeback. For the report on the work of party fractions see, "O rabote kommunistov v sovetakh narodnykh deputatov," *Izvestiia TsK KPSS*, No. 8, 1991, pp. 15-17.

67. Douglass C. North develops this argument in *Institutions, Institutional Change, and Economic Performance*, New York: Cambridge, 1992.

Index of Names

Afanasev, Iu.N., 28, 75–76, 80, 86n, 104, 138, 214

Alekseev, S.S. 92, 98, 110, 118, 127, 137, 236

Alksnis, V. 58–59, 139, 157

Andreev, Iu.E. 97, 135

Andropov, Iu.V., 23, 50

Anweiler, O., 18, 19, 33

Avakian, S.A., 34n, 234n

Barabashev, G.V., 69n, 70n

Berëzkin, A., 181

Bocharov, M.A., 97, 100, 109, 120, 133, 166, 191

Bokser, V., 177, 183, 187

Boldyrev, Iu.Iu., 109n, 119, 122, 127n, 152n

Breslauer, G., 13n, 34n

Brezhnev, L.I., 21–23, 27, 38, 49n, 210

Burbulis, G.E., 143, 148

Burlatskii, F.M., 13, 49, 79, 118, 123, 154, 227, 237n

Chernenko, K.U., 23, 35, 38,

Chernichenko, Iu.D., 75, 87, 178, 219

Cohen, S.F., 3

Colton, T., 164, 176, 177, 182, 184, 215

Di Palma, G., 4, 9, 29–32, 211–213, 216–218, 225–228, 234n

Emelianov, A.M., 83, 97, 101

Filatov, S.A., 199

Geraschenko, V.V., 117

Gorbachev, M.S.
    the soviets, 2, 32, 37–39, 232
    demokratizatsiia, 1–2, 210–213
    19th Party Conf., 44–47
    election as Chairman of Supreme Soviet, 78–79
    committees in Supreme Soviet, 78–79, 91–92
    and IRDG, 105, 137
    the presidency, 136–140

Gromyko, A.A., 41, 42

Gustafson, T., 12n

Hahn, J., 51n

Hammer, D., 14n, 34n, 49n

Hill, R., 13n, 35n, 50n, 155

Hough, J., 13n, 48, 69, 224, 236n

Huntington, S., 3, 6, 7, 237

Kaiser, R.C., 102

Khasbulatov, R.I., 197, 204

Khrushchev, N.S., 20-21, 210-211

Kurashvili, B.P., 50n, 236n

Kutafin, O.E., 34n, 35n

Lenin, 1, 3, 17-19, 26-28

Ligachev, Y.K. 4, 51n, 234n

Linz, J., 4, 7, 231, 237n, 238n

Loewenberg, G., 235n

Lubenchenko, K.D., 96, 133, 149, 152n, 155

Lukianov, A.I., 34n, 35n, 42, 49, 74-77, 80, 85n, 91, 94-95, 107n, 115, 124, 128n, 129-132, 147, 152n

Migranyan, A., 14n, 236n, 237n

Minagawa, S., 33n

Murashev, A.N., 99, 116, 177

Nishanov, R.N., 42, 98, 99, 101, 123, 154

North, D.C., 238n

O'Donnell, G. 4, 7, 14n, 28, 31, 36

Patterson, S., 235n

Polozkov, I.K., 155n, 193, 195, 205

Popov, G.Kh., 76, 80, 104, 111n, 113, 143-145, 156n, 166, 176, 230, 237n

Primakov, E.M., 42, 96, 98, 99, 101, 102, 105, 107, 119, 130, 154, 105, 107, 119, 130, 154

Przeworski, A., 4, 9, 11, 29, 237n

Remington, T., 13, 153n

Ryzhkov, N.I., 35n, 78, 83-84, 113, 117, 139

Ryzhov, Iu.A., 107, 132, 134, 149, 154

Sakharov, A.D., 65, 66, 72, 77, 104, 175

Schapiro, L., 3, 18

Schmitter, P., 4, 7, 14n, 28, 29, 31, 36

Shakrai, S., 186, 190, 197, 227

Sheinis, V.L., 72, 178, 182, 197, 198, 231

Shneidr, M.Ia., 162, 177

Siegler, R.W., 24, 33

Index of Names

Smyth, R.A., 204n

Sobchak, A.A., 69n, 75, 86, 144–145, 153n, 215, 233n

Stalin, 19–20

Stankevich, S.B., 63, 94, 99, 100, 105, 156, 162, 166, 177, 225

Starovoitova, G., 178, 194

Suslov, M., 38

Teague, E., 154n, 157n, 233n

Travkin, N.I., 143, 144, 184, 190–91, 198–199

Urban, M., 42, 48, 50n, 172

Vanneman, P., 33

Yanaev, G.I., 141

Yeltsin, B.N.
   1989 elections, 12, 63, 71n, 175, 213
   and IRDG, 104, 219
   in USSR Supreme Soviet and CPD, 81, 86n, 92–93, 115, 133
   1990 elections, 178
   Chairman of RSFSR CPD, 192–196, 202–204, 227–228
   Russian President, 203, 207n

Yakovlev, A.N., 4, 51n

Zlatopolskii, D.L., 33n